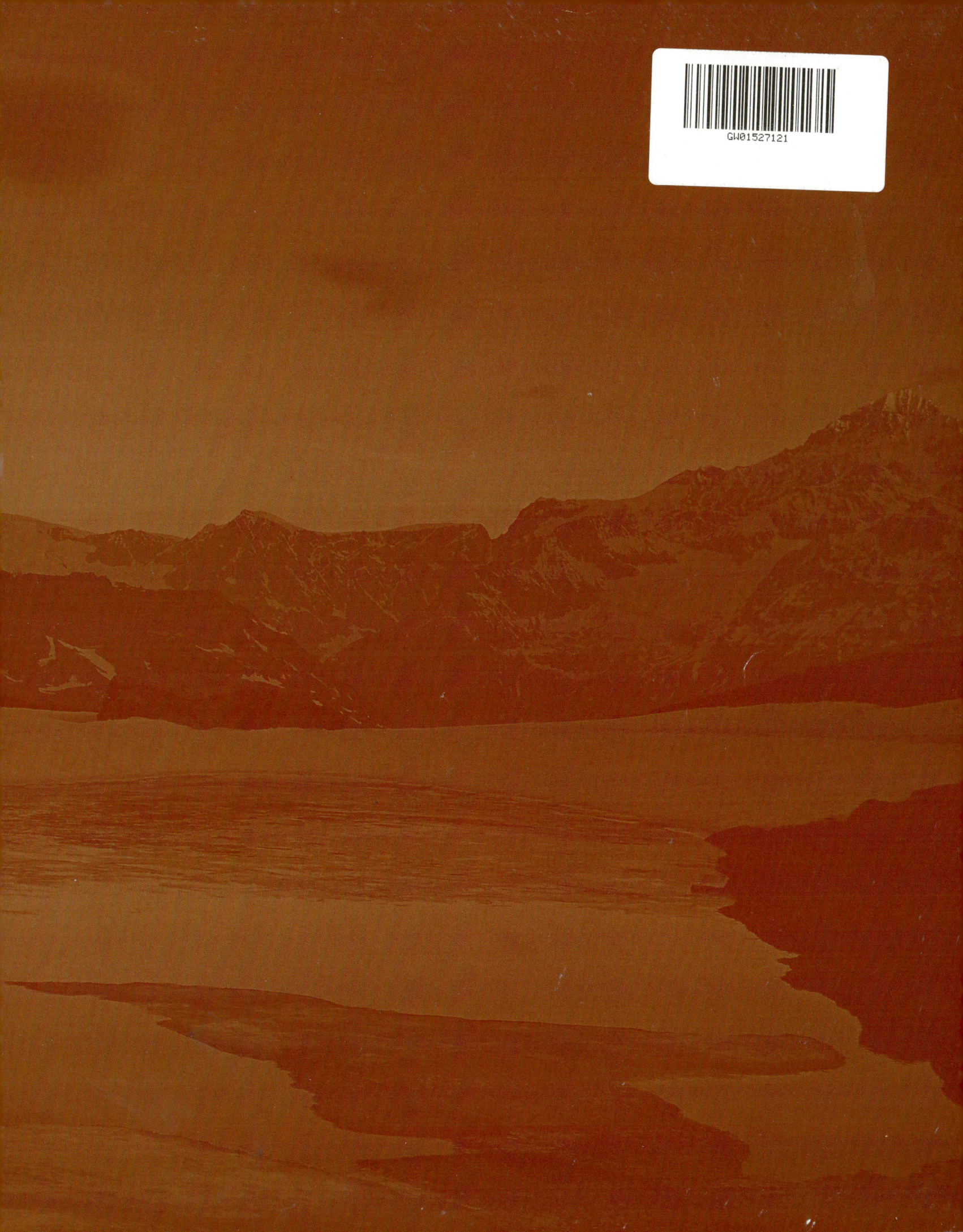

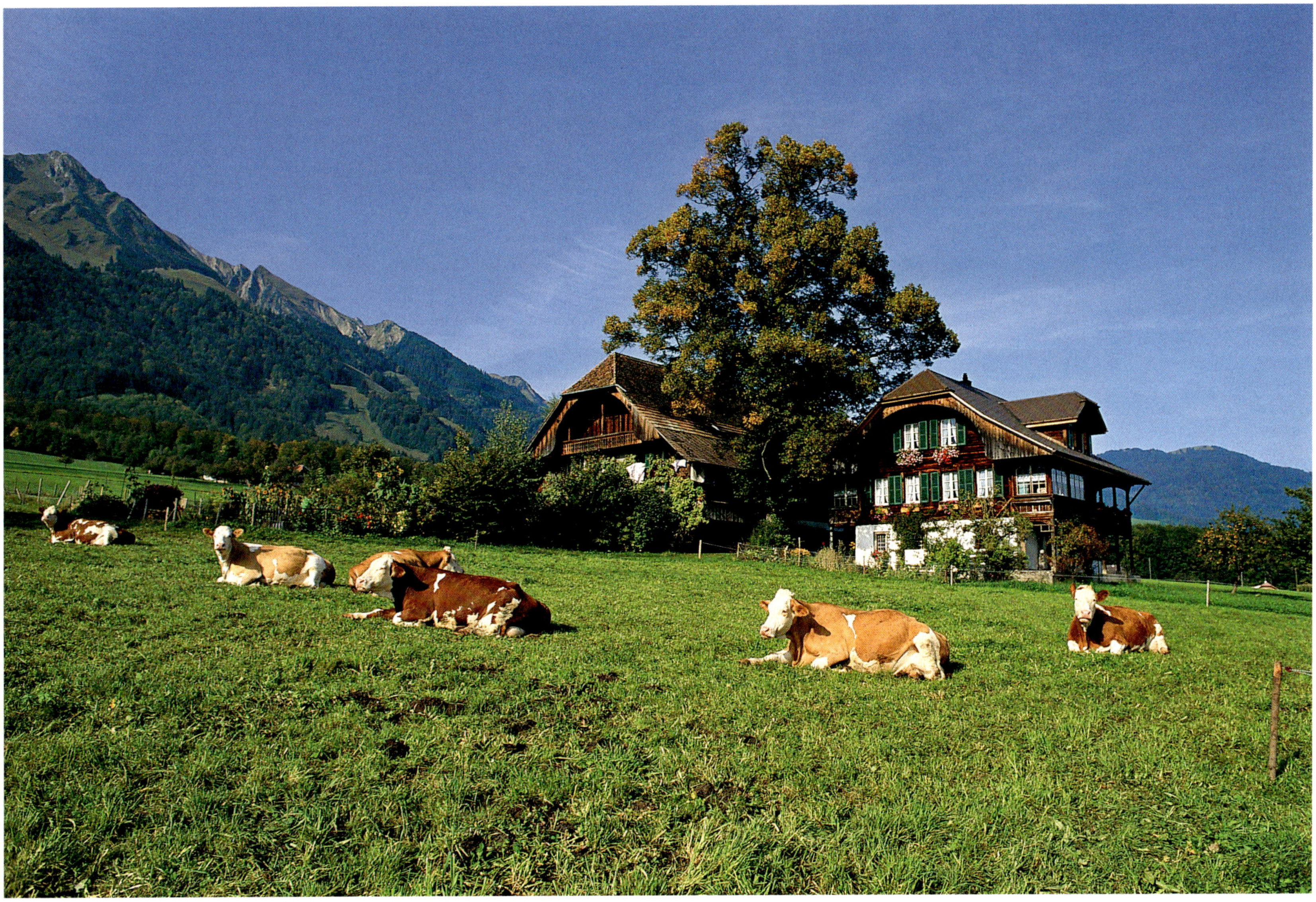

Fascinating

Switzerland

Photos by

Roland Gerth and Christian Heeb

Text by

Jost Wolf

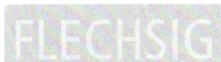

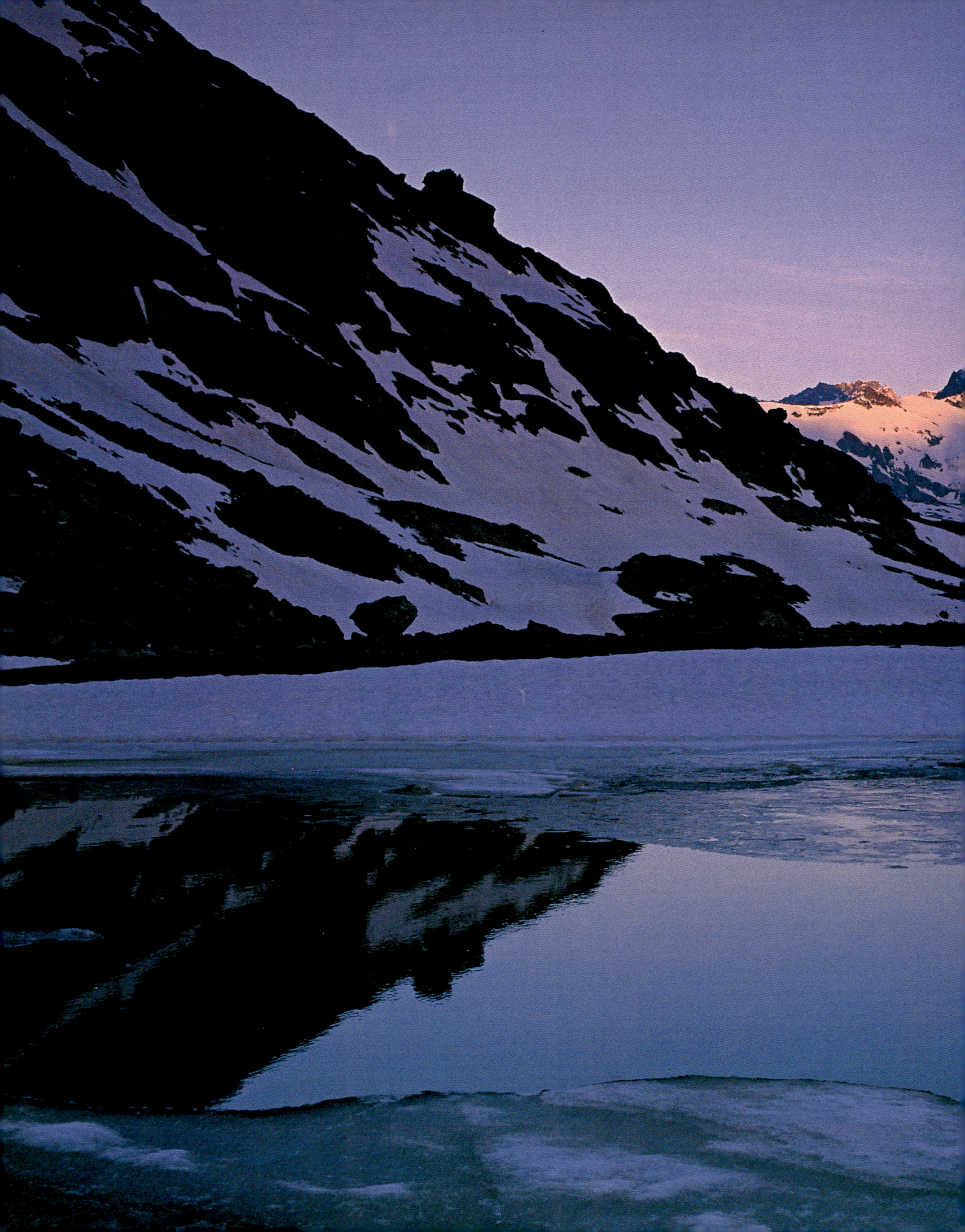

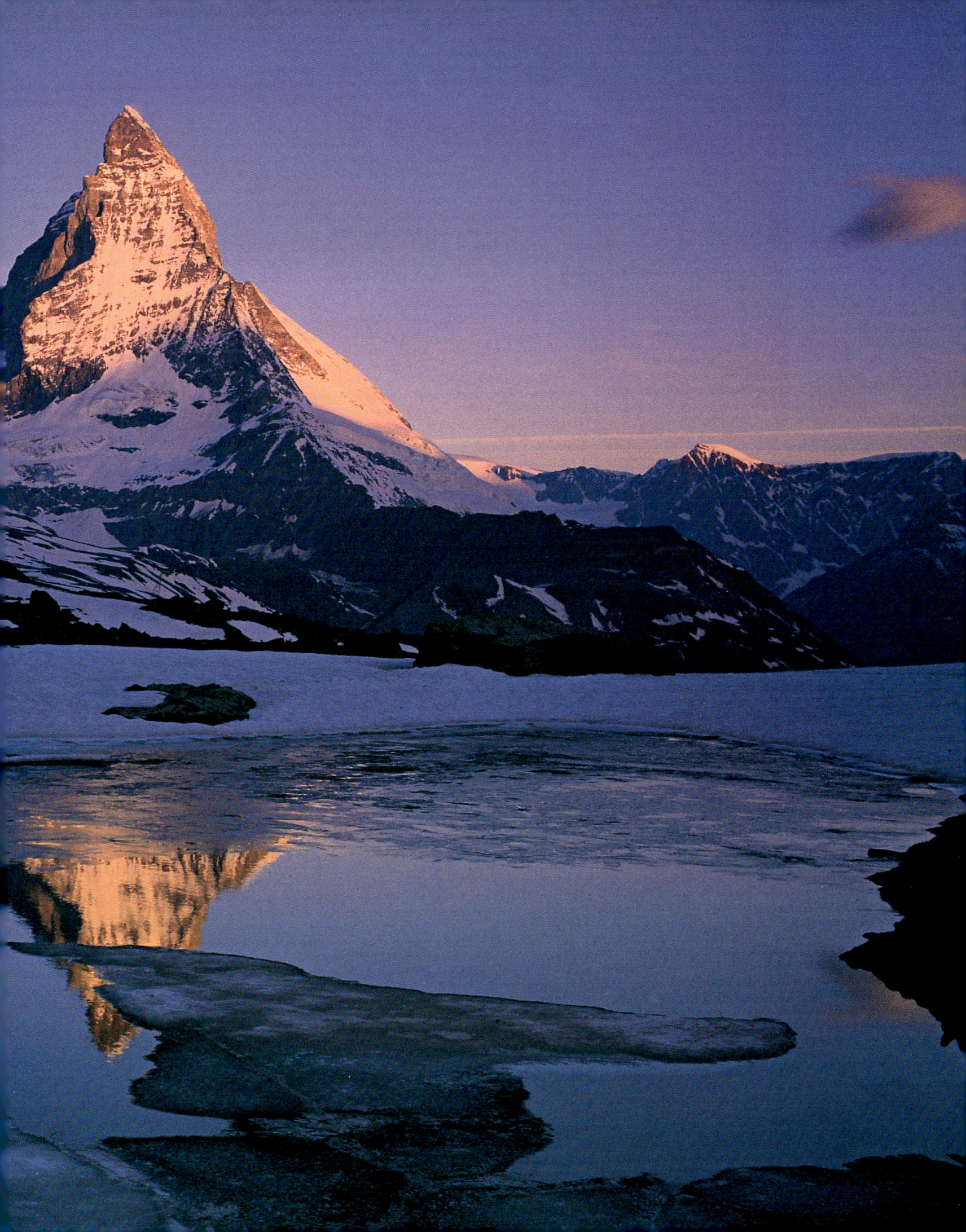

First page:
Jagged mountains, blue skies, Swiss chalets and brown cows happily chewing the cud: this and much more is Switzerland, here near Pohlern on the edge of the Bernese Oberland.

Previous double spread:
The Matterhorn appears almost mystical in the red glow of the sun. The north face, visible here, belongs to Switzerland; the south face is Italian. Its distinctive shape has not only made the seventh highest mountain in the Alps famous the world over but also Switzerland's national landmark, the symbol of which has travelled the globe on millions of boxes of Toblerone chocolate.

Right:
All done up for the yearly parade into the mountains, here on the Schwägalp in the canton of Appenzell-Ausserrhoden. Details are important when in May or June the village cattle is herded up to its lush summer pastures; the colours of the local dress and the pitch of the cowbells are all carefully coordinated to ensure that the procession is a success.

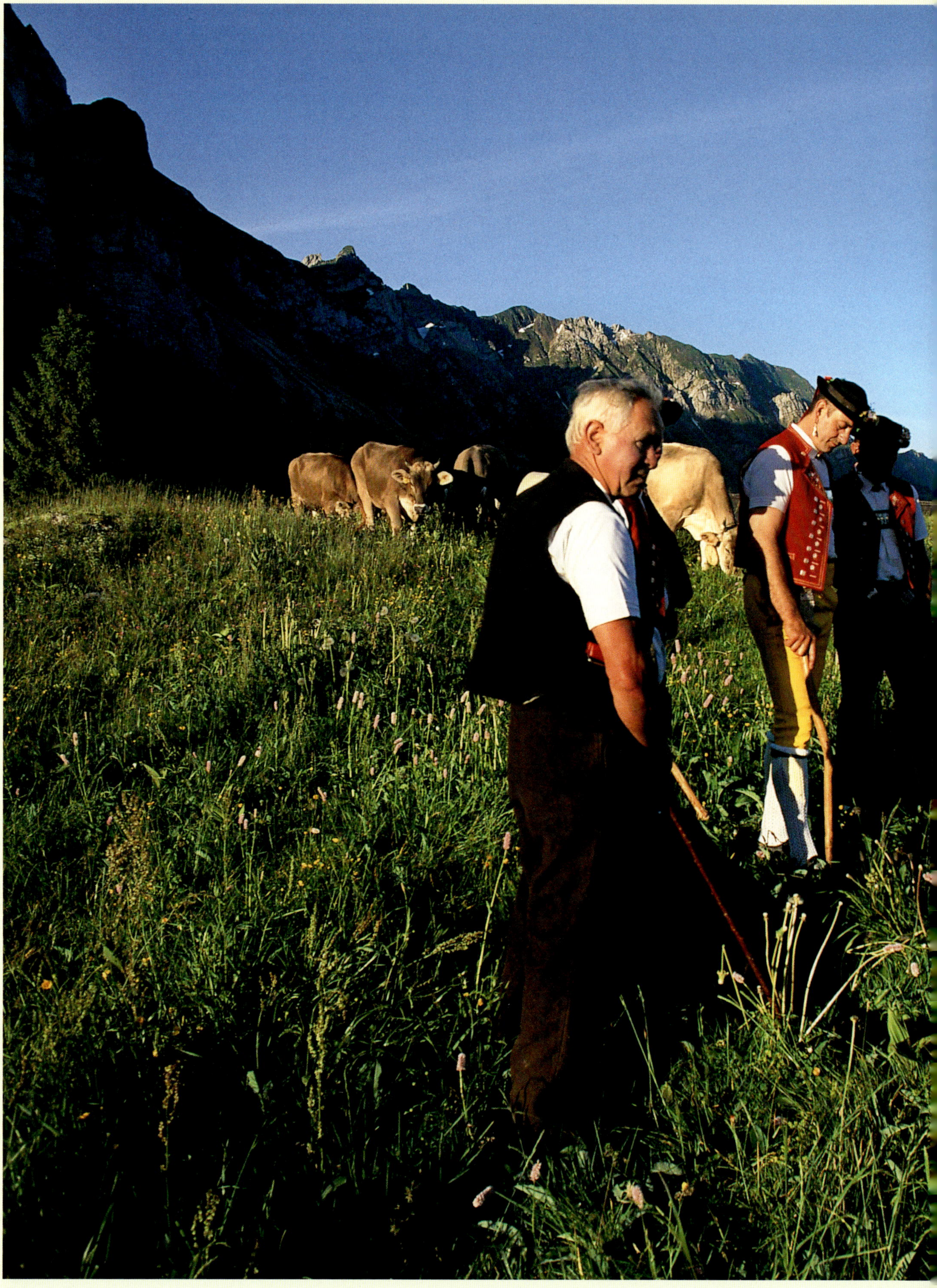

Page 10/11:
The mighty towers of Zürich's minster are visible for miles around. It's thought that the church goes back to the Carolingians; scientists have dated its foundations back to before 1100.

Contents

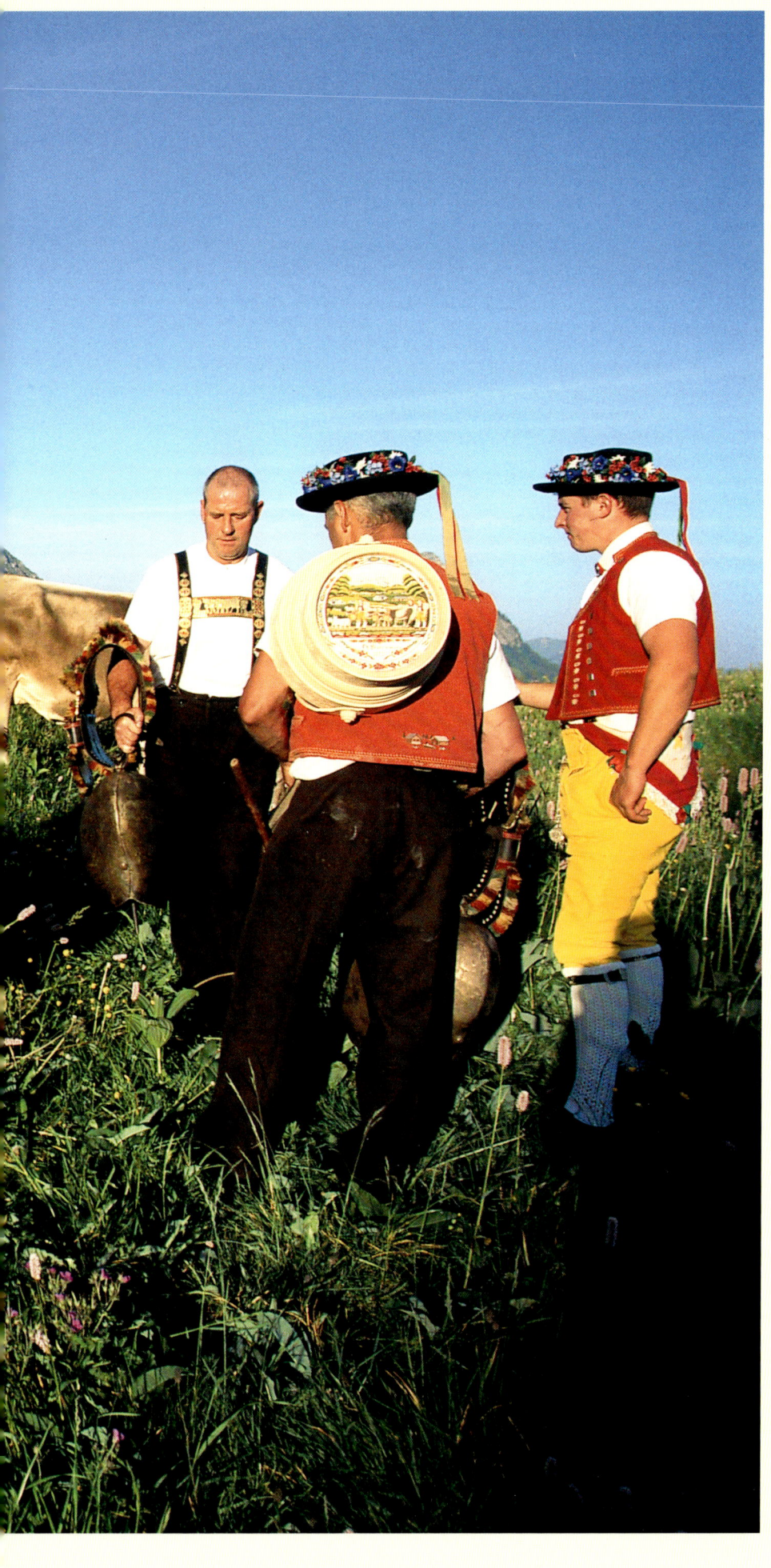

12

SWITZERLAND – DIVERSE YET STRONG

20

WESTERN SWITZERLAND – WHERE THE SWISS SPEAK FRENCH

36

THE SWISS HEARTLANDS – BIRTHPLACE OF THE CONFEDERATION

66

SVIZZERA ITALIANA – WHERE THE CONFEDERATION GOES MEDITERRANEAN

PAGE 90:   INDEX
PAGE 91:   MAP
PAGE 92:   CREDITS

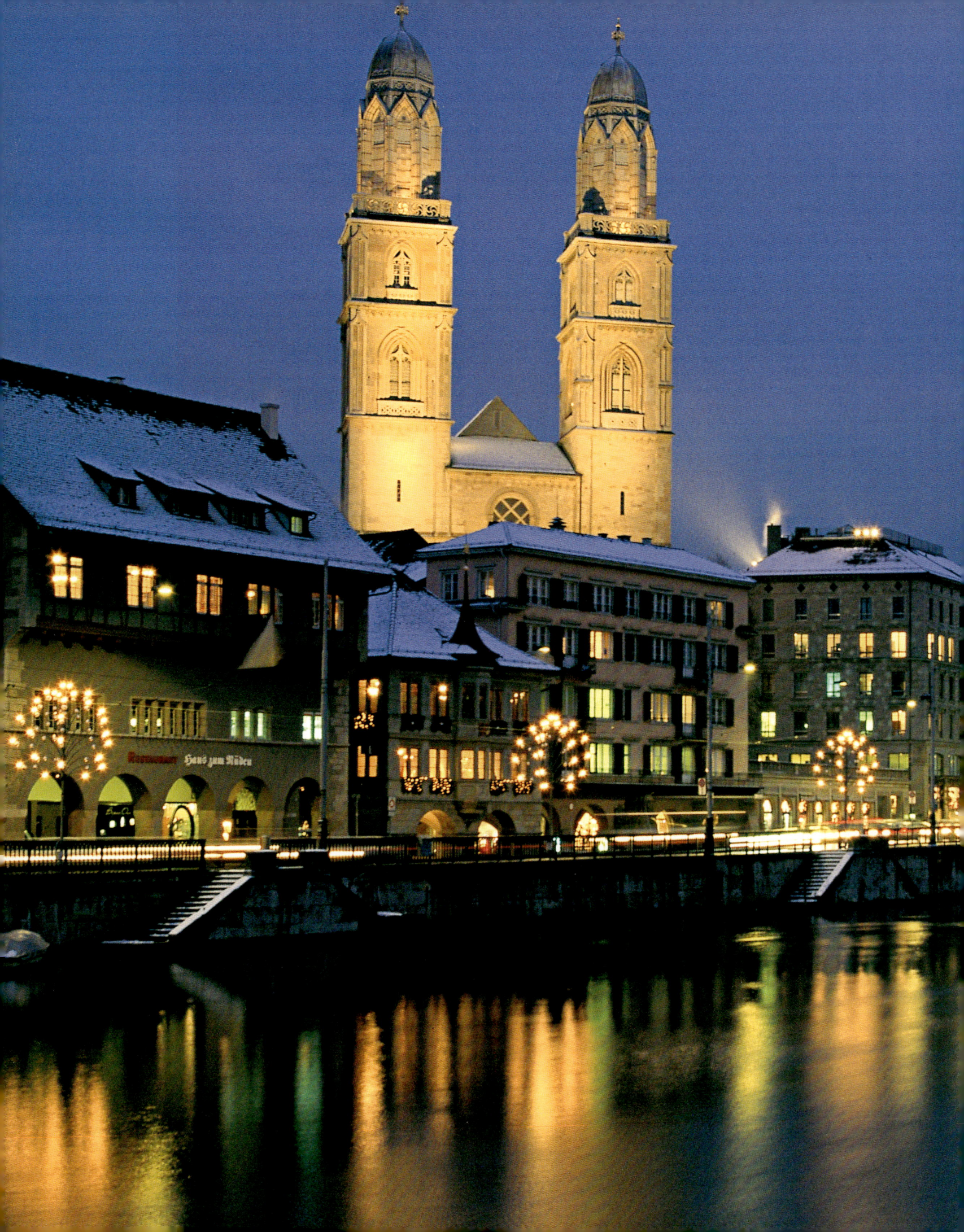

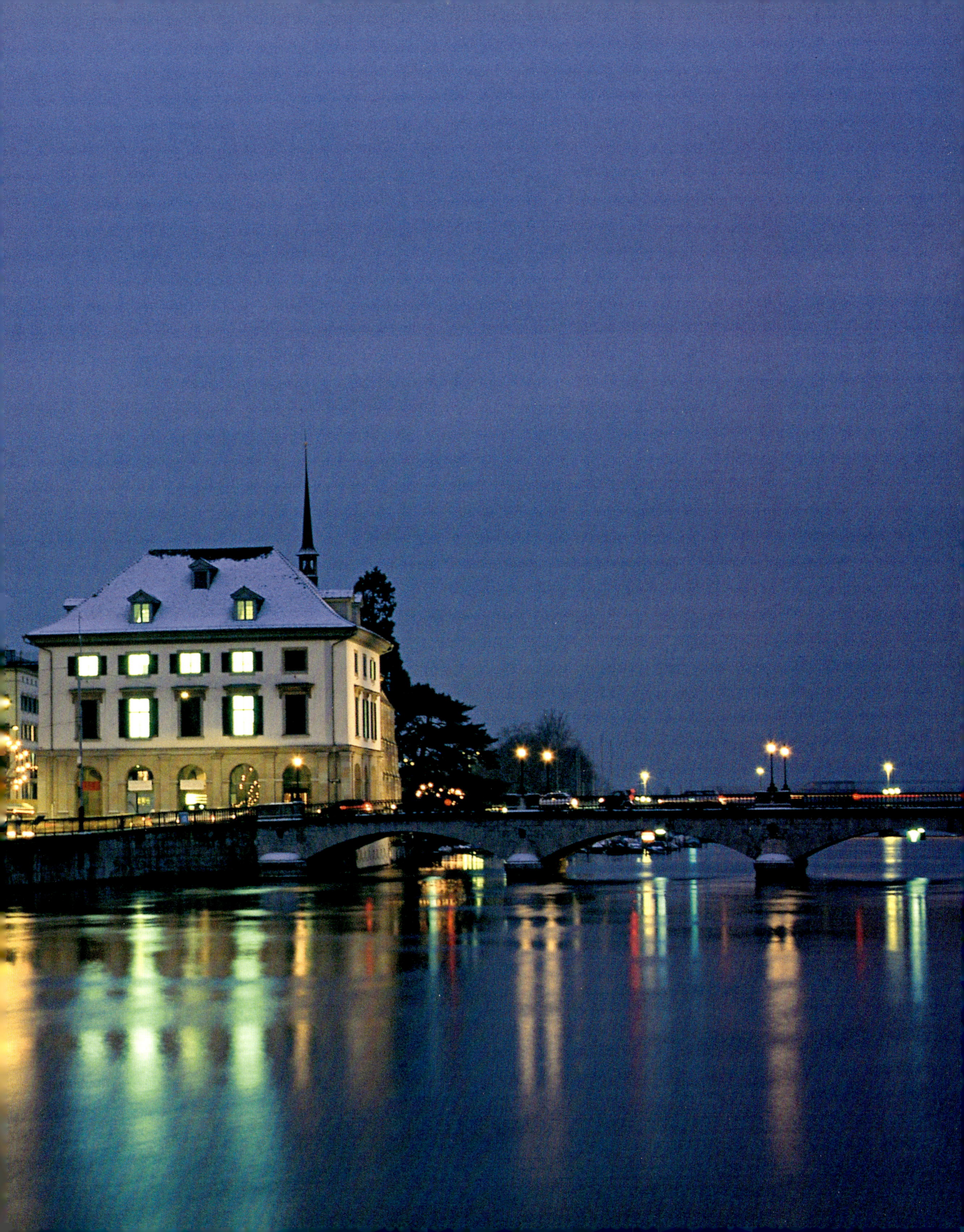

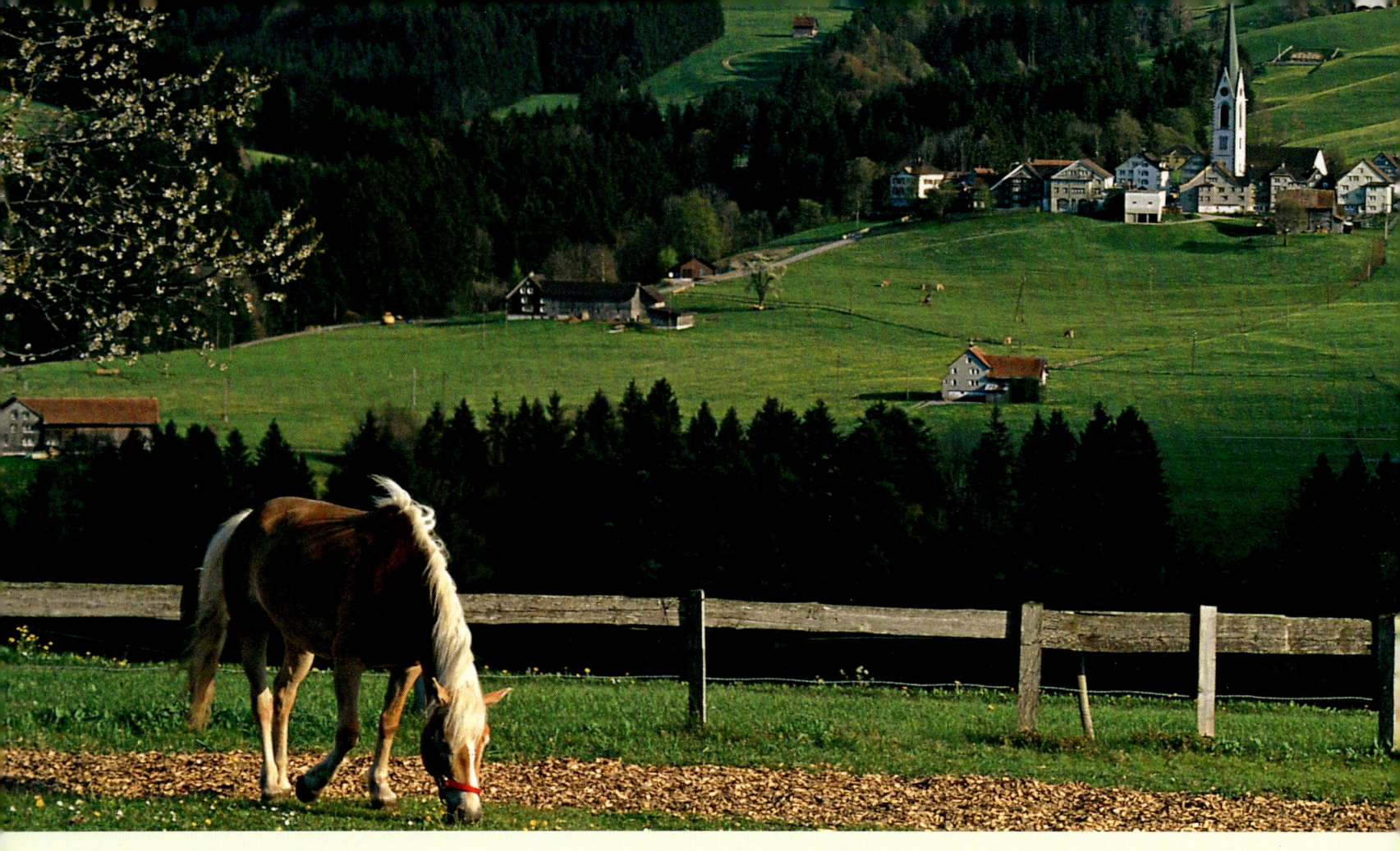

Switzerland – diverse yet strong

Chocolate, Swiss bank accounts, cuckoo clocks, mountains, political neutrality, precision tools and timepieces, round cheese with holes in it ... Be honest: what first springs to mind when Switzerland is mentioned? Just a lot of stereotypes? Maybe. But even these show that Switzerland is extremely diverse. As the much-cited legends will have it the three forest cantons of Uri, Schwyz und Unterwalden laid the foundations of the Swiss Confederation on a remote meadow high up above Lake Lucerne on August 1, 1291. Other regions soon joined them, many of them very different in their ethnological, religious and linguistic makeup. Each of these new Confederates contributed not just its own identity but also its particular strengths and skills to this loose alliance of states. Both have turned Switzerland into one of the most heterogeneous and economically powerful countries in the world, reflected in the healthy pride the Swiss have for their great little country.

Under the sign of the cross

Everywhere you go you are accosted by a white cross on a red background: the Swiss flag. This national emblem has become a cult symbol and can be found adorning designer clothes, penknives and fashion accessories. Swiss pride even has its own word: Swissness. And the strange thing about it is that it's directed inwards. The Swiss are delighted that the Confederation is still alive and kicking but don't particularly wish to force their national convictions on anybody else. The spirit of political neutrality most definitely lives on.

50 rounds for every Swiss man

Switzerland's neutrality is self-imposed, long-lasting and armed for conflict and has existed in practice since the defeat by France in the battle for the duchy of Milan in 1515, the last major military conflict in which Switzerland took part. Switzerland's neutral role has been internationally recognised since 1815. Unlike Austria, however, it has never been written into the national constitution – which has done nothing to curb its contribution to the Swiss consciousness. On the contrary: neutrality plays a significant part in the solidarity of the Swiss league and is a strong bond which unites the Swiss. Whether they still need to be armed, however, is often the subject of debate. There are frequent campaigns to abolish the army. In 1989 and 2001 plebiscites were held to this end, in which the Swiss voted to keep their soldiers. And they are well equipped for

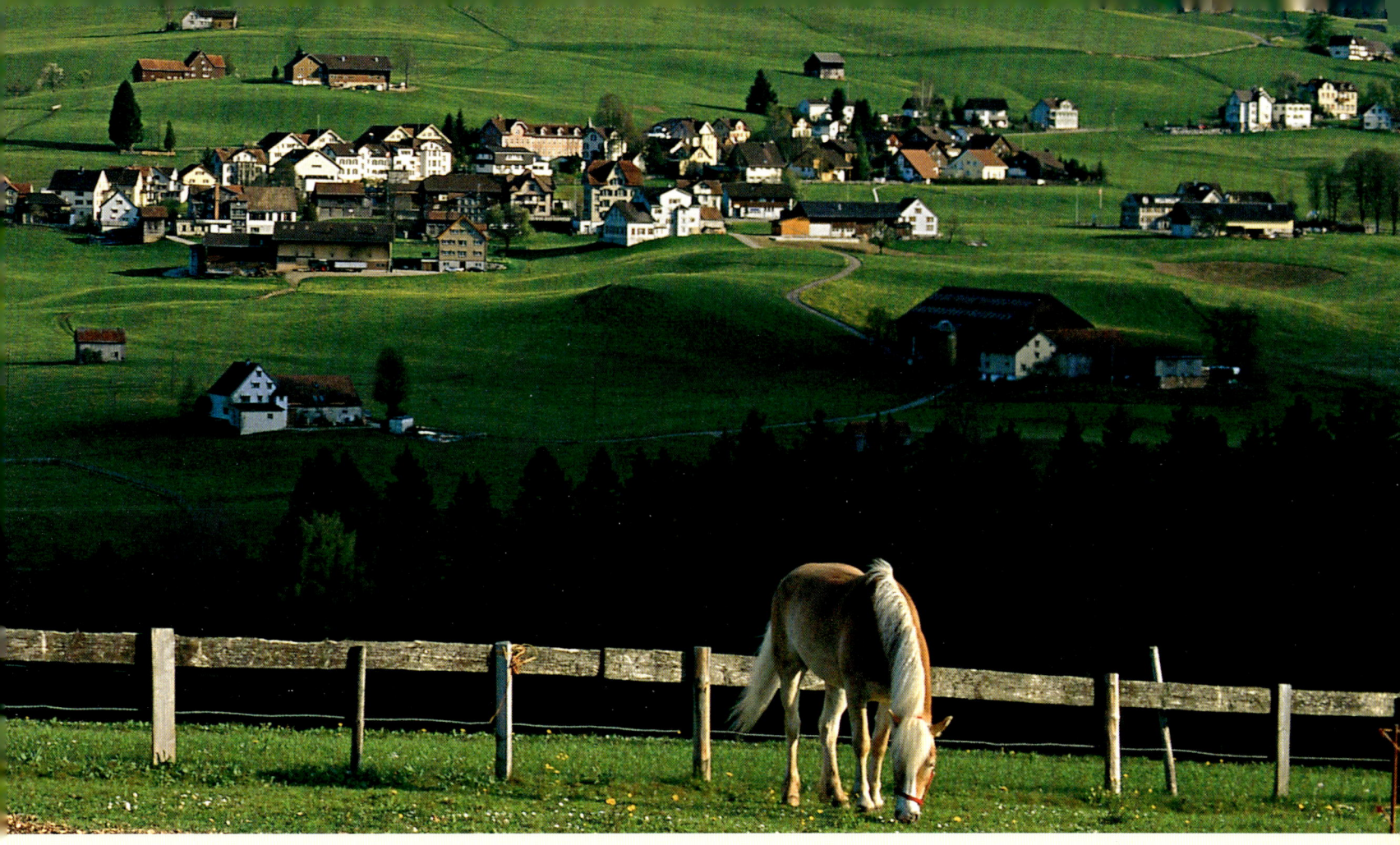

Above:
Hundwil in the hinterland of Ausserrhoden. Schwägalp is also part of the community from whence a lift transports visitors up to the top of the Säntis, the highest mountain in the east of Switzerland at 2,501 metres (8,205 feet) above sea level.

invasion. All those found fit for national service and trained as recruits are given a submachine gun and a sealed tin of 50 rounds of "war ammunition" to take home so that the country can quickly respond to a call to arms.

Referenda under the open sky
Before it came to war, however, there'd probably be the odd referendum or two. An army ever ready to jump to its defence is not the only myth which surrounds Switzerland. The country is also famous for its grass-roots democracy. In Switzerland all those eligible to vote are able to influence the course their country takes through petitions and plebiscites. In theory 100,000 signatures collected over the space of 18 months are enough to trigger a national petition for a change in the constitution. In practice the threat of this alone is enough to wake up the politicians and get them to suggest alternatives. Real grass-roots democracy is, however, only really practised in Switzerland in the cantons of Appenzell-Ausserrhoden, Appenzell-Innerrhoden and Glarus. This is where all those entitled to vote meet out under the open sky on a specific day to discuss and decide on various laws and decrees.

An inaugural document to keep the peace
In Switzerland a national state is not allowed to assume that everybody is the same and has the same concerns; it must instead take into account the local affairs and individual needs of its various citizens. If necessary each inhabitant must be requested to voice his or her opinion personally. This was undoubtedly uppermost in the minds of the three forest cantons of Uri, Schwyz and Unterwalden when they signed the inaugural document of the Confederation at the beginning of August, 1291; there were to be no paid external judges, with the most diplomatic of the gathering negotiating in the event of conflict and the others defending their judgement. Criminals were to be exiled. Following the death of King Rudolf I of Habsburg, upholding the status quo and maintaining peace throughout the land was the chief concern of the new Confederates – whose pact was much more than just a simple defence alliance. Despite their remoteness Switzerland's Alpine valleys were of tactical importance to the rulers of Germany. They coveted the mountain passes which secured their hold over Italy. Certain privileges were thus bestowed upon Inner Switzerland by German potentates in an attempt to curry favour with the Confederates.

The Swiss learn to fight
When in 1314 the Swiss supported the rival Bavarian candidate at the election of the new king, however, the Habsburgs were slightly disgruntled – to say the least. The infamous last straw in the affair was the tussle over Kloster Einsiedeln. The monastery in the canton of Schwyz was under the protection of the Habsburgs and laid claim to lands the Confederates could have put to better use themselves. Raids by the Swiss finally prompted Leopold I of Austria to wage war on the rebels, culminating in the Battle of Morgarten. Despite a clear majority in numbers

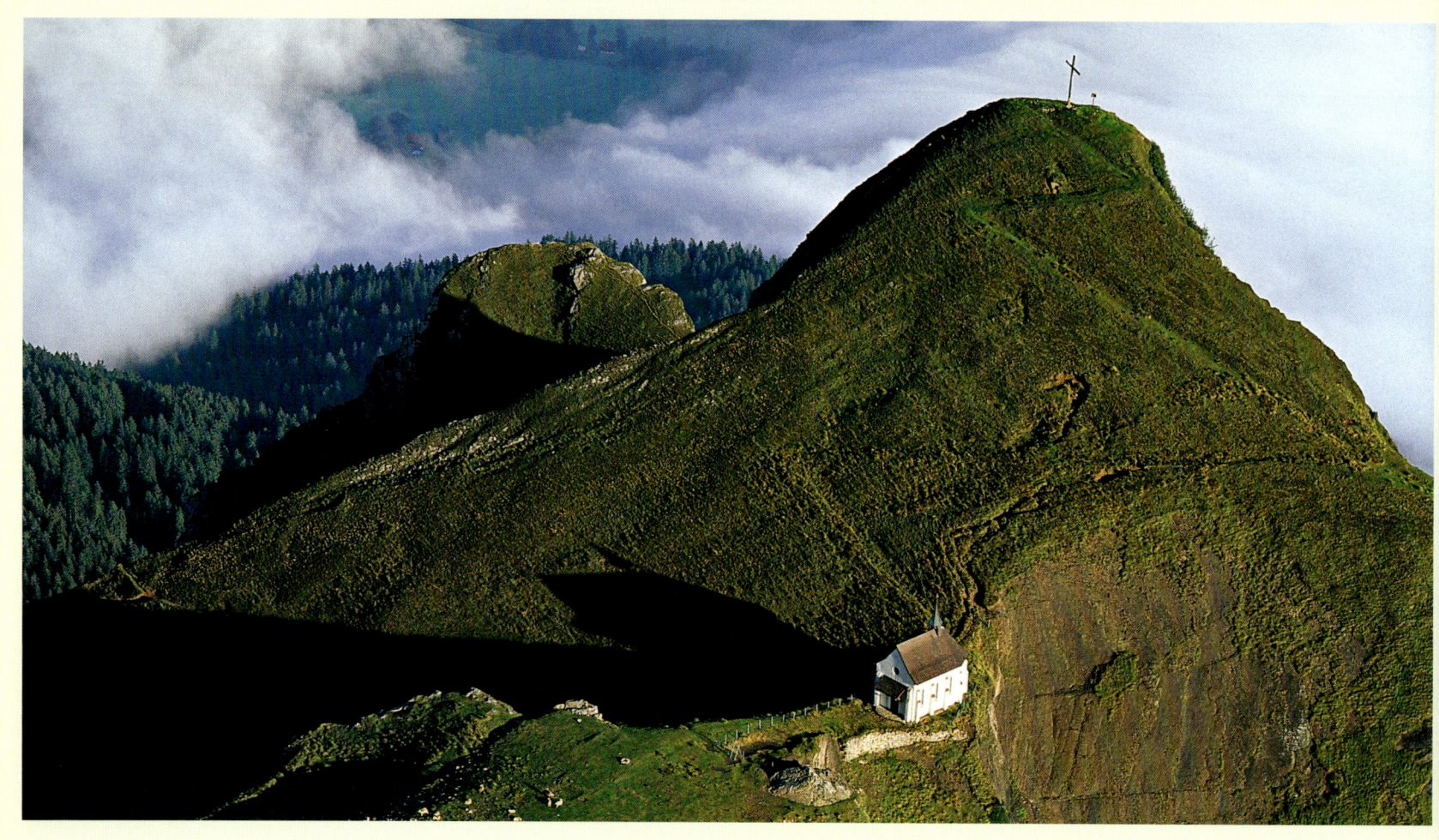

During the Middle Ages the Pilatus Massif near Lucerne was called Frakmont. Legend has it that its present designation stems from Pontius Pilate, the Roman procurator of Judea. On his death mighty storms blew up at each site chosen for burial; Mount Frakmont, constantly weathered by storms, was thus deemed the perfect place of interment. The Roman is said to have found his final resting place in the lake on the summit, now silted up (Lake Pilatus near Oberalp).

on the Austrian side the Swiss were victorious and the myth of Swiss invincibility was born. Immediately Lucerne, Zürich, Glarus, Zug and Bern joined the alliance, forming a league of the eight ancient cantons. In further battles the Swiss were able to drive the Habsburgs out of Switzerland altogether. In 1415 they even conquered the Habsburgs' ancestral lands. (Their ancestral seat, the castle of Habsburg, is situated near Brugg in the canton of Aargau). Several battles and alliances later, by 1513 the Confederation consisted of thirteen cantons, supplemented by various allies. And then in the religious turmoil which was to follow the political disunity of the cantons made itself felt. Some went with the Reformation, others remained Catholic. The Confederates eventually came to an agreement but were still powerless when on March 5, 1798, French troops marched into the country. In keeping with the ideals of the French Revolution a centralist state, the Helvetic Republic, was founded. It didn't last long. It did, however, form the basis of the Swiss Constitution of 1848 which superseded the formerly loose amalgamation of states built on coalition and alliance, creating a national state in its own right.

The "Rösti divide" splits the country

This, however, has done little to improve the homogeneity of the Swiss. There is even a humorous expression to describe their differing mentalities and opinions: one speaks of a country split by the "Rösti divide". The divide runs along the narrow valley of the River Sarine which forms the boundary to French-speaking Switzerland in the canton of Fribourg. Here the German *Röstigraben* becomes the French *Rideau de röschti* or the "iron Rösti curtain" – and on either side opinions differ, reflected in the way each party votes. Switzerland's Francophones are more open-minded towards other countries and the European Union when it comes to matters of foreign policy. Regulations by the state are met with less criticism here than on the German-speaking side of the invisible border. The Swiss Italians, on the other hand, are relatively impartial. They tend to go with French Switzerland on foreign affairs but share Swiss German opinions on other issues. And the *Rösti* themselves? These are the Swiss version of hash browns and used to be the staple breakfast fare of Swiss Germany's farming community. Today they are a national dish – and a culinary bone of contention. Here the Swiss are also divided: should *Rösti* be made with raw or cooked potatoes?!

High German on the decline

While we're on the subject of German-speaking Switzerland ... Many a tourist from Germany would laugh at the combination of the words "German-speaking" and "Switzerland". When the Swiss start talking in what they class as German, most 'real' Germans don't understand a word. In German Switzerland people speak *Schwytzerdütsch* or Swiss German – everywhere. On the radio the news and travel announcements are read in dialect, employees complain to their bosses in *Schwytzerdütsch*, in offices and even at school High German is often never spoken. Swiss High German is only written down on paper – and then often

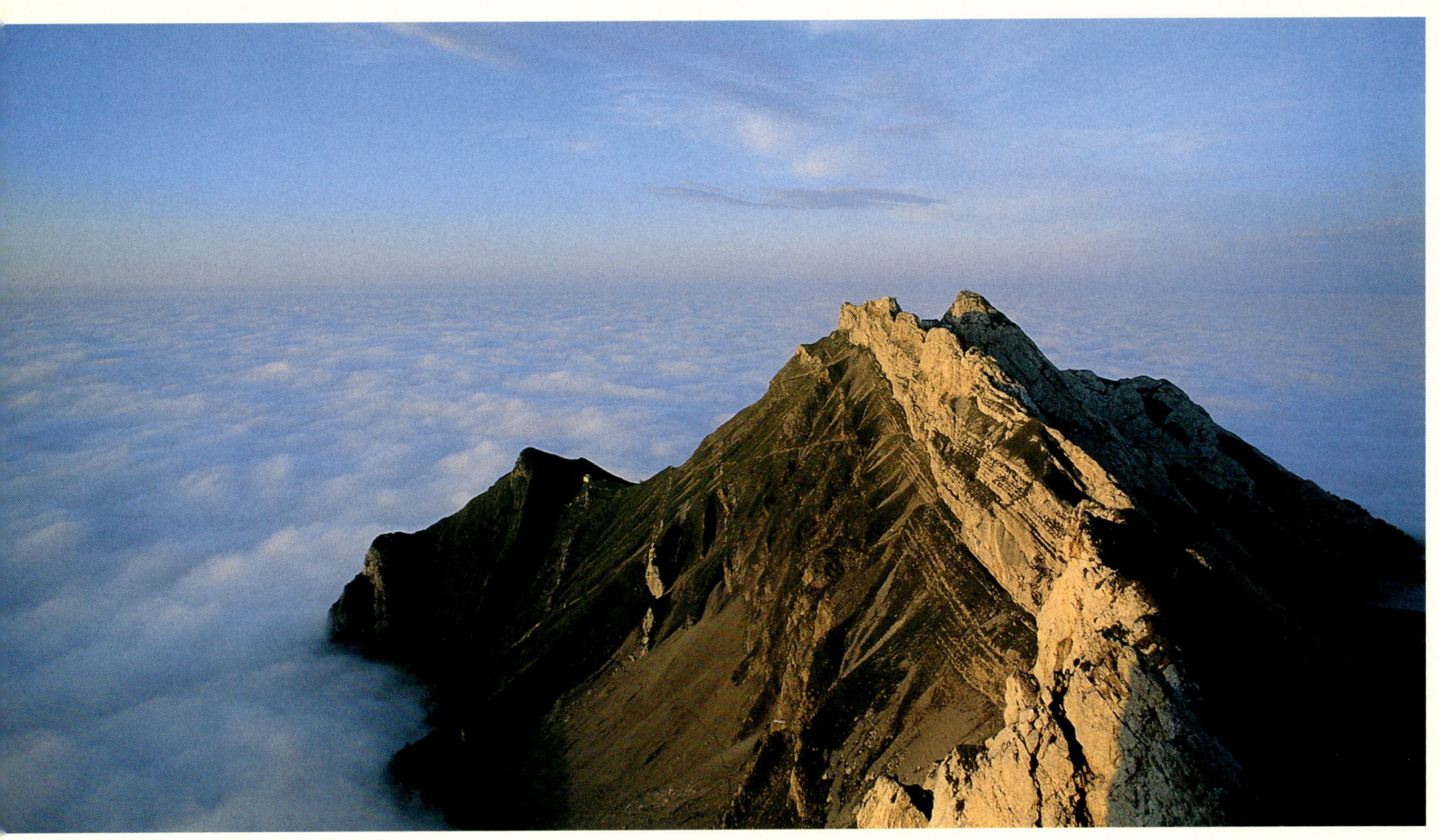

automatically converted into dialect when read aloud. Where in Germany the news on the radio is read in standard German even in the remotest parts of Bavaria, where people switch easily from dialect to High German, often in mid-sentence, for the Swiss this is a problem. They don't particularly like speaking High German and think of it as a foreign language. This often leads to conflict when it comes to communicating with their Swiss French, Italian and Romansch neighbours who learn standard German at school and can't understand *Schwytzerdütsch*. In the business world English has thus recently become the accepted common language.

Wrestlers, batters and stone throwers

One area where English or even High German are definitely not required are Switzerland's more unusual national sports with very Swiss designations, such as *Hornussen*, *Schwingen* or *Steinstossen*. The latter, "stone throwing", is exactly what it says; in heavyweight or 'king' class a stone weighing 83.5 kg (184 lb) is thrown in competition, with the burliest competitors able to hurl the rock four metres (13 feet) or more. *Schwingen* is another word for *Ringen* or wrestling, where the ring is a circle of sawdust up to 14 metres (46 feet) in diameter. *Hornussen* is a cross between cricket and baseball. A disc or *Nouss* weighing 78 grams (ca. 3 ounces) is hit by a batter from one team as far as possible across the trapeziform pitch while the opposite team tries to stop it in mid-flight with wooden slats held or thrown up in the air.

Access through the mountains

Of the ca. 41,000 square kilometres (15,830 square miles) which constitute Switzerland today 60% are in the Alps, making the country absolute paradise for nature lovers. The scenic spectacles which cause them to utter cries of delight and wonder, however, pose something of a challenge to the modern Swiss state. With every valley needing to be made accessible some clever engineering is called for. One such feat is the Great St Bernhard Pass, once a major Roman transit route, which negotiates a giddy climb of over 2,400 metres (7,870 feet). Today there are few villages which are not linked up to Switzerland's dense network of roads. With 3,652 kilometres (2,269 miles) of standard-gauge track the country also has the densest railway network in the world – with only 11 kilometres (7 miles) not electrified. The network is so efficient that in places not reachable by road access is provided by rail – and in some cases only by cable car!

Feats of engineering for faster connections

In recent years more and more importance has been attached to the railways in an attempt to spare man and his Alpine habitat further pollution through car exhausts. This is one reason why the Swiss are currently devoting all of their engineering skills to the NEAT project (the Neue Eisenbahn-Alpentransversale or NRLA, New Railway Link through the Alps). Major tunnels through both the Lötschberg and Gotthard are to provide the Swiss with fast connections to

Pilatus Mountain is not only of interest as the subject of legend; the Pilatus-Bahn, the steepest rack railway in the world, climbs a gradient of 48% to the summit at 2,070 metres (6,791 feet). The Pilatus can be reached from Lucerne by two cable railways. On a clear day there are grand views of Lake Lucerne from the top – where there is also good paragliding, a summer toboggan run and the longest playable alpenhorn in the world.

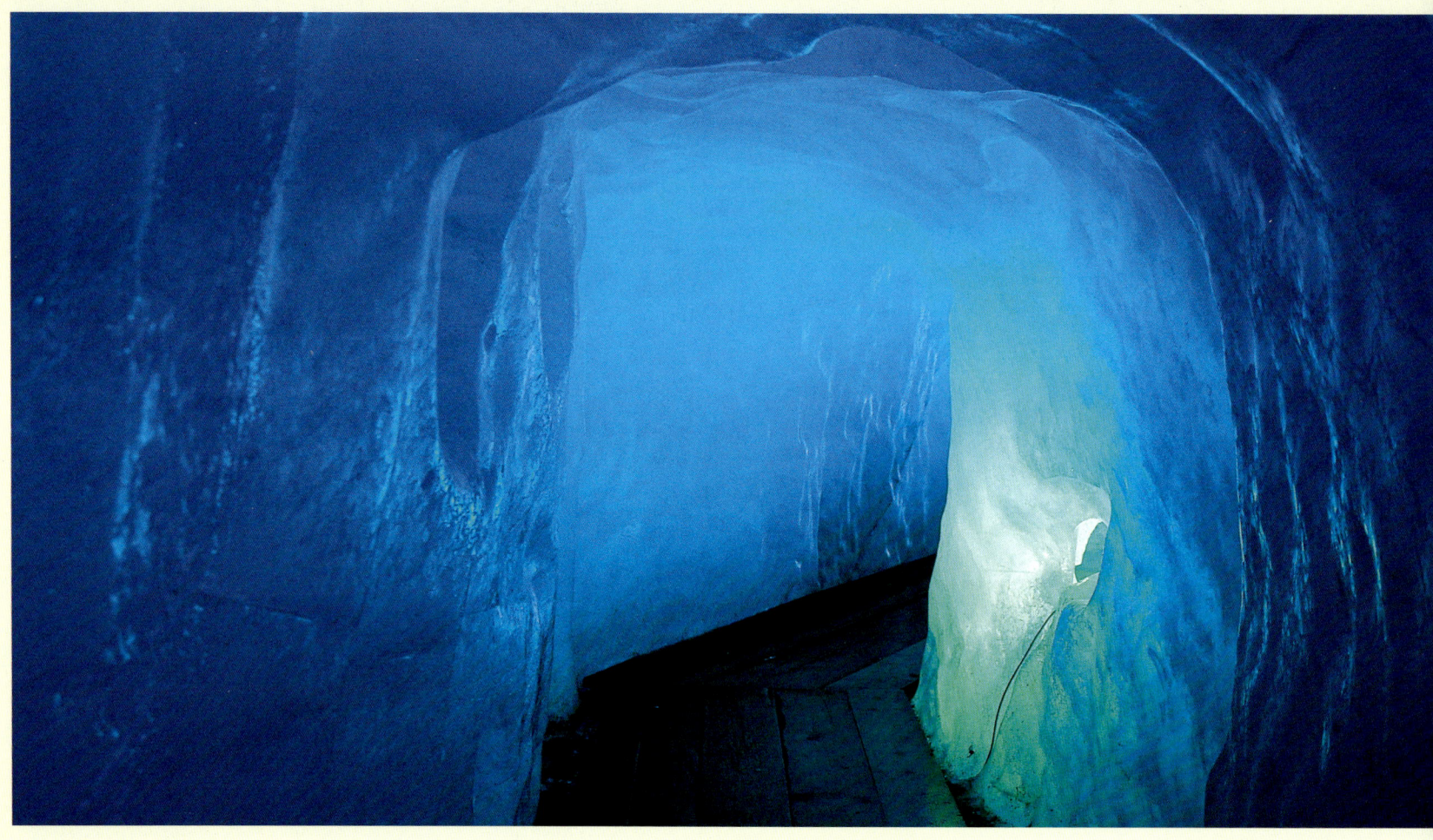

Above:
The brilliant blue ice grotto in the Rhône Glacier is ca. 2,300 metres (7,546 feet) above sea level and was first carved out of the ice over 120 years ago. The ice moves ca. 30 to 40 metres (100 to 130 feet) per annum, calling for the grotto to be renewed once a year.

Right page:
Lake Sils is reliably windy, making it popular with surfers. In Sils in the Engadine where the lake can be found both German and Romansch are spoken, the lake's Romansch name being Lej da Segl.

Page 18/19:
The Bernina Express, here near Morteratsch, is the pride and joy of the Rhätische Bahn. It was launched in 1973 as an independent rail service geared towards tourists.

Italy in the hope that in ten years heavy vehicle traffic will have been shifted from road to rail. At 57 kilometres (35 miles) long the new tunnel underneath the Gotthard Pass will be the longest in the world. The date of completion is set for 2015 when trains will be able to zoom through the mountain at up to 250 kilometres (155 miles) an hour. In the narrow bends of the old Gotthard Tunnel speeds are limited to 80 kilometres (50 miles) an hour and the narrow curve radii and steep gradients mean that goods trains may not be too heavy. 41 railway tunnels and 38 road tunnels already cut through Switzerland's mountains, with five more for trains and 13 for cars currently under construction. It's almost as if the Swiss were bent on making their mountains as holey as their cheese.

Milk – and what the Swiss make from it
And they don't come much holier than Emmental cheese, the holes made by bubbles of carbon dioxide emitted during the maturation process which can take anything from three to twelve months. The more symmetrical the holes, the better the cheese. It gets its flavour from fodder munched by contented cows on Alpine pastures: lush green grass and wild flowers and herbs. Cheese manufacture is tradition in Switzerland. Even the Romans had cheese with holes in it sent to them from the far side of the Alps. Today about half of Switzerland's milk production is used to make cheese. Much of the other half is the chief ingredient of something much sweeter: chocolate. The confectionery trade may not be as old as Switzerland's cheese dairies but like the cheese industry it was certainly a trend setter, with Swiss chocolate being rapidly acclaimed the world over.

Precision and innovation
Besides cheese and chocolate there is another top, typically Swiss export which is still very much up to the minute; Longines, Rolex, Omega and IWC are just a few of the country's famous watchmakers. The precision of Swiss timepieces is legendary. Neil Armstrong took his first steps on the moon in 1969 with a Swiss watch on his wrist: an Omega Speedmaster Professional. NASA had chosen it for its reliability even in extreme conditions. The clockmakers of Switzerland have also given us the watch as a fashion accessory in the form of the Swatch. Vibrant designs in plastic positively called for more: a second watch to go with your favourite shirt, jeans or dress. Hence the name Swatch which stands for Swiss Watch or Second Watch.
Eccentric innovation coupled with tradition and a keen nose for business: the Swatch seems to exemplify everything which is Swiss. This small country in the heart of Europe knows how to use its assets and abilities to its best advantage – and in doing so will always confidently go its own way.

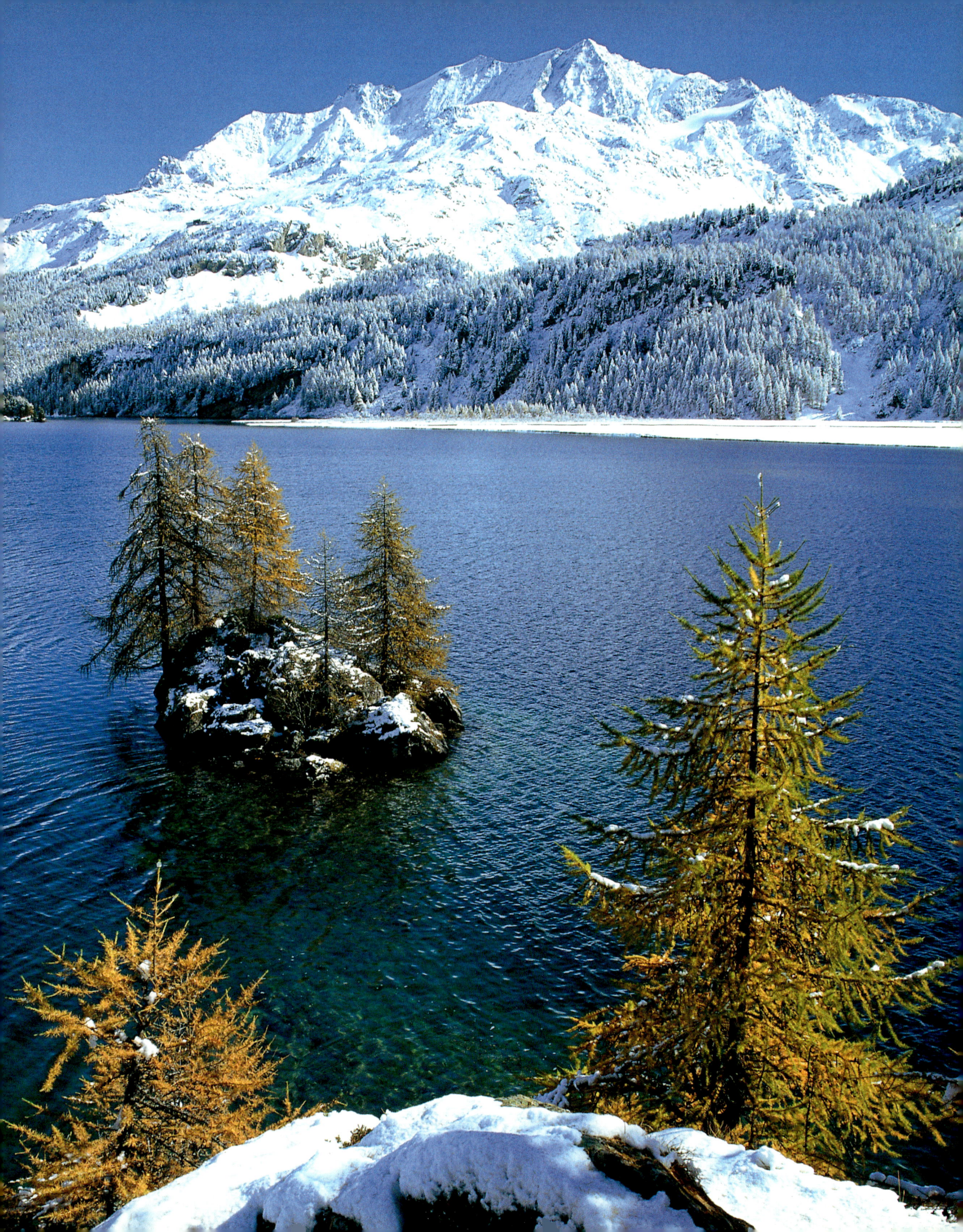

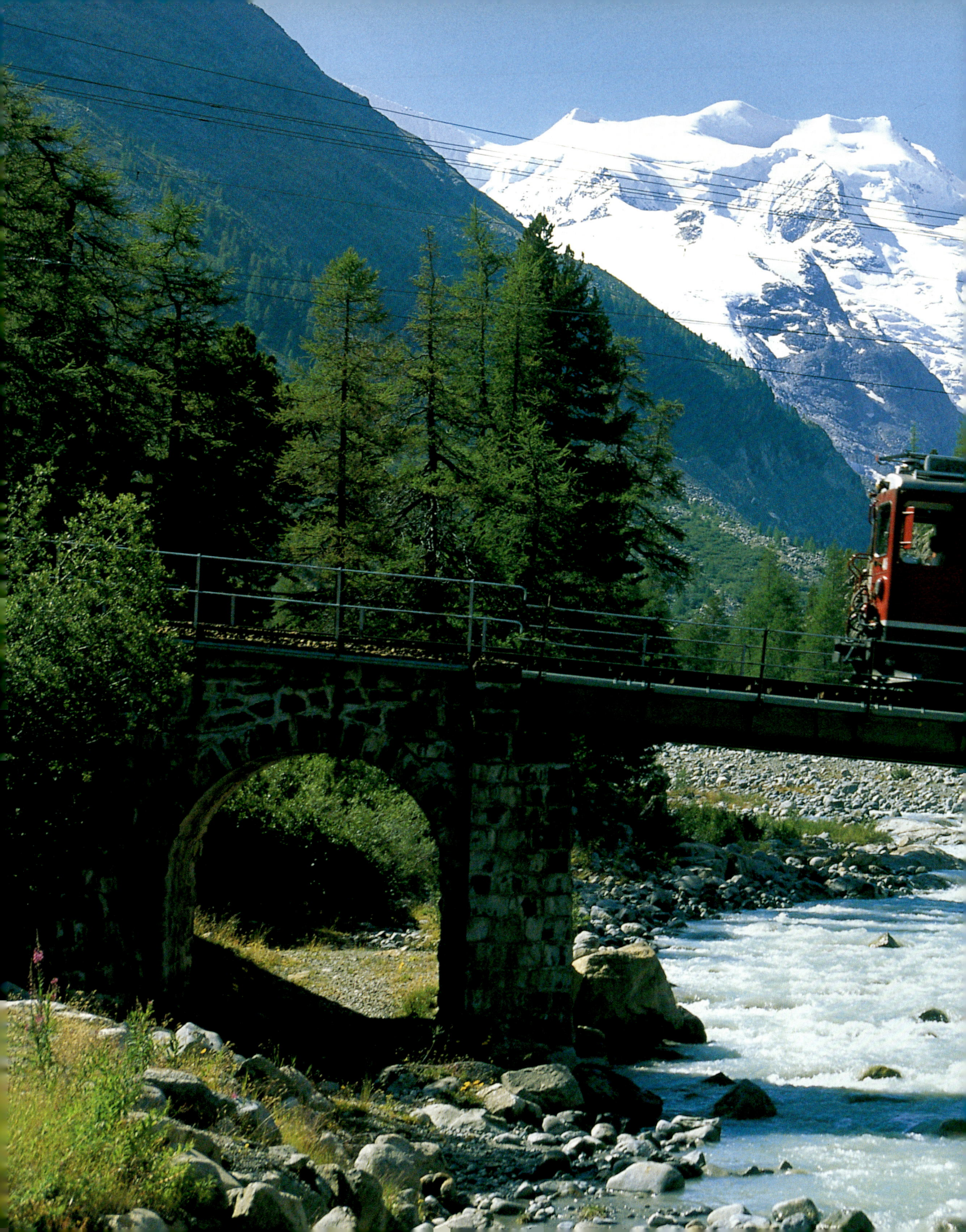

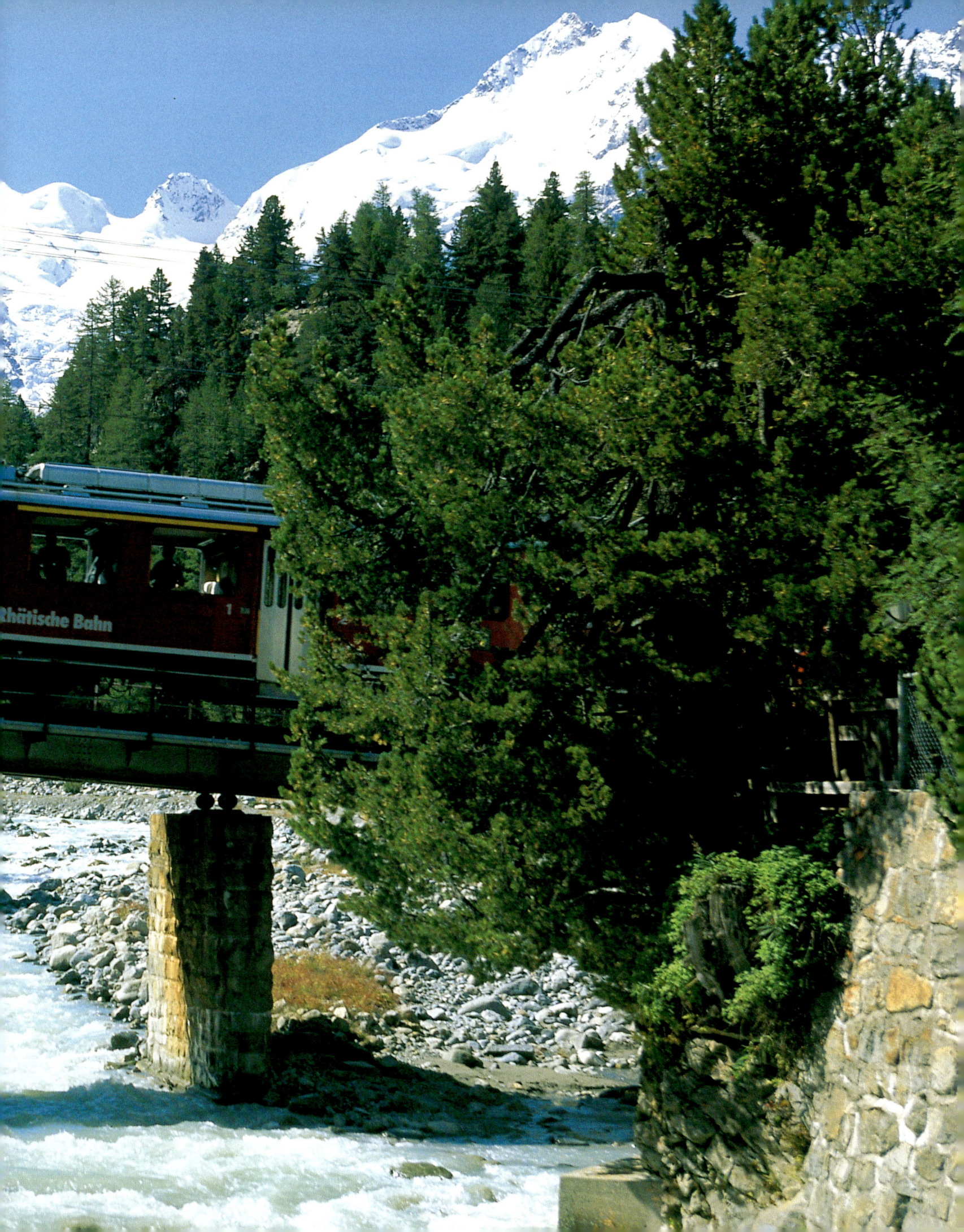

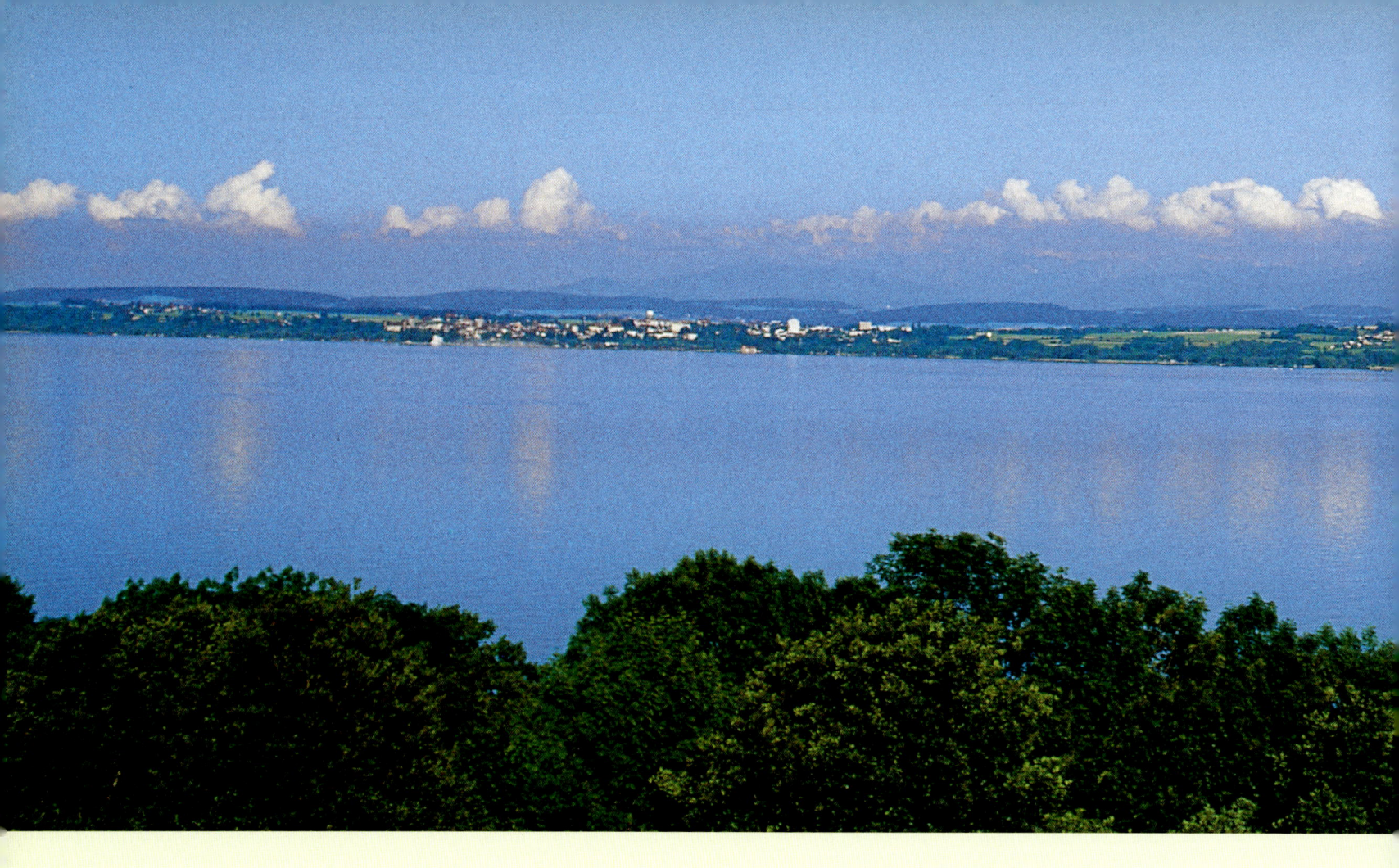

Western Switzerland – where the Swiss speak French

It's eerie how quickly you cross the invisible border. Just a minute ago the ads on the billboards were in German; now they're touting their wares in French. And once you get to Fribourg in the valley of the Sarine, asking the way to the nearest public toilets in your best school German will only earn you a uncomprehending shrug of the shoulders. 63.6% of the inhabitants of Fribourg have French as their mother tongue and call themselves *Suisses romands*. The people of western Switzerland clearly distinguish themselves from their German-speaking Swiss neighbours – yet do not identify with France. For many years much of French Switzerland belonged to the kingdom of Burgundy which had a strong Catholic culture. French-speaking Switzerland is no longer so homogenous. The differences between the cantons of Genève and Valais are considerable, as are those between Fribourg and Neuchâtel. The linguistic boundary runs through the middle of Valais; north of the Rhône it hugs the course of the Raspille and to the south the contours of the Finges Forest. France almost completely engulfs the French-speaking canton of Genève, which is considered liberal – despite its 45 administrative districts enjoying less autonomy than their counterparts in the rest of French Switzerland. Another anomaly is the Protestant majority of Vaud, the canton next to Genève. Yet both profit equally from the tourism on Lake Geneva, the largest lake on the edge of the Alps (the second largest is Lake Constance) whose French name Lac Léman dates back to the Roman word for the country surrounding it, Lemanus.

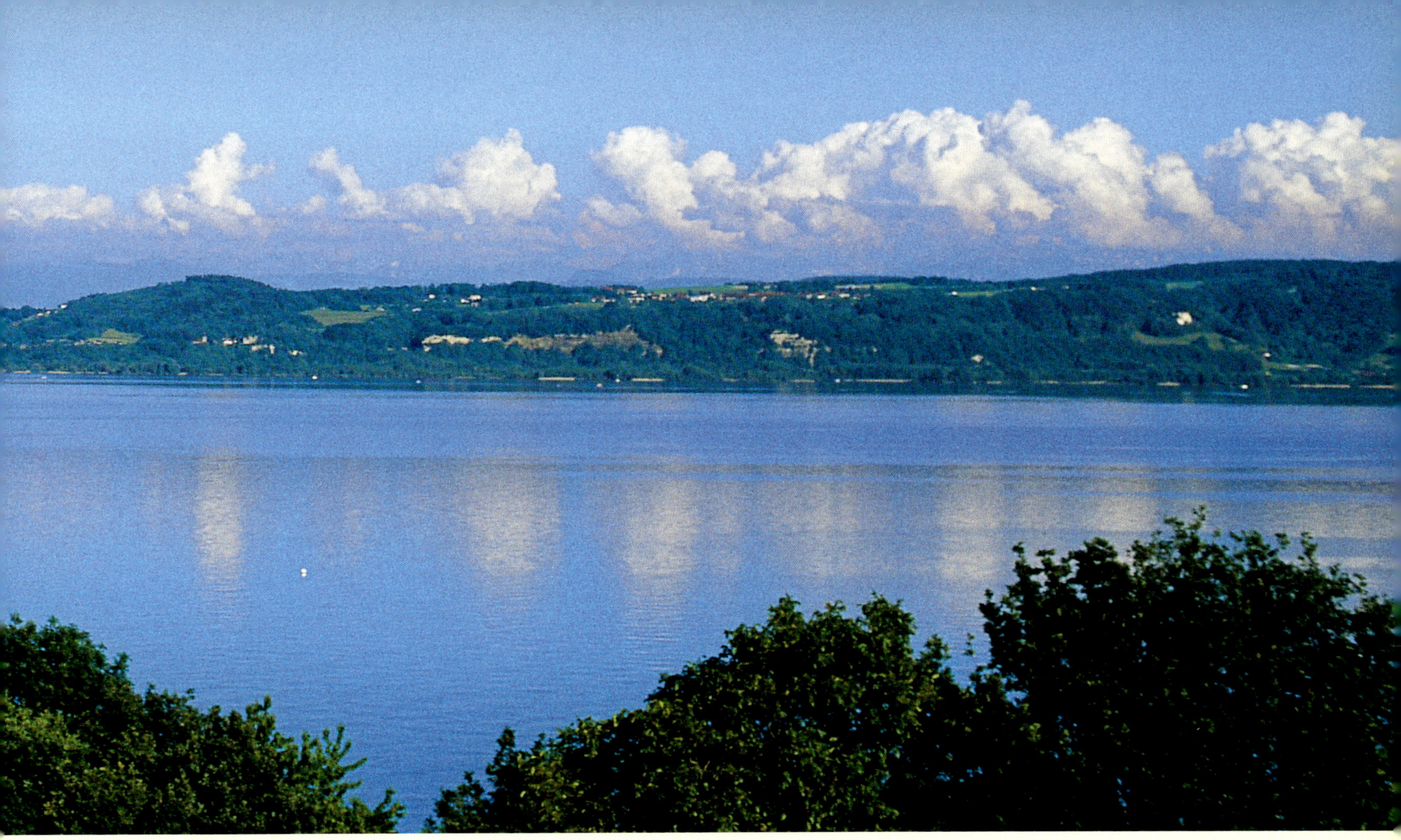

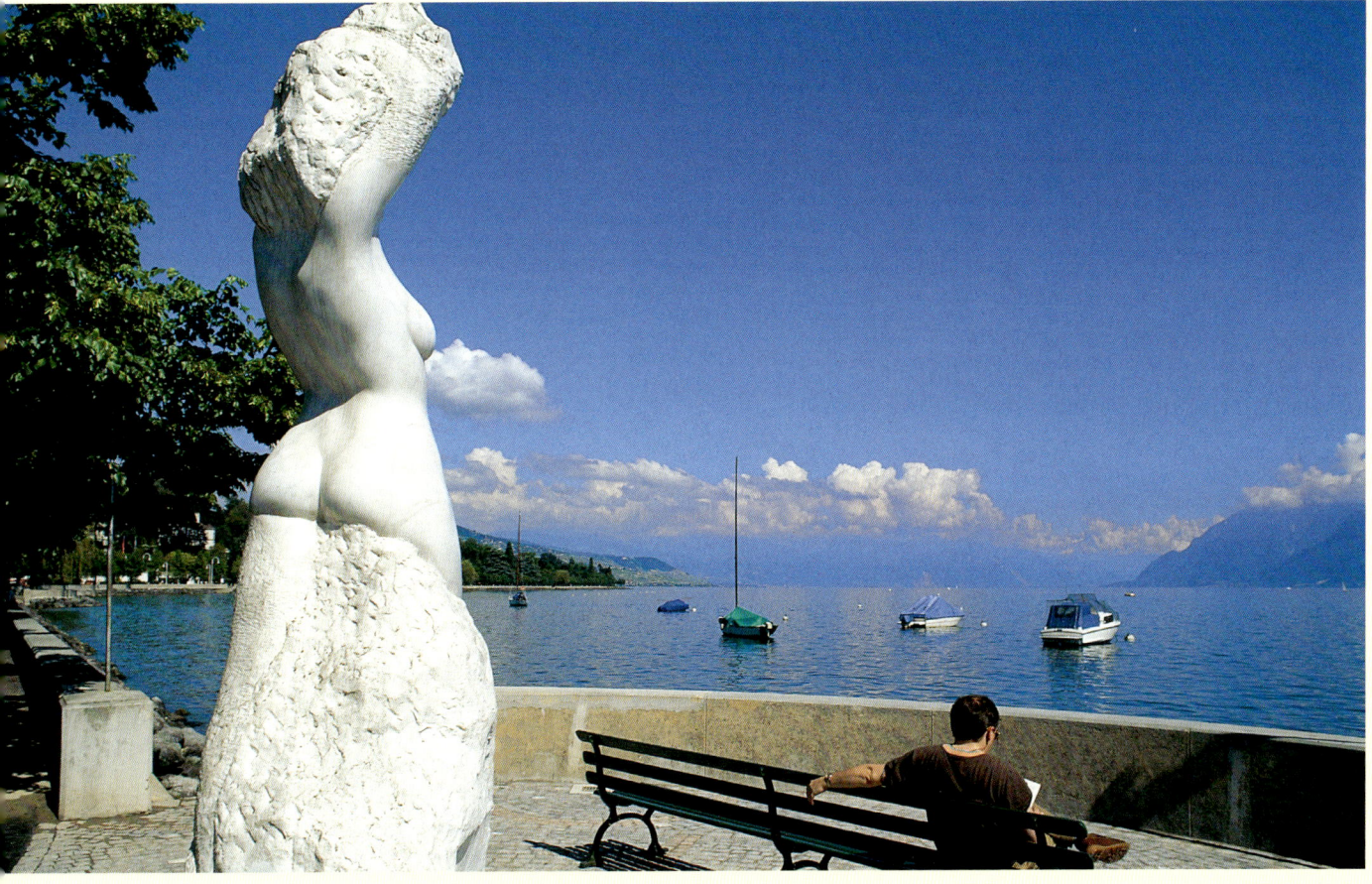

Above:
At 218 square kilometres (84 square miles) Lac de Neuchâtel is the biggest lake to lie entirely in Switzerland. It's so large that it stretches across the three French-speaking cantons of Neuchâtel, Fribourg and Vaud and also the multilingual canton of Bern.

Left:
Lac Léman is the French name for Lake Geneva. At up to 310 metres (1,017 feet) deep, Lake Geneva is the lake with the most water in Central Europe.

21

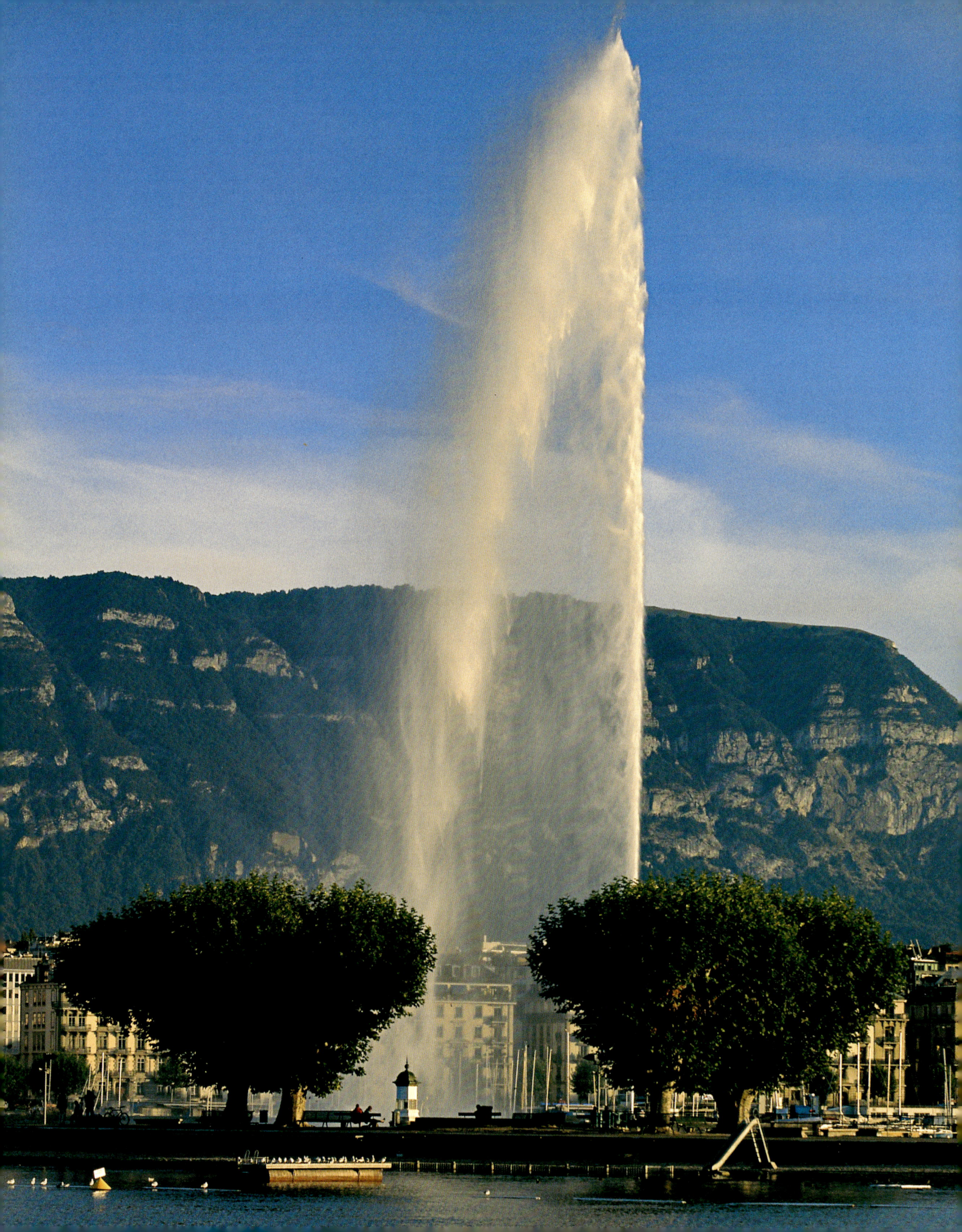

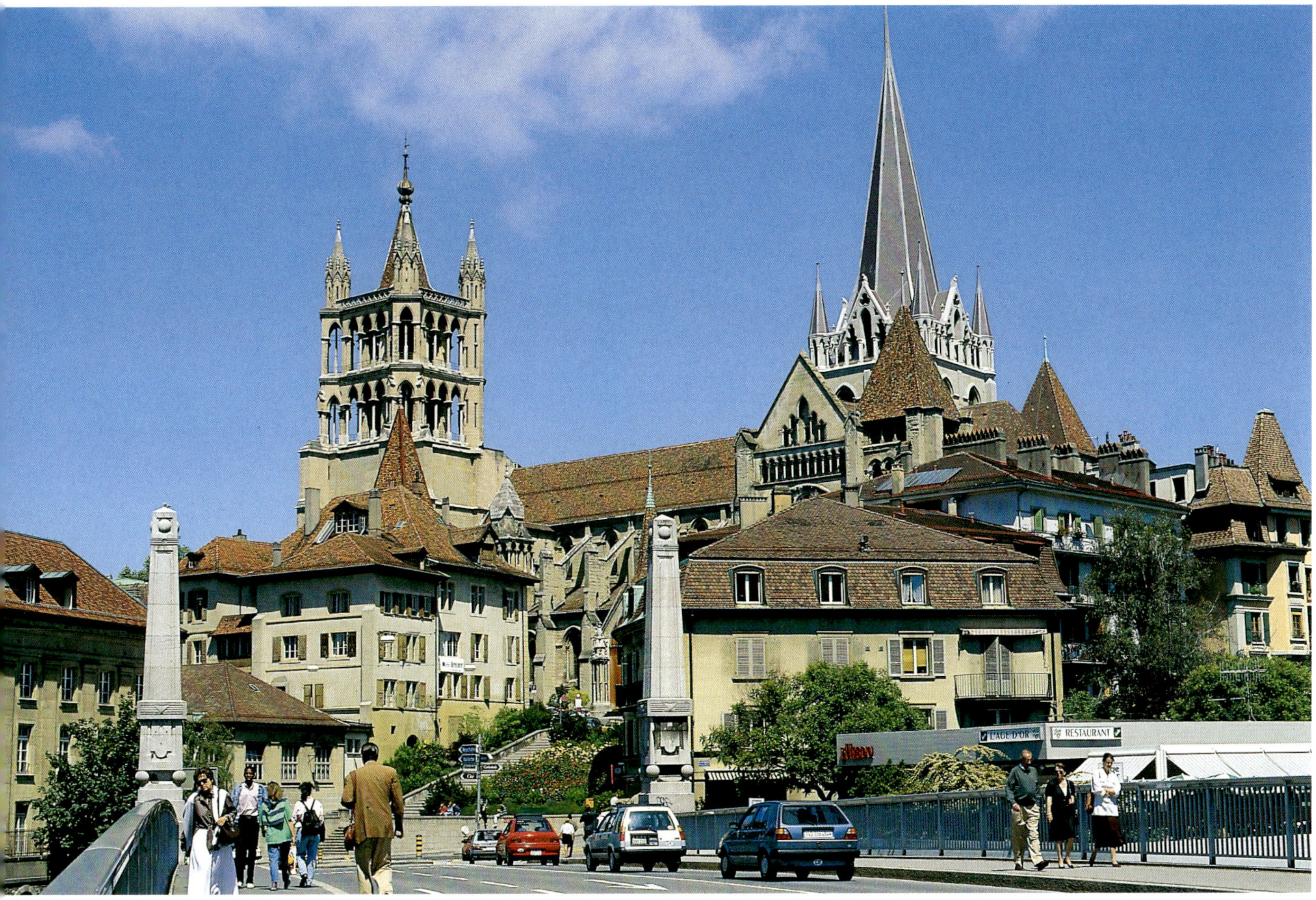

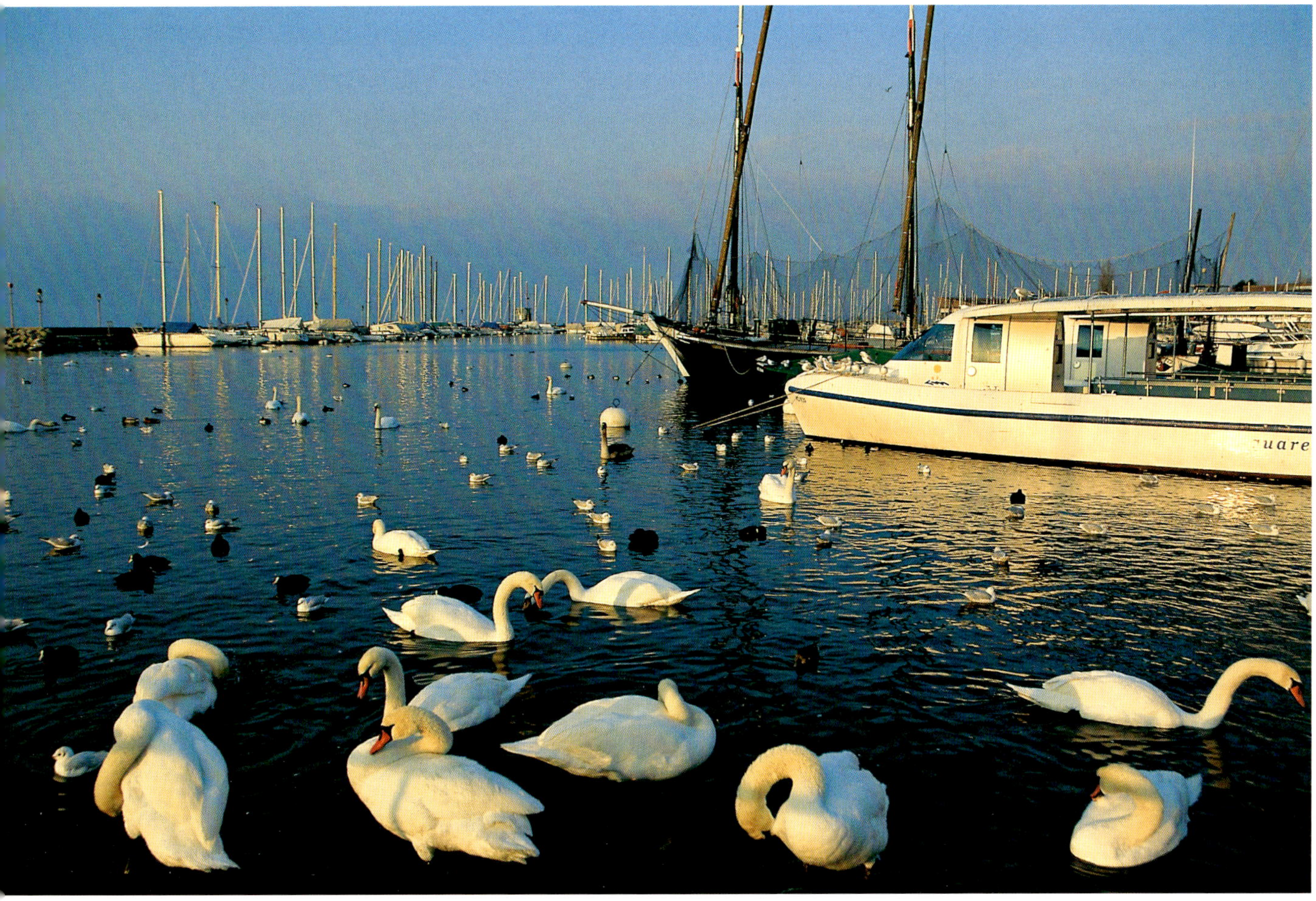

Left page:
UNO, CERN, ICRC, WHO, ILO, ITU, WIPO, WMO, WOSM and UNHCR: countless international organisations with cryptic acronyms have chosen Geneva as their headquarters. The second largest city in Switzerland after Zürich, Geneva's local landmark is its giant Jet d'Eau fountain.

The International Olympic Committee (IOC) and various other world associations are based in Lausanne, making the city the unofficial capital of sport. Up above the town its enormous cathedral straddles a hill where in the 3rd century AD a small community of craftsmen became established.

Ouchy is Lausanne's traditional harbour on the shores of Lake Geneva, flanked by grand hotels put up in the 19th century.

Page 24/25:
Le Châtelard takes its name from the castle of the same name. The amalgamation of 17 villages and hamlets is now part of the political community of Montreux. Montreux itself is synonymous with music, famous the world over for its annual jazz festival and also its mild climate which allows subtropical plants to thrive along the shores of Lake Geneva.

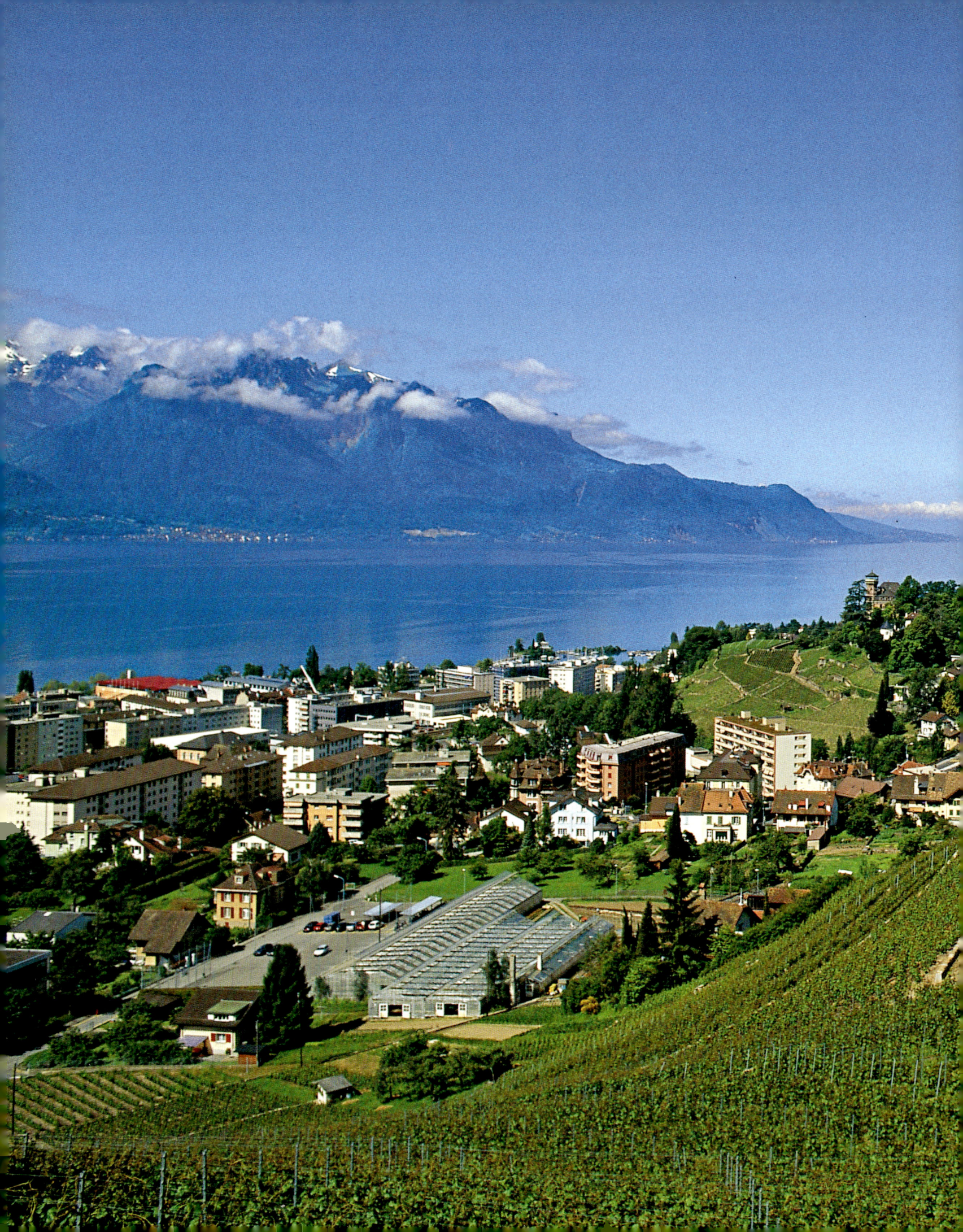

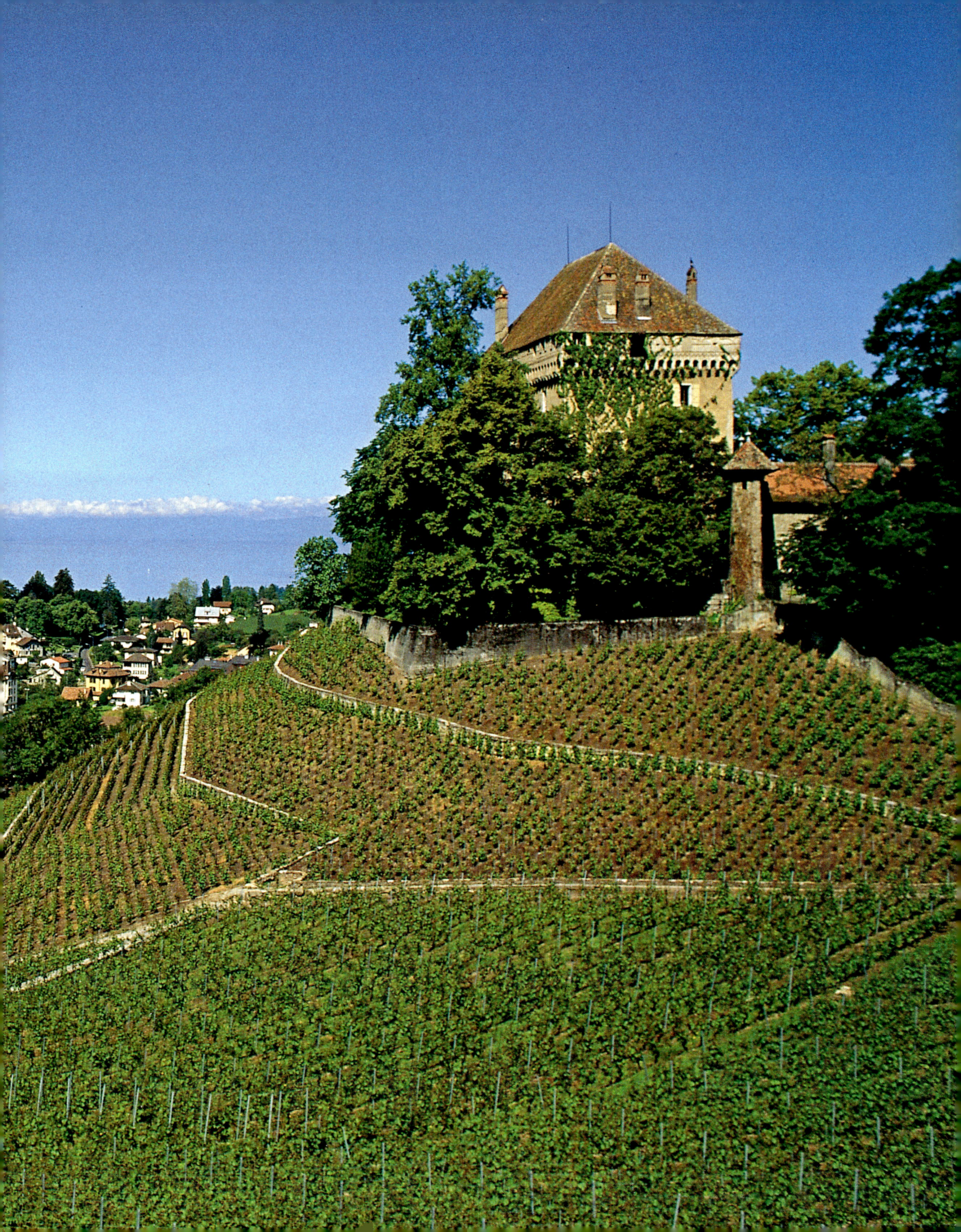

Château Chillon clinging to a rocky spur on the edge of Lake Geneva is a popular and picturesque motif, the oldest visible parts of which date back to the 11th century. The castle was almost torn down during the 19th century and used in the building of the railway. Only the indignant protest of a historically minded politician saved the edifice from destruction.

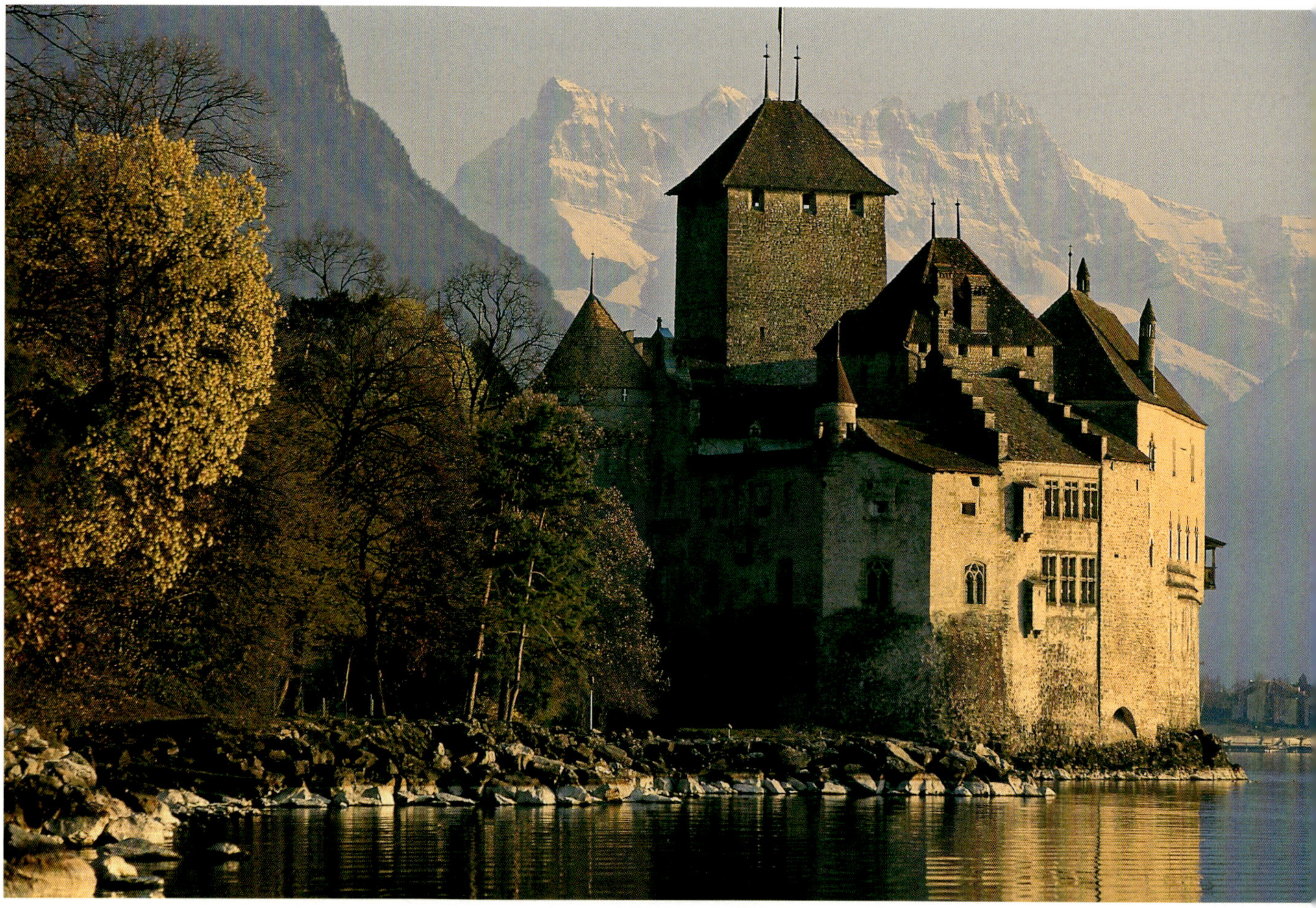

The appealing old town of Le Landeron (Landern) in the canton of Neuchâtel has been almost completely preserved and boasts a 15th-century town hall. The traditional wine village straddles the linguistic boundary between the German- and French-speaking parts of Switzerland.

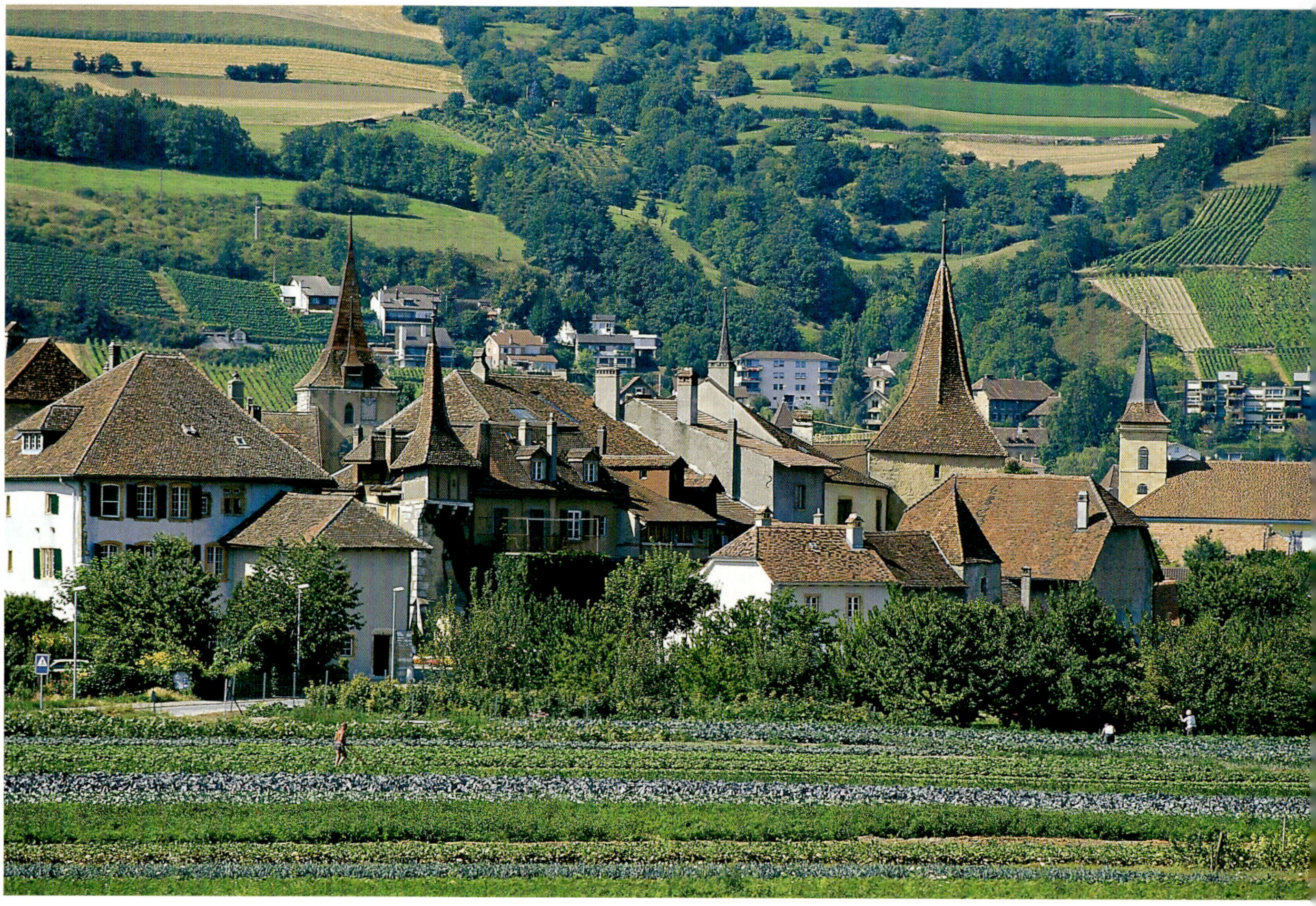

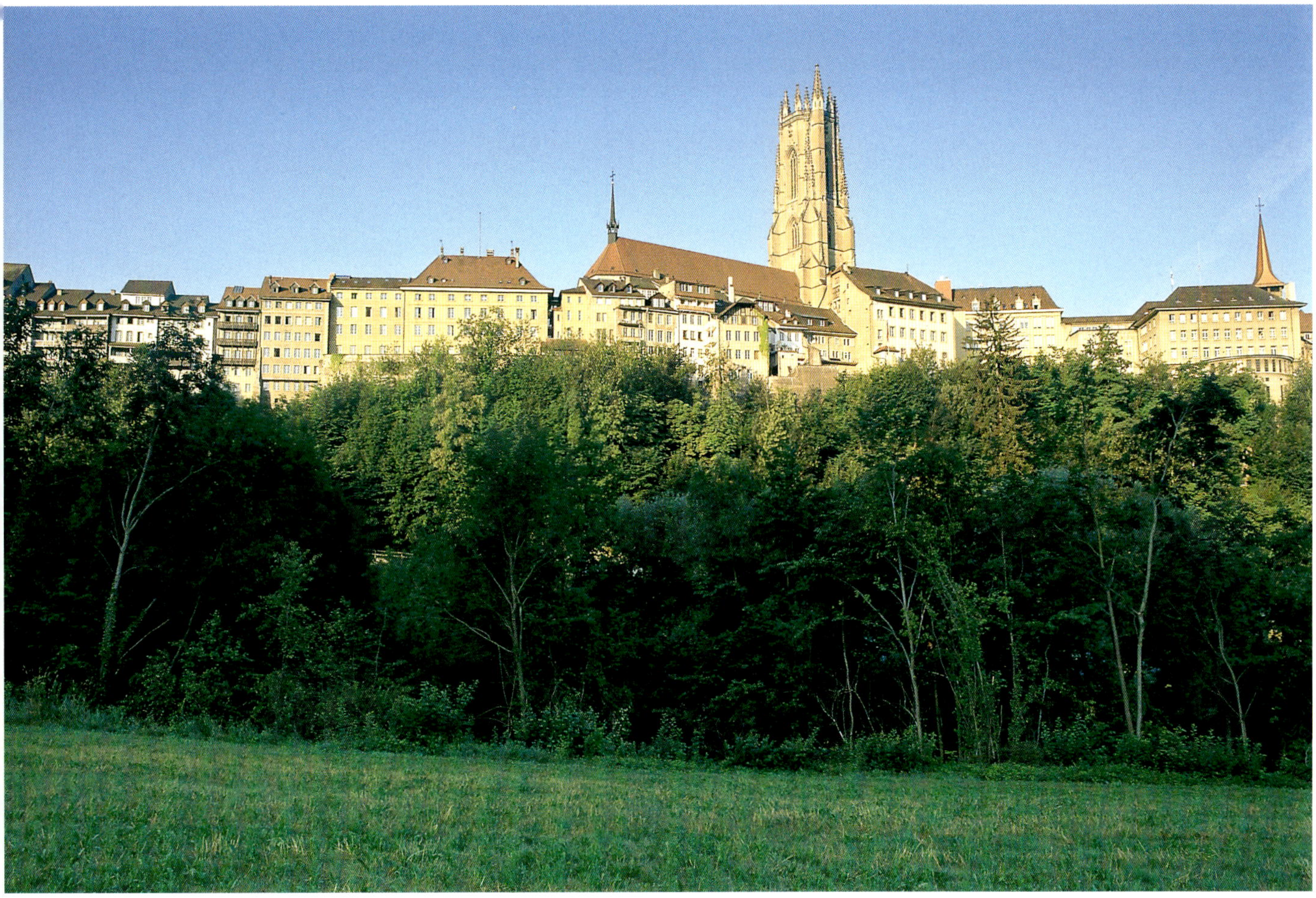

Not to be confused with Freiburg im Breisgau, which is on the edge of the Black Forest in Germany, the ancient settlement of Fribourg in Switzerland is situated on a rocky outcrop high up above the valley of the River Sarine. The town forms the boundary between German and French Switzerland, reflected in the fact that even its university is bilingual. Like Germany's Freiburg, Swiss Fribourg was also founded by the Zähringen dynasty.

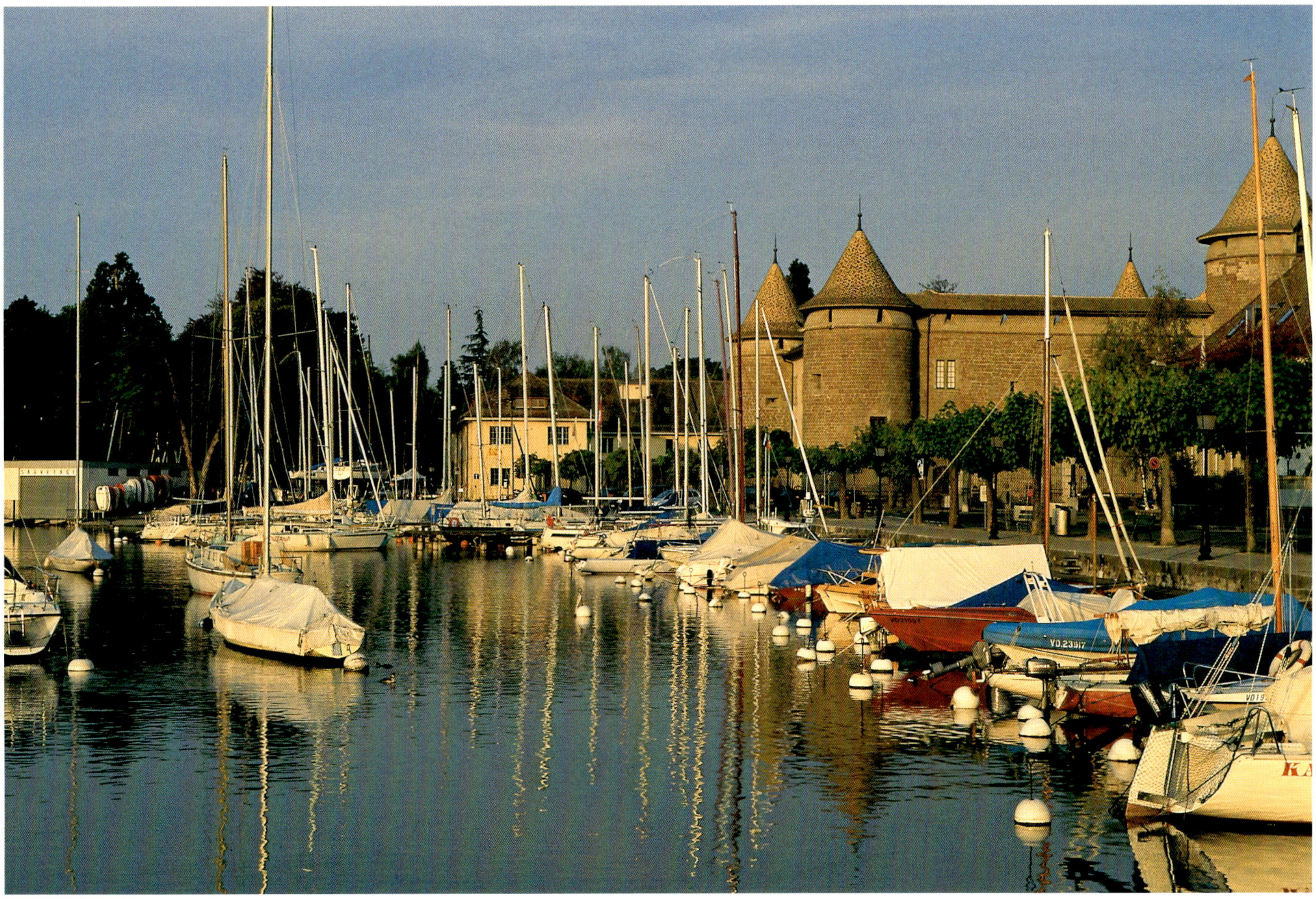

About ten kilometres (six miles) west of Lausanne on Lake Geneva lies Morges with its romantic little harbour and delightful medieval town. In the background is its mighty fortress, the Château de Morges, which was last extended during the 16th and 17th centuries.

On a slight elevation on the western shores of Lake Neuchâtel is Grandson, its most prominent building the castle of the same name first mentioned in 1050. It took on its present quadratic form during the 13th century on the extension of the first defensive structure erected on the site. An enormous menhir on the road to Fiez demonstrates that the Grandson area was inhabited very early on.

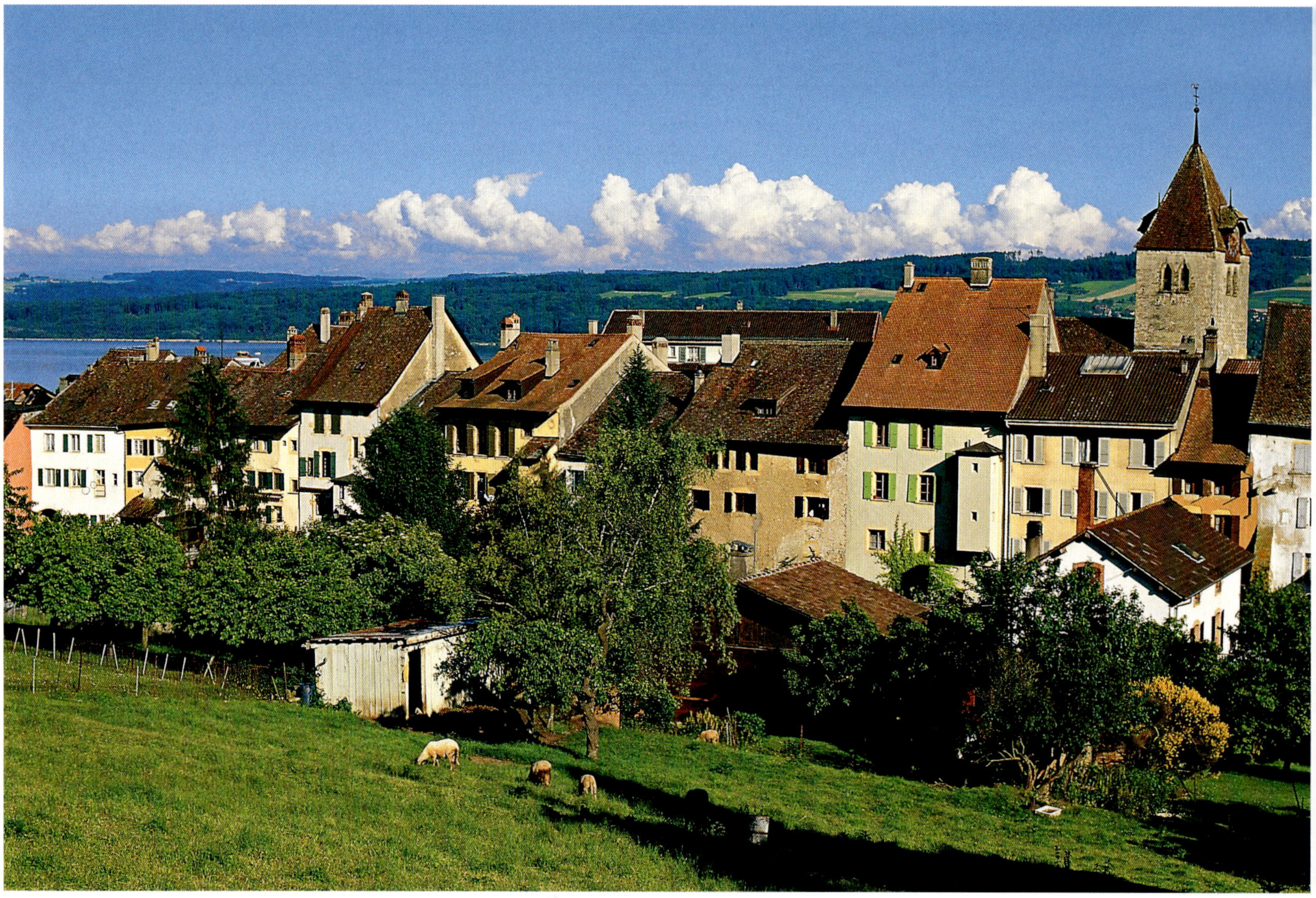

Moudon probably dates back to the Celts who founded the refuge of Minnodunos here. The name Minnodunos refers to a hill dedicated to the god Minnos. Originally a farming community, the advent of the railway gradually brought industry into Moudon and in 1899 the establishment of what was to become a roaring trade in cheese.

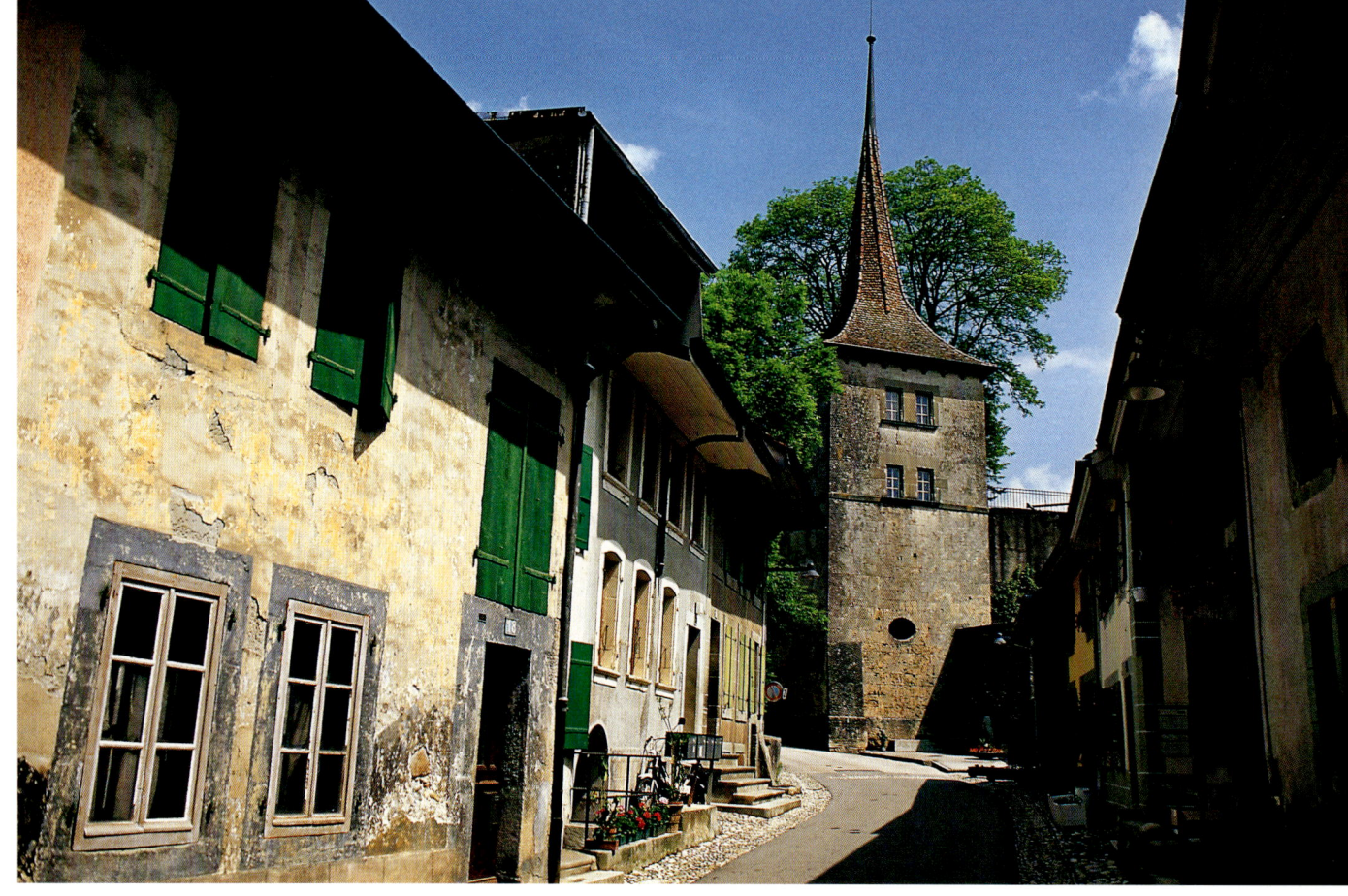

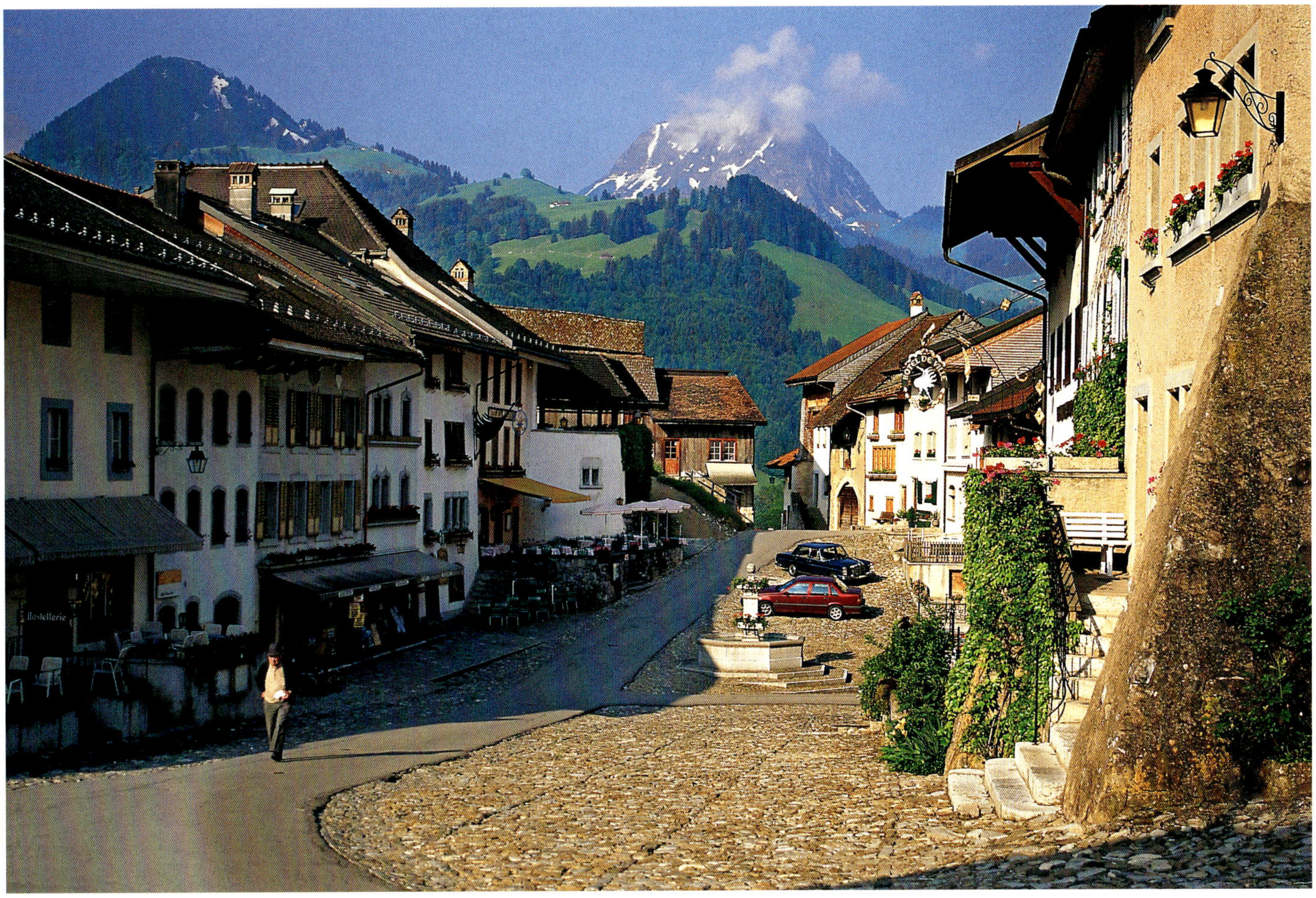

The medieval town of Gruyères in the canton of Fribourg is also famous for cheese. At a local museum dairy visitors can see how the tasty cheese is made.

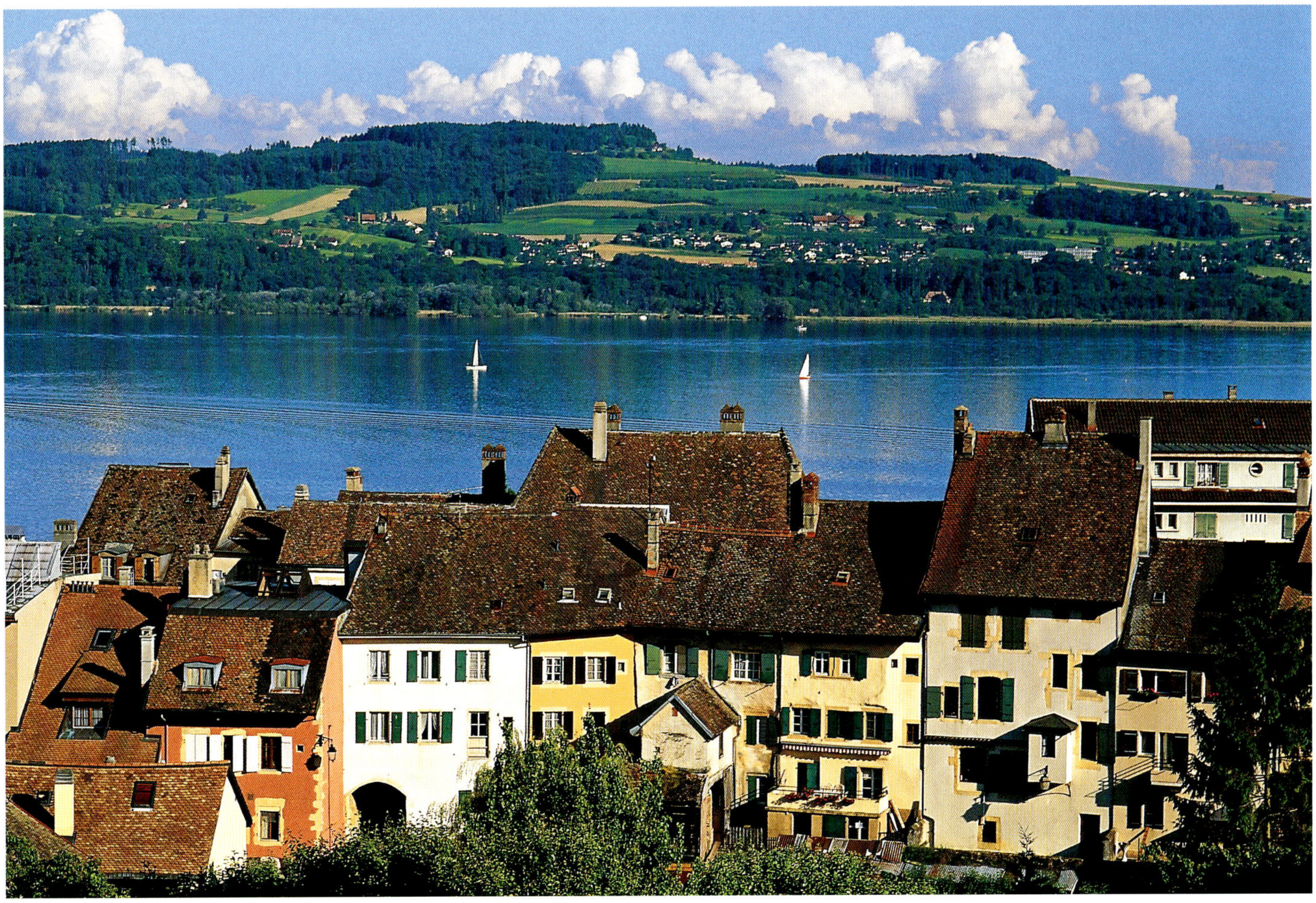

The southern slopes of the Jura Mountains on Lake Neuchâtel are planted with fertile vineyards growing Chasselas (Gutedel), Pinot noir and the internationally acclaimed Oeil de Perdrix, a rosé wine.

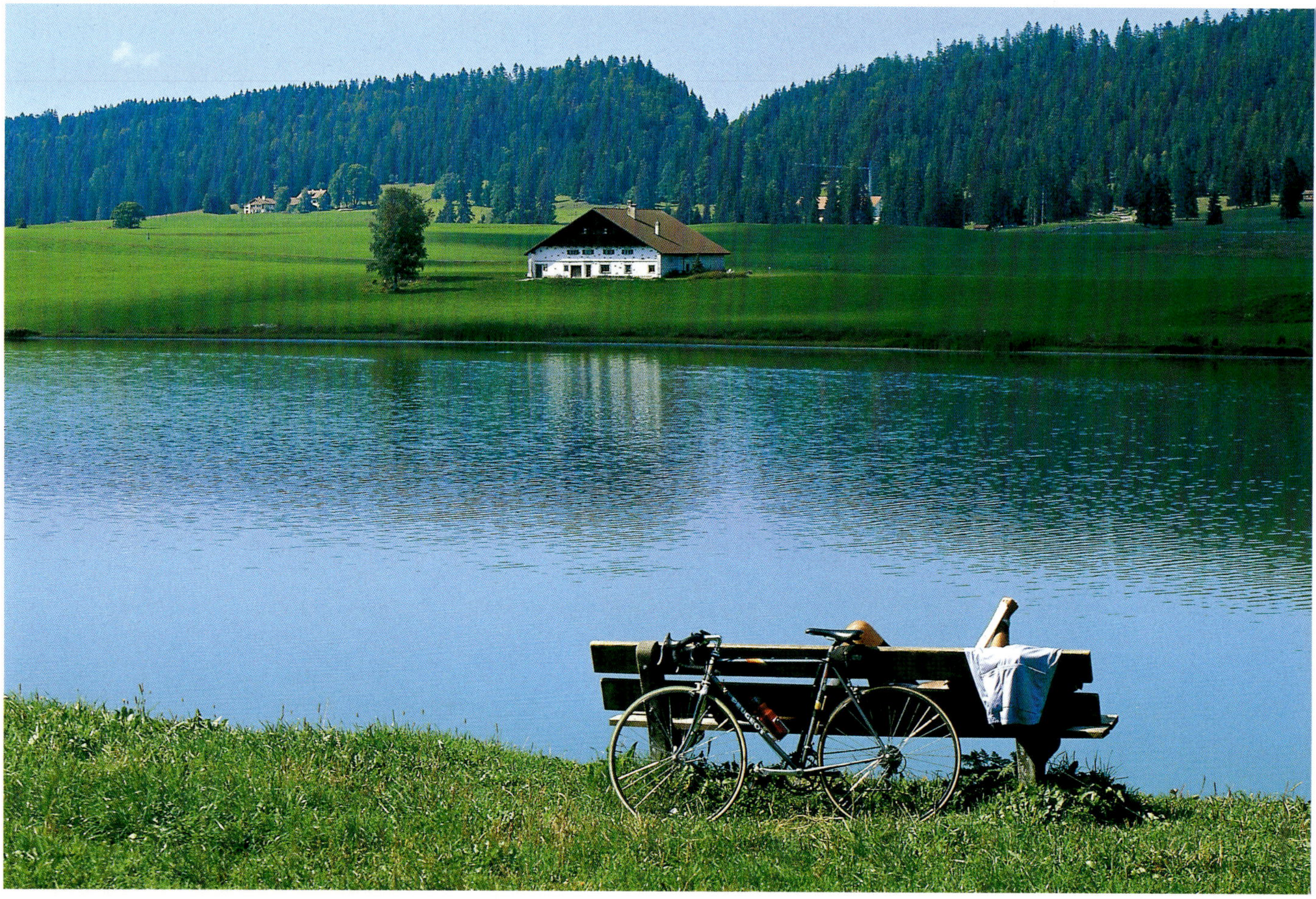

In the high-lying Vallée de la Brévine in the Jura of Neuchâtel is the Lac des Taillères, 1,036 metres (3,399 feet) above sea level, fed by rainwater, rivulets and sources in the lake. Excess water drains away through the porous, chalky bottom of the lake to resurface a few miles further south in the Areuse karst. In winter the flat water freezes over very easily, making it extremely popular with ice skaters.

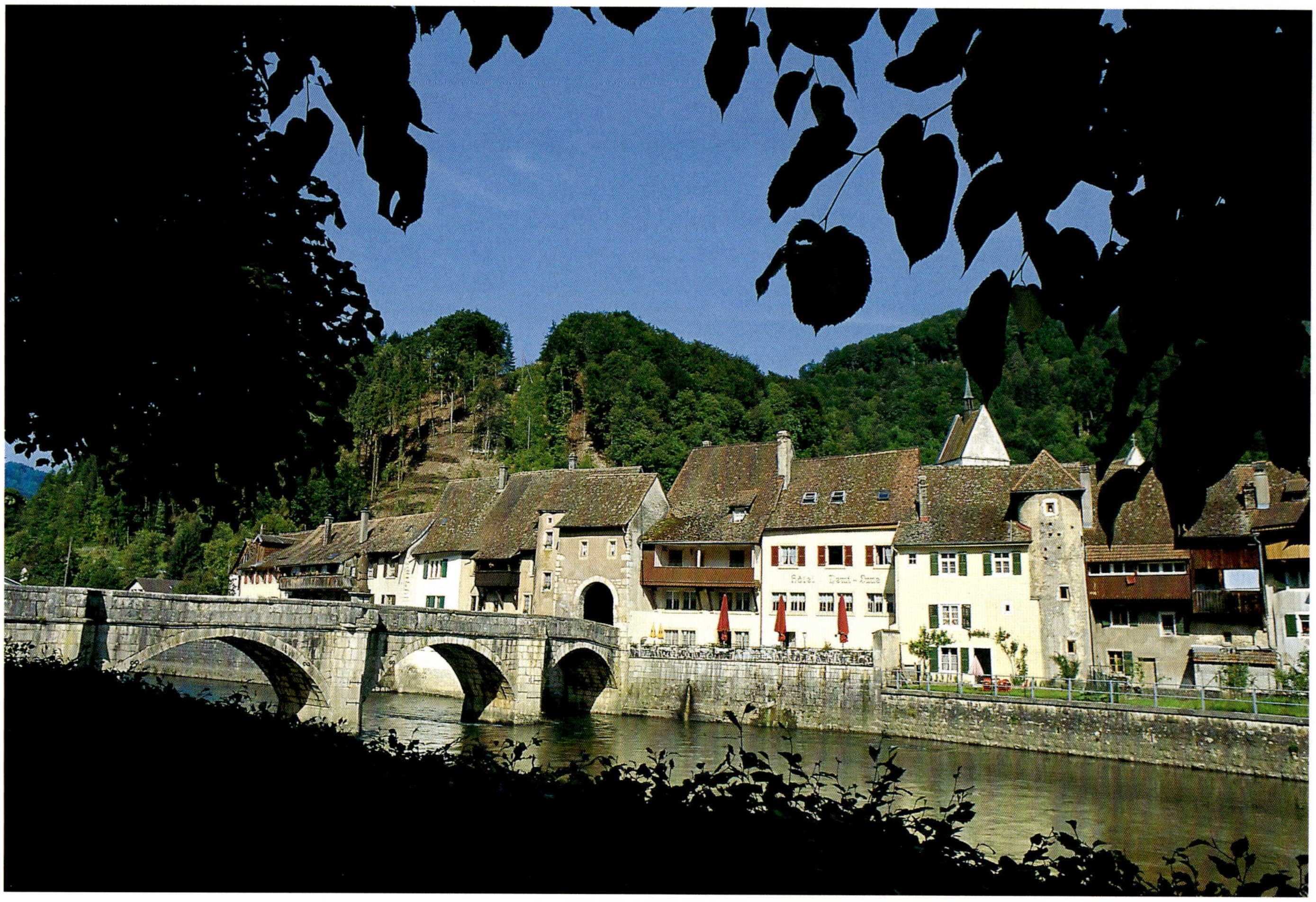

The historic little town of Saint-Ursanne has squeezed itself into the narrow valley of the Doubs in the canton of the Jura. The arched bridge leading up to the south gate was built in 1728.

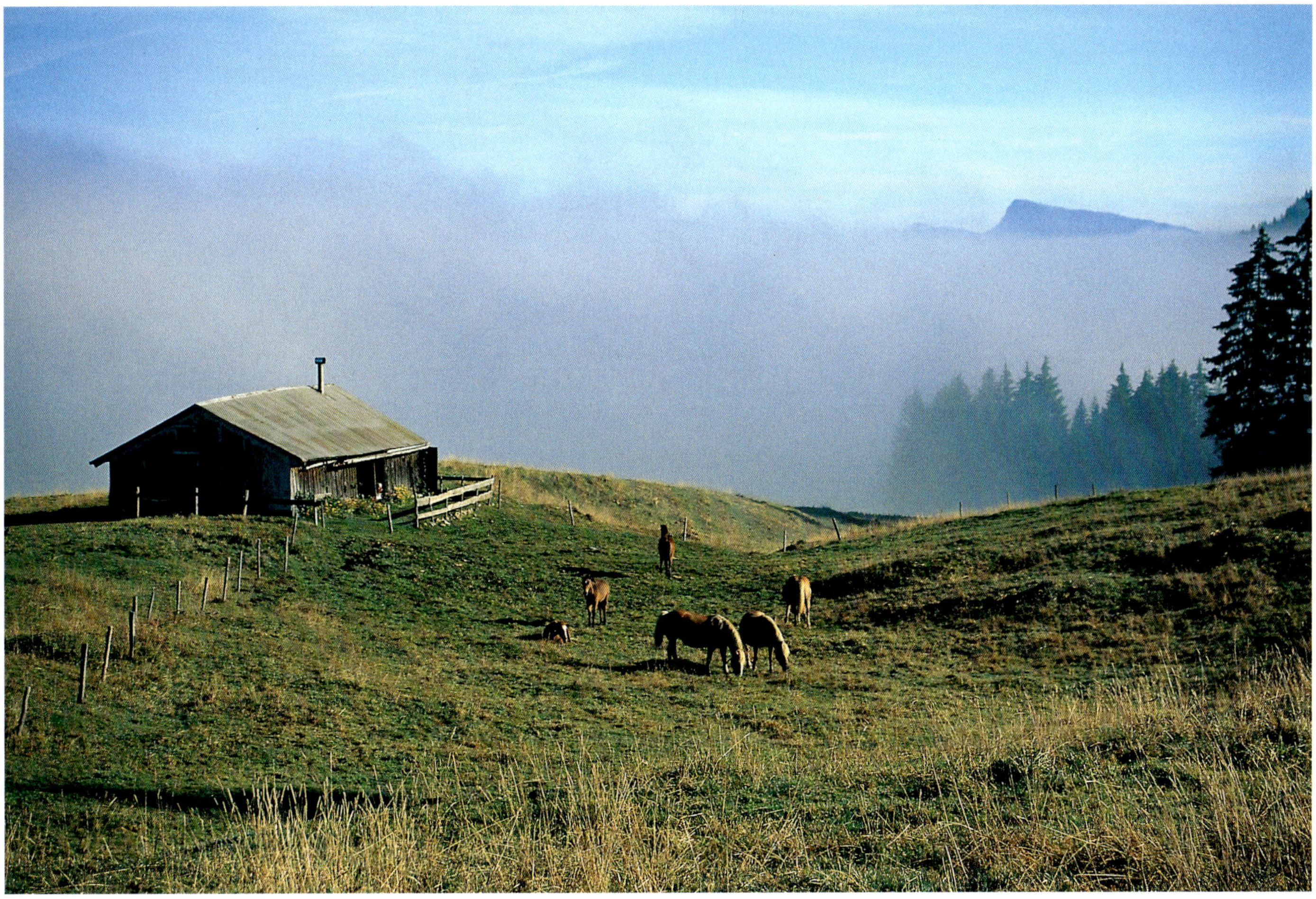

The Vallée de Joux is an isolated high-lying valley in the Vaud Jura, its climate suitably harsh for its height of 1,000 metres (3,280 feet) above sea level. In winter the area is perfect for cross country skiing.

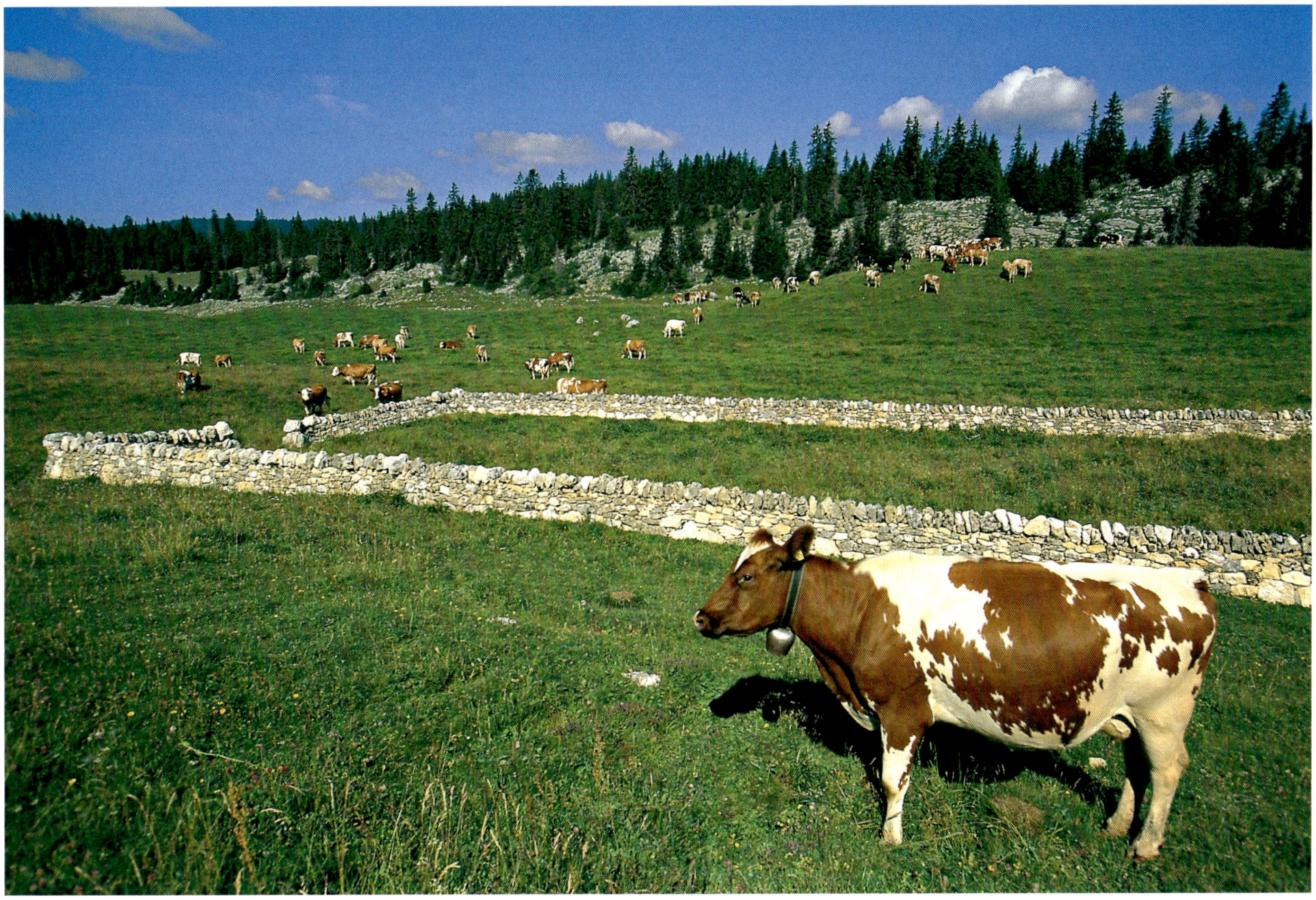

Lush high-lying pastures in the canton of Vaud. Not far away the Col du Marchairuz mountain pass links the two villages of Le Brassus and Bière, the pass climbing up to 1,447 metres (4,747 feet) at its highest point.

Right:
The Great Aletsch is the biggest and longest glacier in the Alps. 23 kilometres (14 miles) long and 118 square kilometres (45 square miles) in area, it creeps in icy silence through the canton of Valais. Its 27 million metric tonnes of ice originate in the Jungfrau region 3,800 metres (12,470 feet) up. The glacier was made a UNESCO World Heritage Site in 2001.

Right page:
The primeval beauty of the Riffelalp with the unmistakable peak of the Matterhorn in the distance.

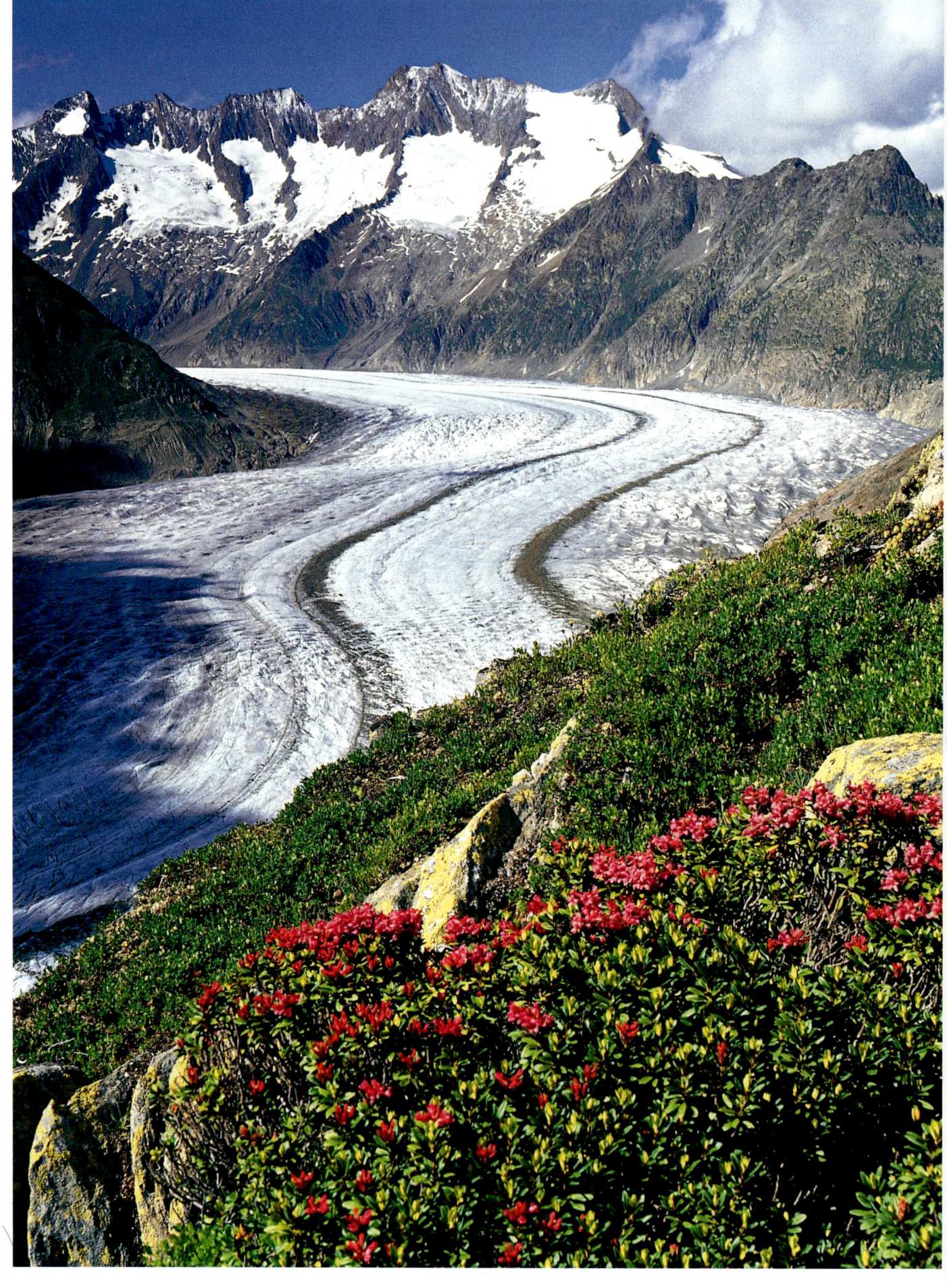

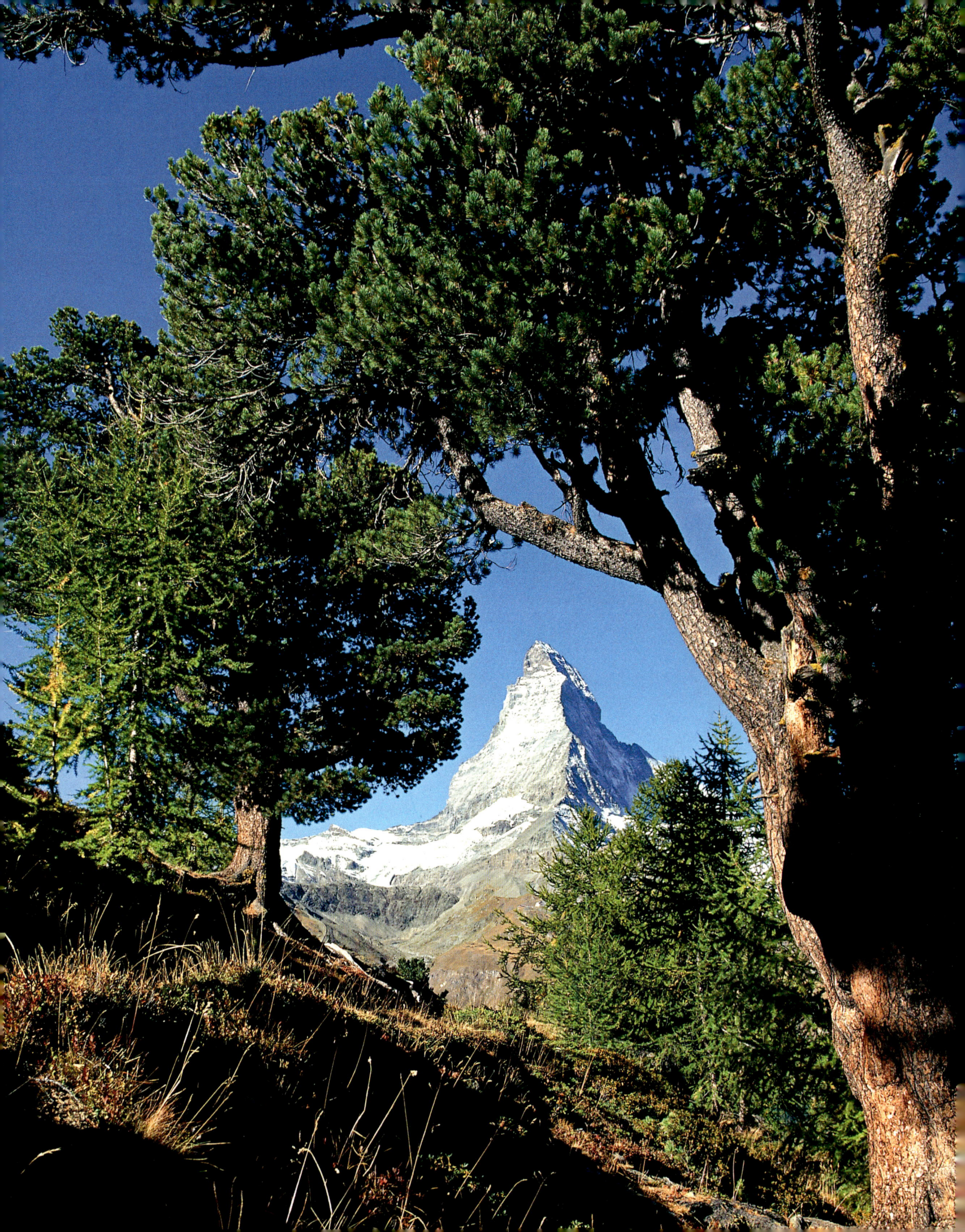

Between the tree line and the eternal snows at heights of up to about 3,500 metres (11,480 feet) is where the ibex feels most at home. Ideal conditions are provided by the Gornergrat in the canton of Valais, for example. At the beginning of the 19th century the ibex was almost extinct. Down to just about 100 animals it was carefully reintroduced and now again happily populates its natural habitat, with around 14,000 of the species in the Swiss Alps alone.

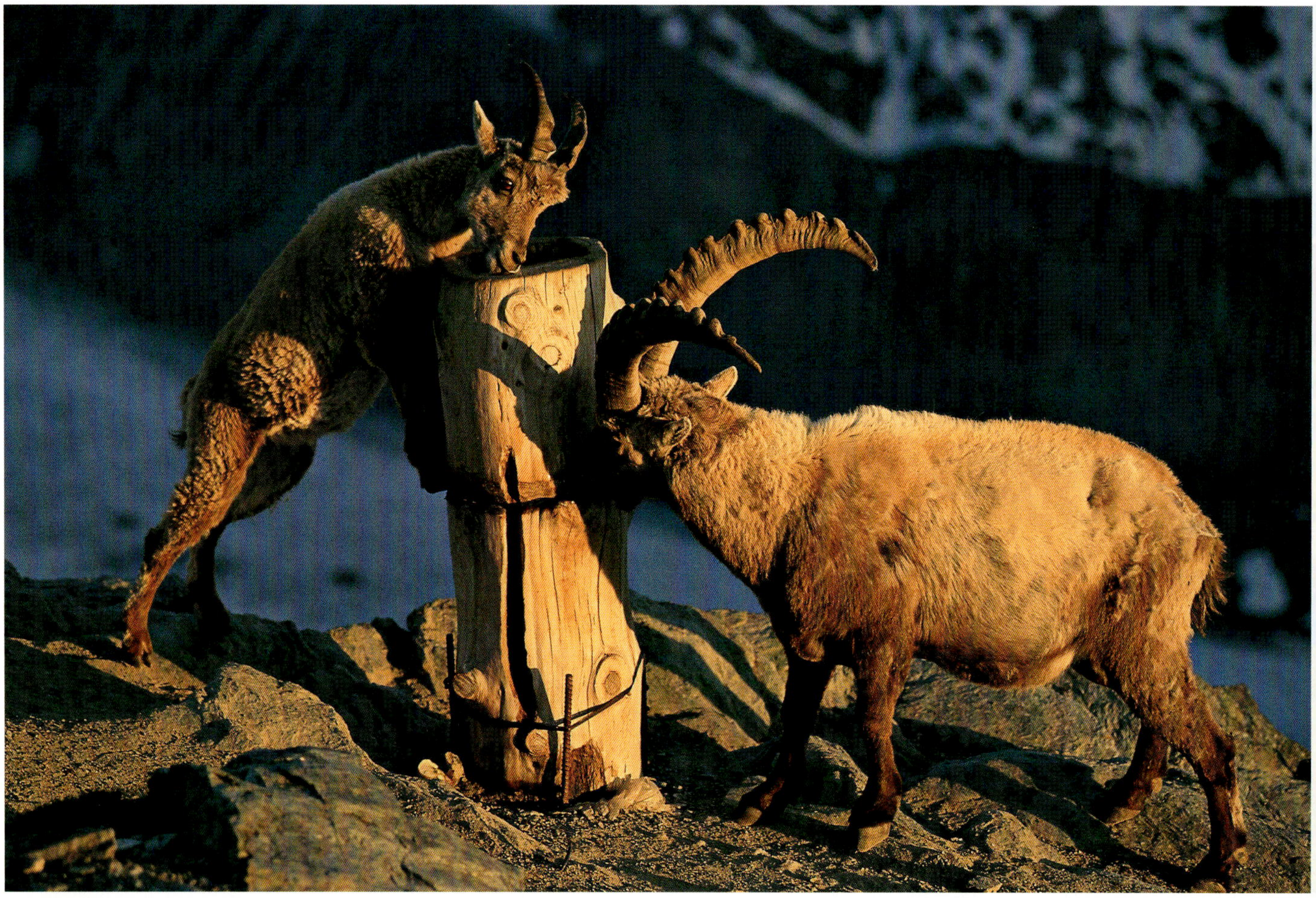

Lac de Moiry lies embedded between the lofty heights of the Garde de Bordon, the Corne de Sorebois and the Sasseneire in the canton of Valais.

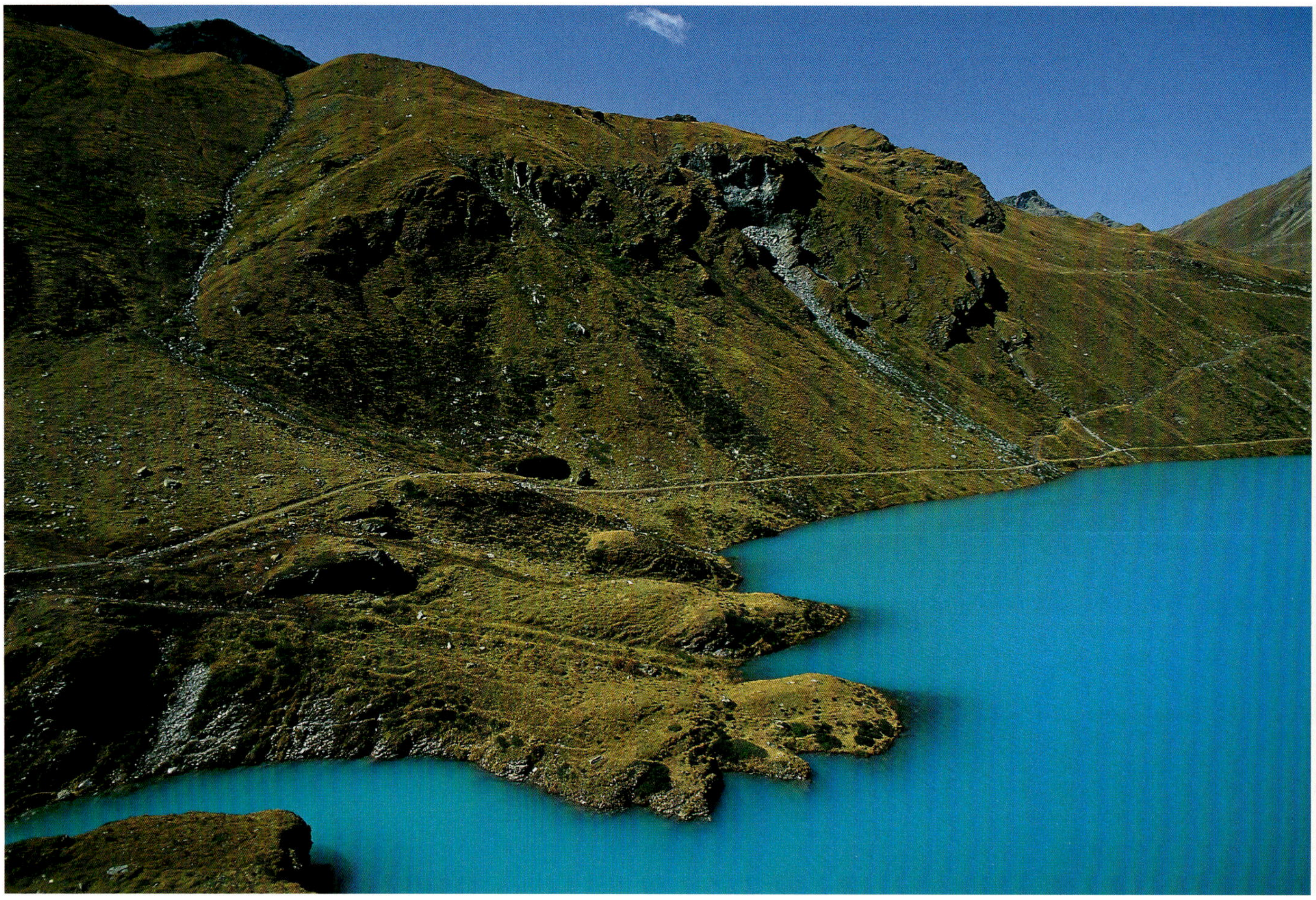

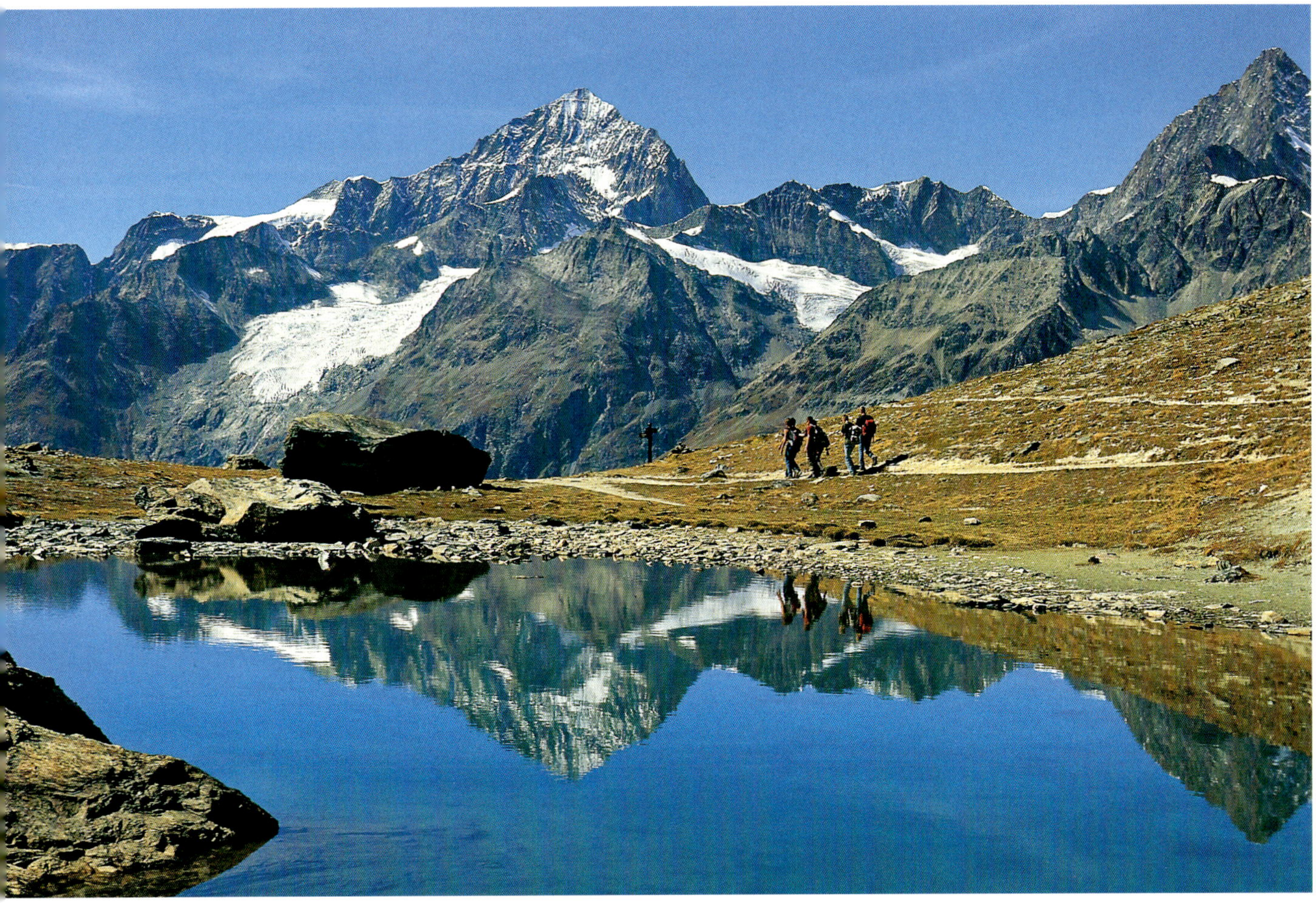

Seeing double: the Matterhorn Range reflected in the brilliant blue waters of Lake Riffel.

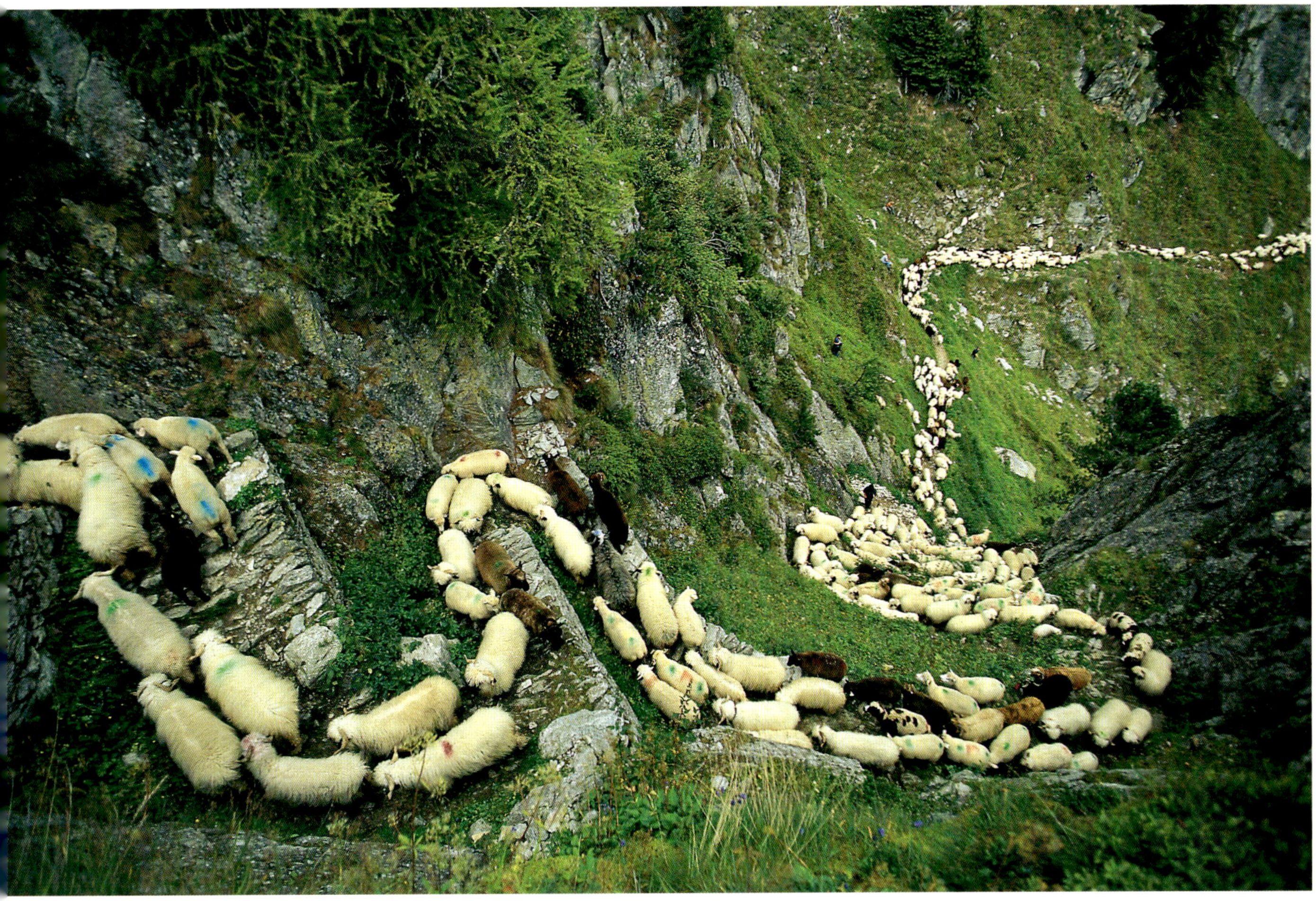

Driving the cattle down from the Belalp near Naters. During the summer sheep and cattle are grazed on the mountain pastures and their milk processed in an Alpine dairy, one of the delicious products of which is unpasteurised cheese.

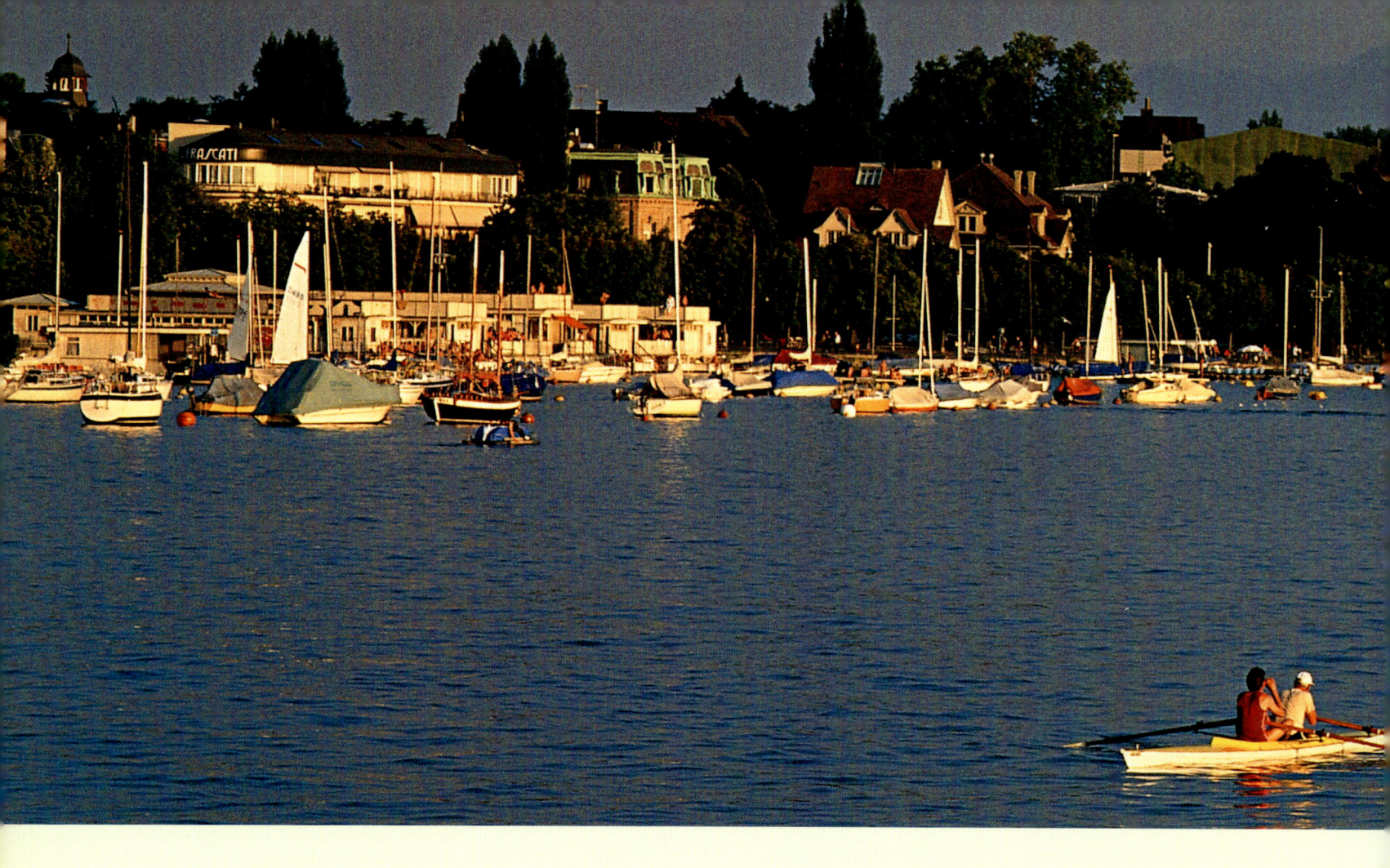

The Swiss heartlands – birthplace of the Confederation

Central Switzerland, and particularly the original three forest cantons of Uri, Schwyz and Unterwalden, still considers itself the birthplace of the Swiss Confederation. This is where the Reformation feared to tread; even today the majority of its inhabitants are Catholic. During the 19th century Uri, Schwyz and Unterwalden continued to bitterly fight the founding of a national state, preferring instead to uphold the less restrictive league of states; today they like to remind the rest of Switzerland of their special status by categorically voting "No" in Switzerland's not infrequent referenda. Bordering on the central Swiss canton of Lucerne are the canton and Swiss capital of Bern. East of Bern is Emmental where the famous cheese comes from. The forest cantons are bordered on the other side by the rolling hills and orchards of eastern Switzerland – where the city of Zürich is kept firmly at arm's length. Nobody here sees Zürich as the "secret capital of eastern Switzerland" – a term generally applied to it by both the general public and the media who are under the misconception that Zürich is in the east. The northwest of Switzerland provides a buffer zone between the Swiss heartlands and Germany. As the canton boundaries around Basle are by tradition extremely arbitrary, for many years politicians have been talking about creating a new canton of Northwest Switzerland. As yet nothing has materialised – which is surprising, as the area around Basle is considered to be very liberal. The neighbouring canton of Aargau is characterised by its many small towns, one of them Brugg with the nearby Habsburg, the ancestral seat of the dynasty of the same name.

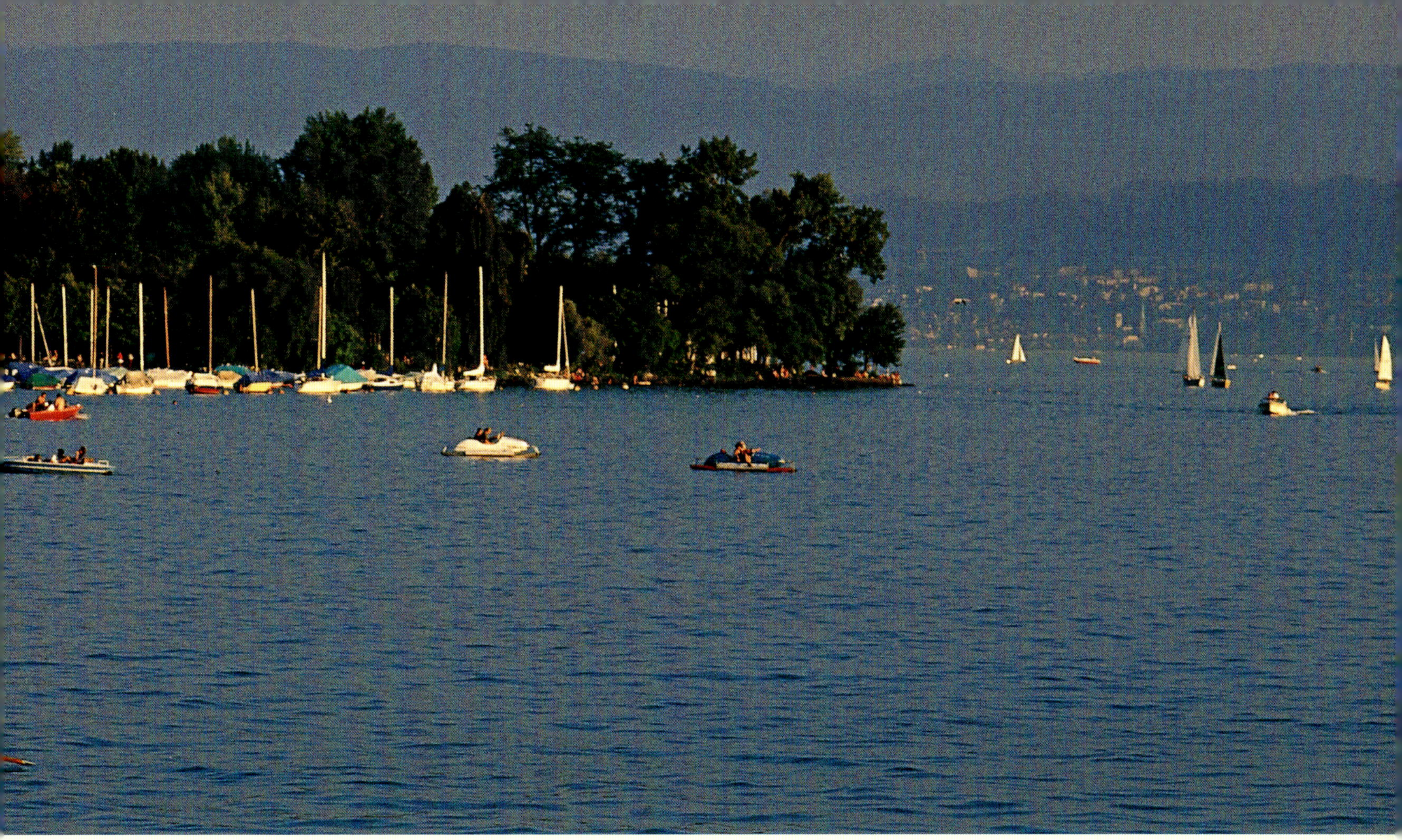

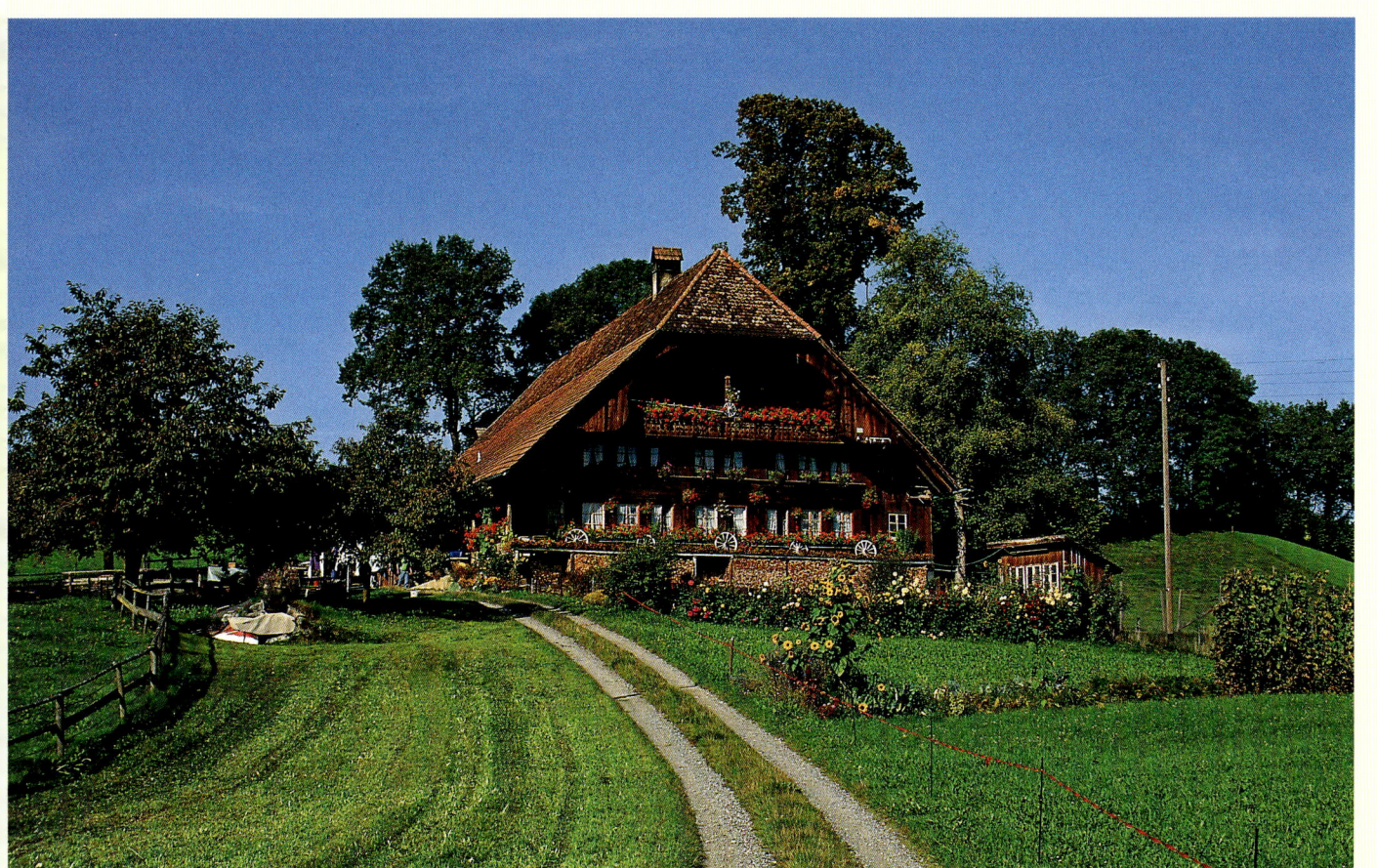

Above:
At the end of the last ice age the Linth was dammed by the terminal moraine of the Linth Glacier to form the elongated waters of Lake Zürich. The lake last froze over in the harsh winter of 1962/63. Nowadays it's often so mild here that palms and figs thrive in the lakeside gardens.

Left:
A farmhouse near Riggisberg. The region in the Bernese Oberland is popular with daytrippers and hikers from Bern and Thun.

Page 38/39:
A strong current and steel rope ensure safe passage for the ferries zipping across the River Rhine in Basle. They have provided an important foot passenger link between Grossbasel on the left bank and Kleinbasel on the right since the mid 19th century.

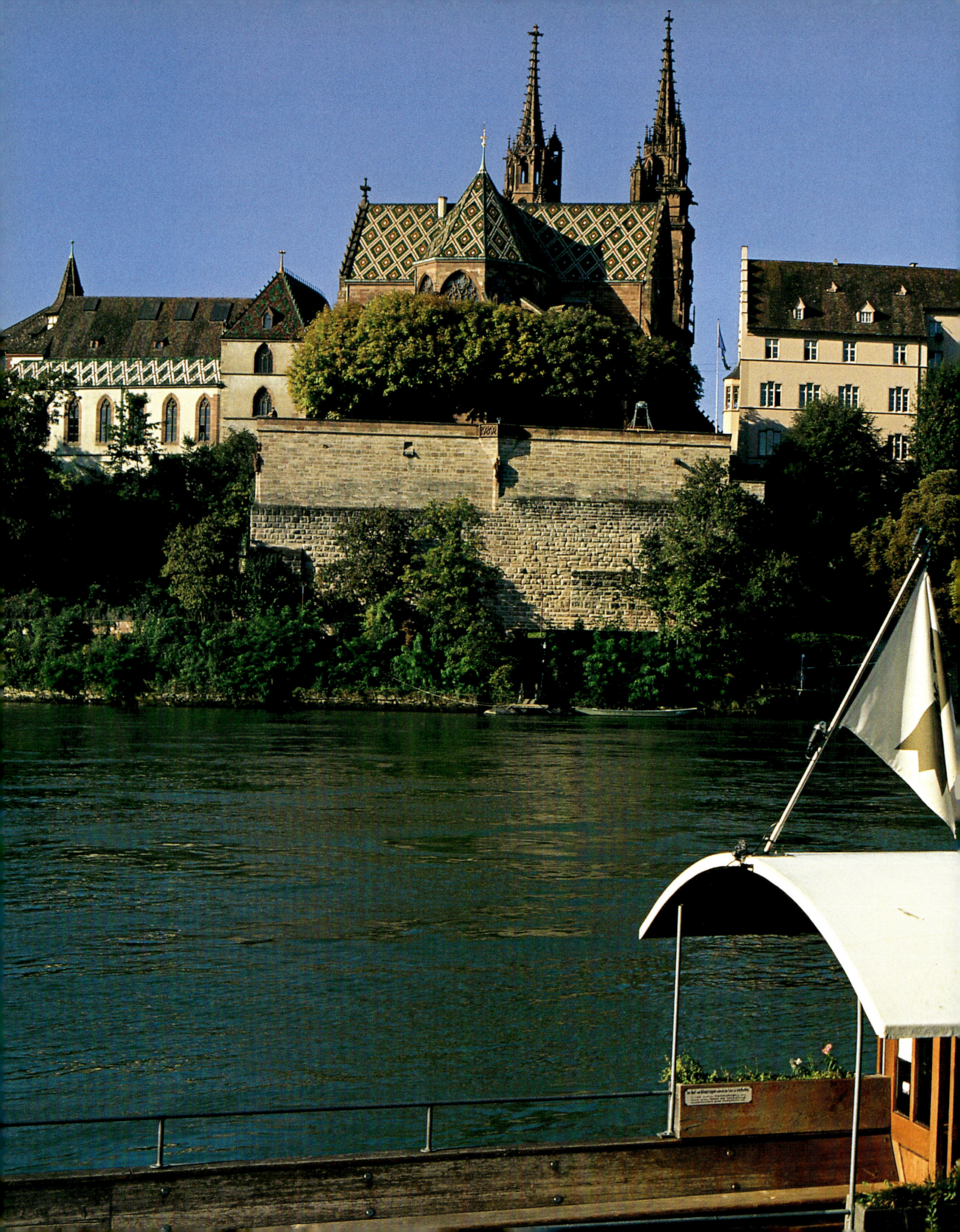

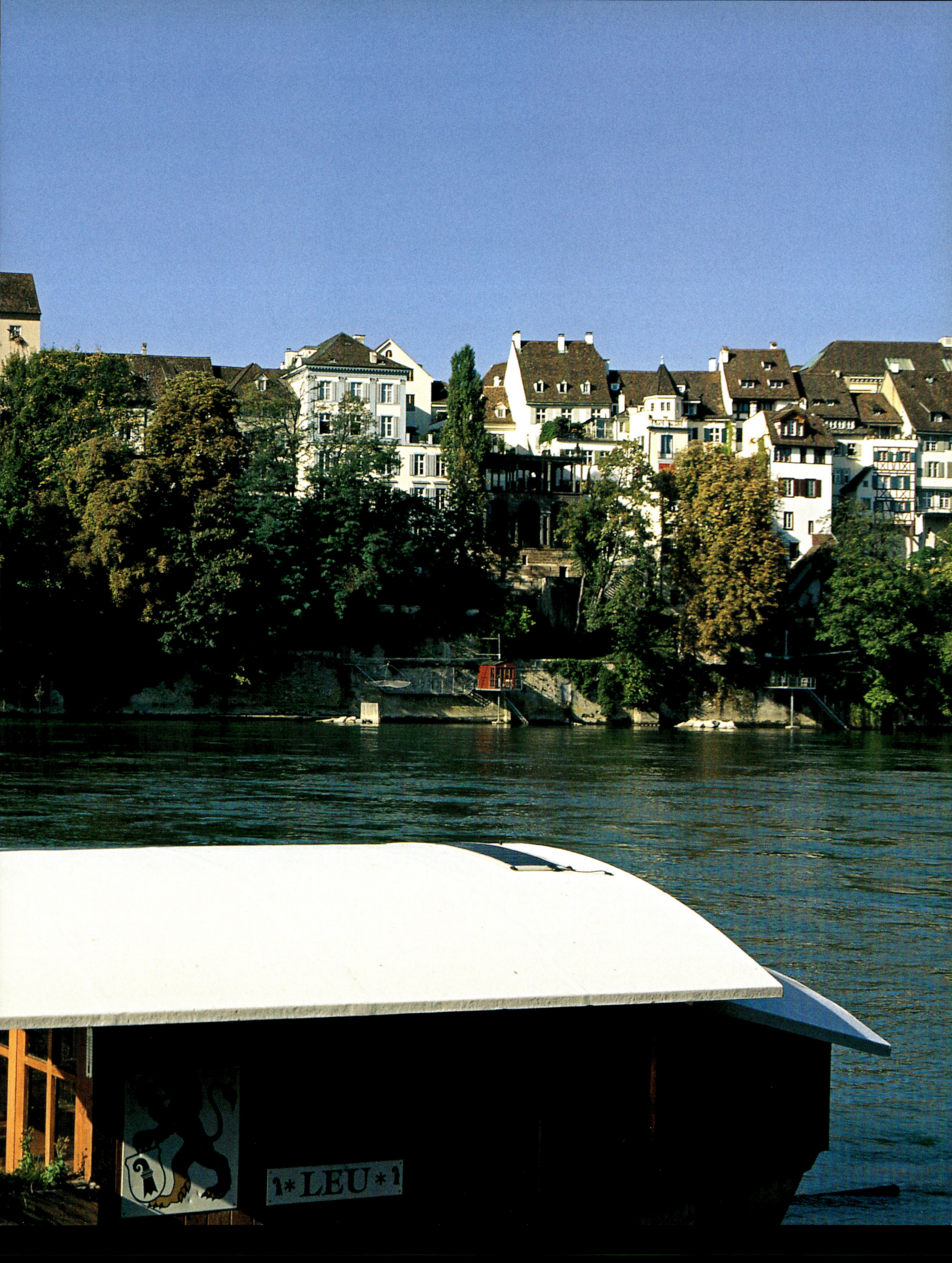

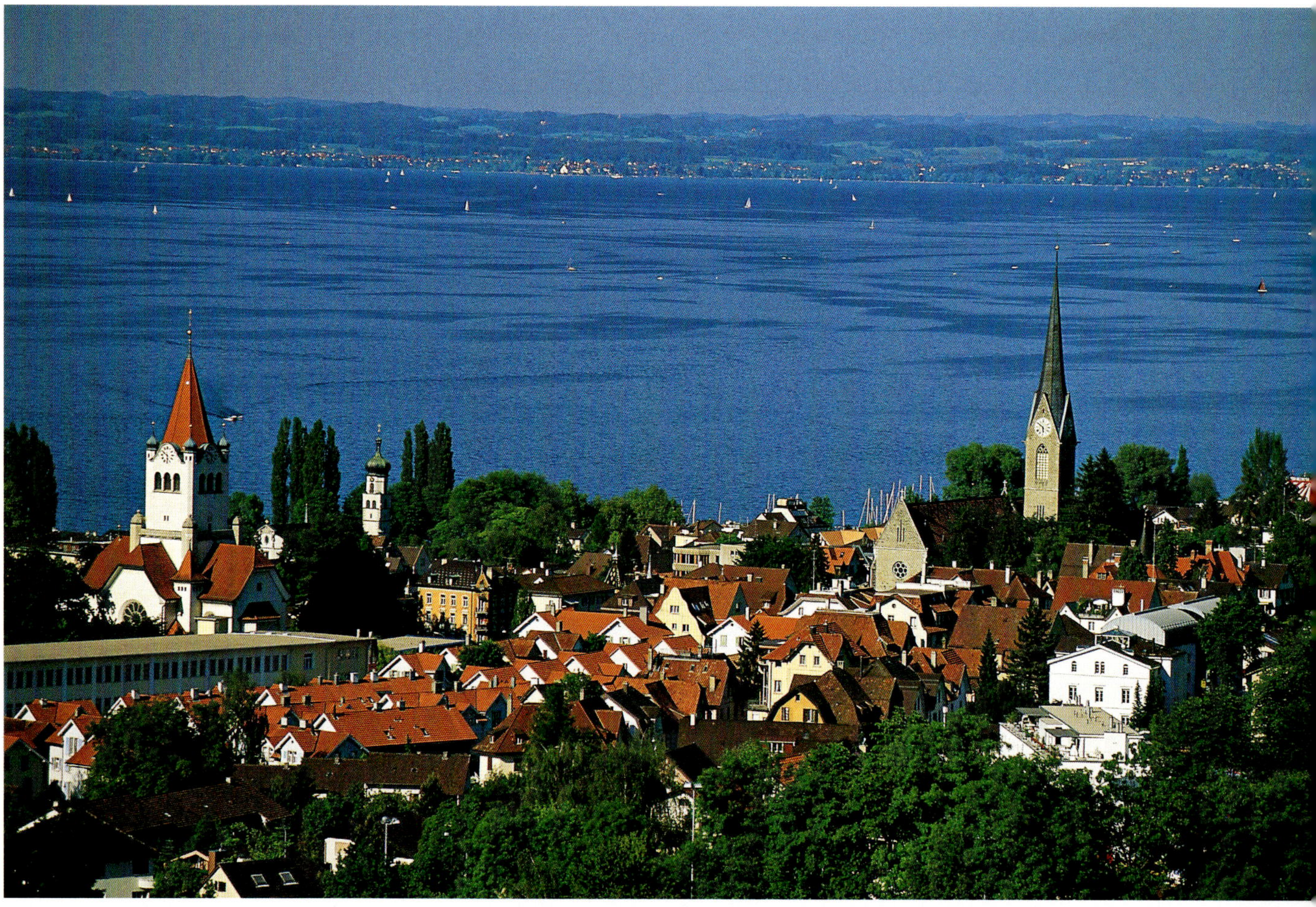

Lake Constance bordering on Switzerland, Germany and Austria is the third-largest lake in Central Europe. It is in fact two lakes, joined at Constance by the Seerhein. Some of the cities hugging its shores, such as Rorschach in the canton of St Gallen, date back to ancient Alemannic settlements.

The division of territory regarding Lake Constance is not conclusive. Only the Überlinger See in the north completely belongs to Germany. Contracts split the ownership of the Seerhein at Constance between Switzerland and Germany; all other waters over 25 metres (80 feet) deep are managed jointly by the three countries. To date the lake has not yet been recognised by international law as a national boundary.

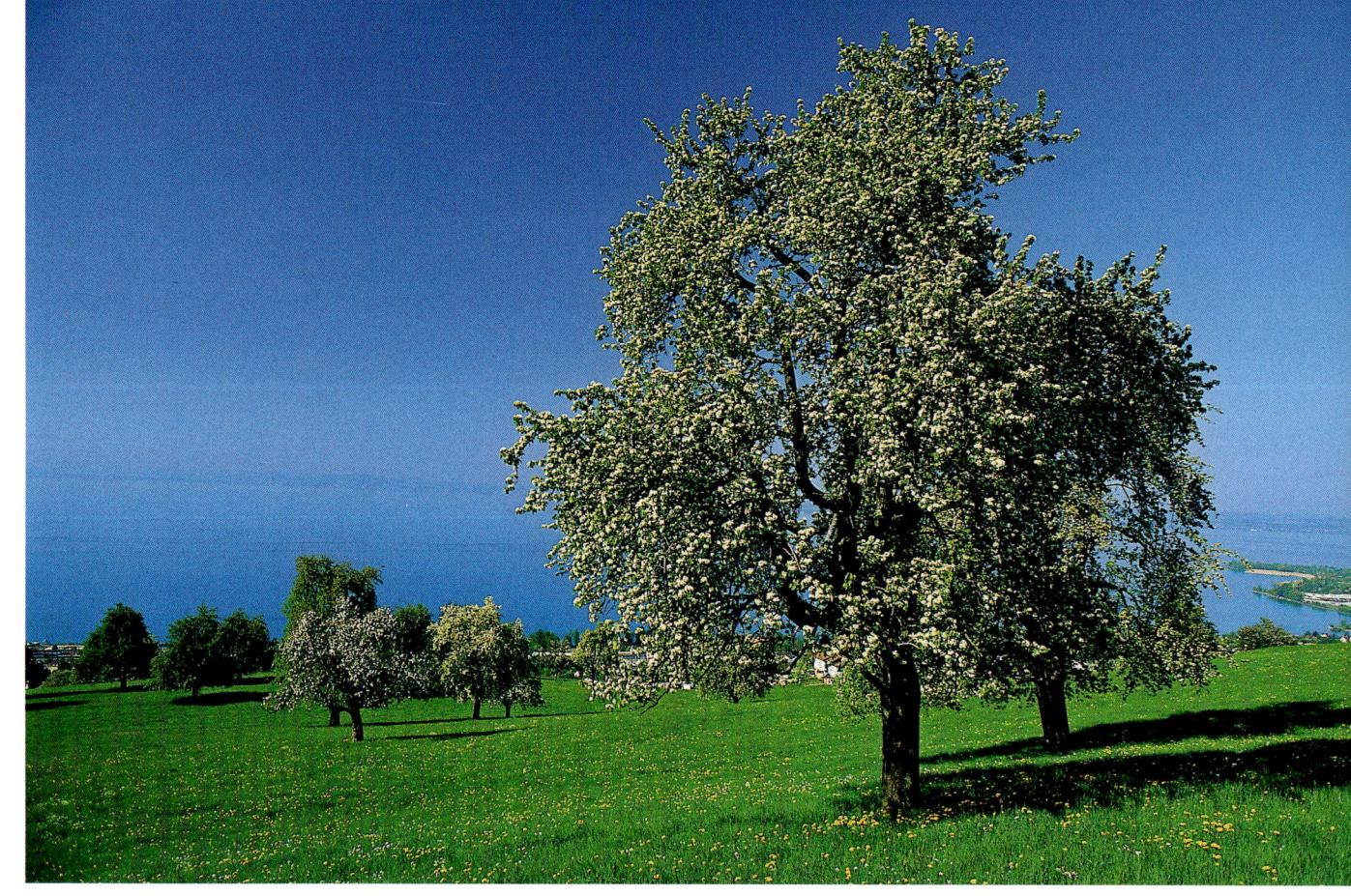

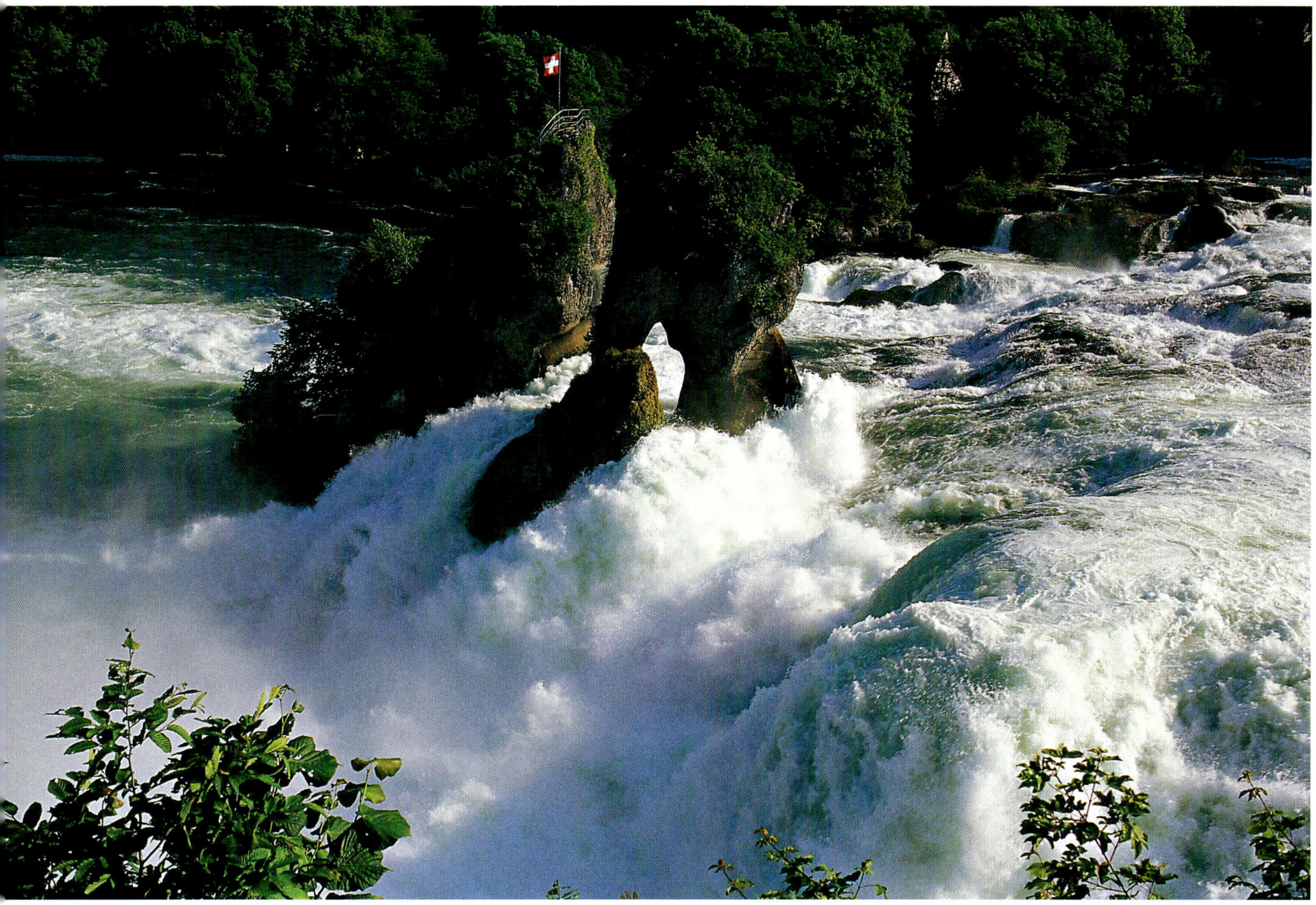

Between Lake Constance and Basle the powerful Rhine Falls crash 23 metres (75 feet) down into the depths in a fury of spray. The spectacle attracts thousands of visitors each year, many of whom are transported by boat to the central rock from whence they can marvel at the sheer mass of water angrily churning past them.

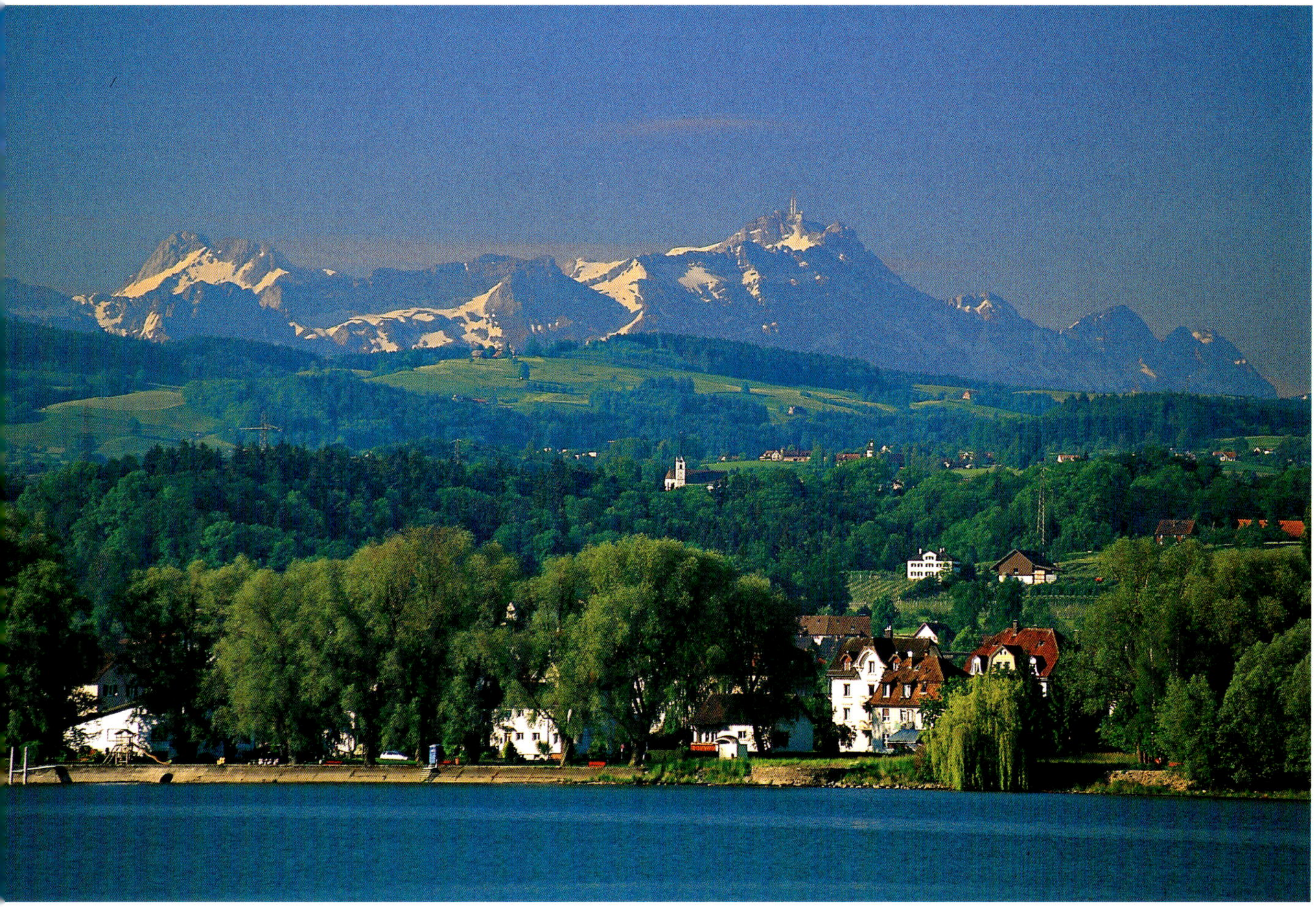

Mountains and lakes, the epitome of Switzerland, are again found in the mighty Mount Säntis and serene Lake Constance, depicted here. On a clear day the television tower in Stuttgart can be seen from the summit – a good 170 kilometres (110 miles) away!

St Gallen's baroque monastic church marks the spot where in 612 Irish monk Gallus ensconced himself in his hermitage. The abbey is now a UNESCO World Heritage Site.

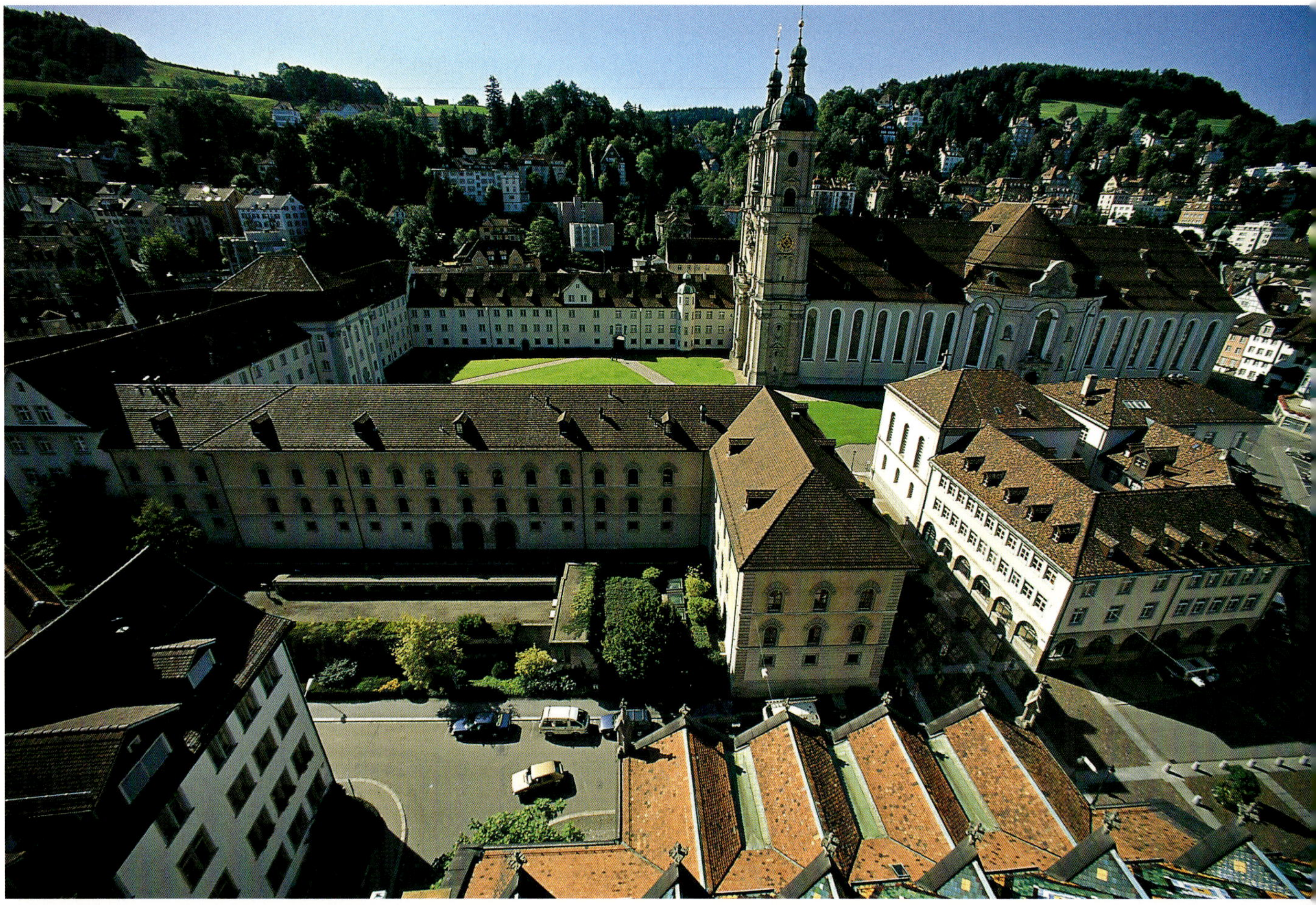

The abbey library in St Gallen is considered to be the most beautiful secular baroque room in Switzerland. The library houses around 2,000 valuable manuscripts, 400 of which were produced during the monastery's heyday over 1,000 years ago.

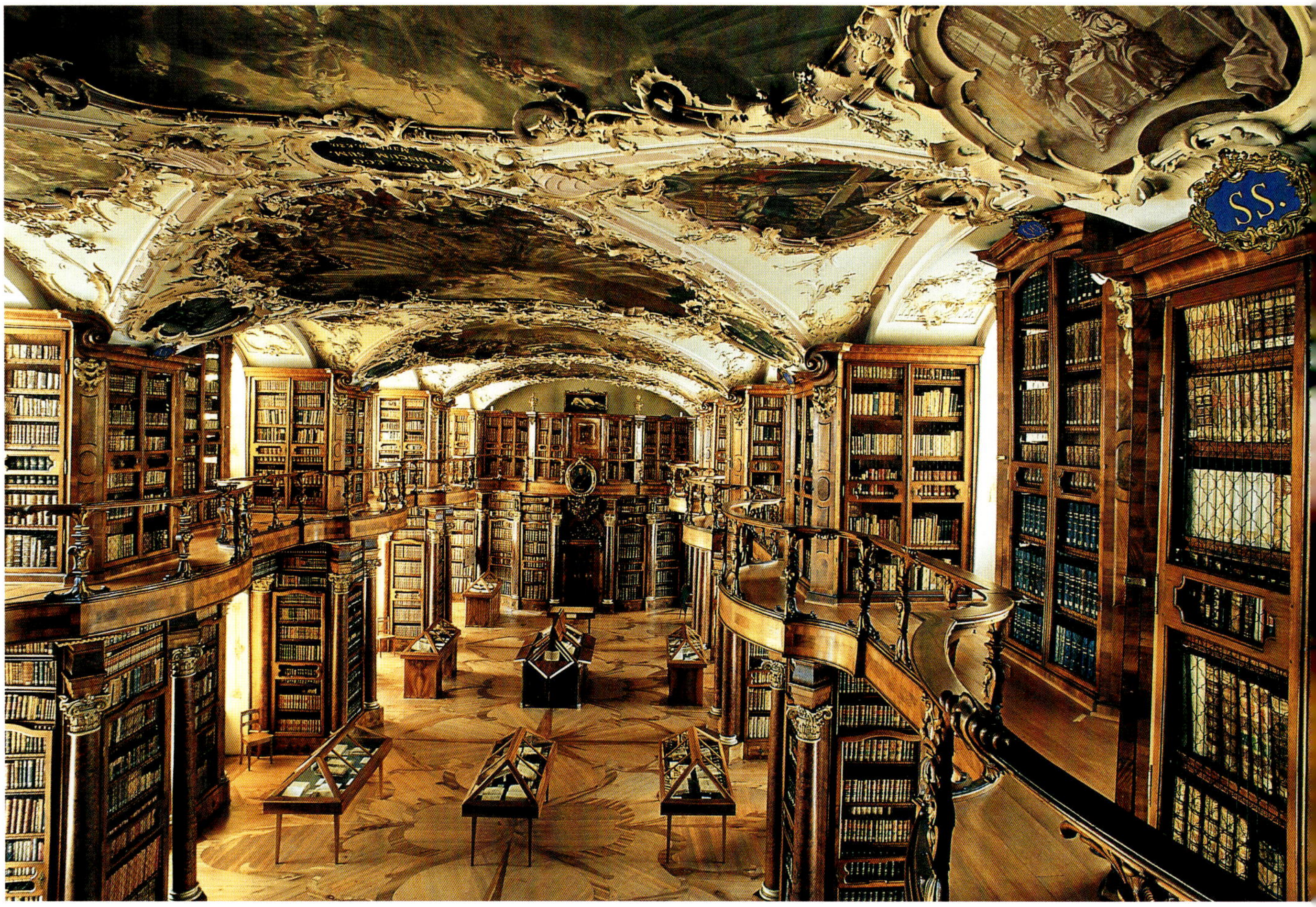

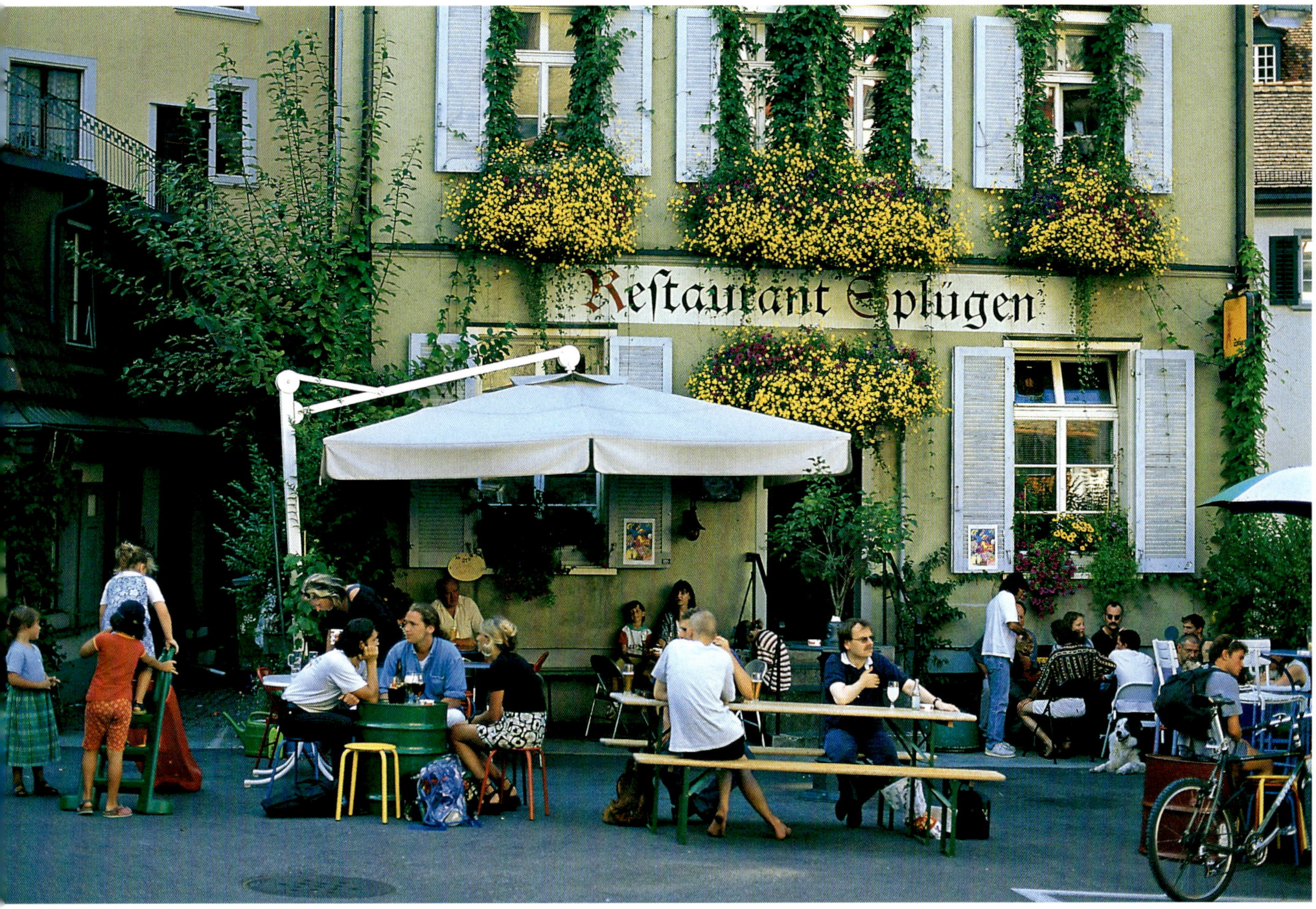

Tucked into a narrow high-lying valley in the foothills of the Alps about 15 kilometres (10 miles) southwest of Lake Constance, life in the old town of St Gallen has a distinctly Mediterranean feel to it.

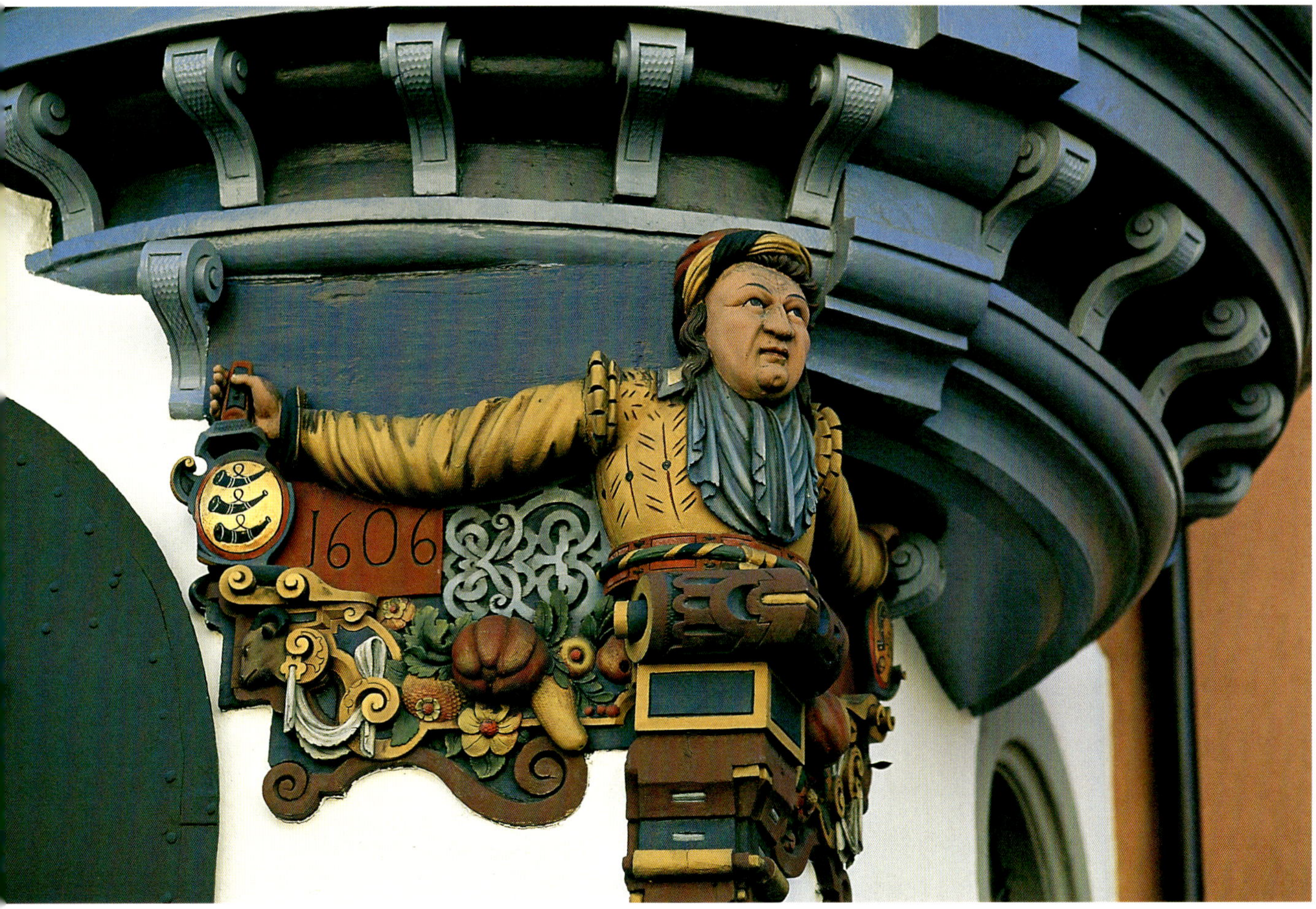

Ornately carved figures shoulder the bulbous oriels which adorn many a historic merchant's dwelling in St Gallen. Linen and cotton manufacture brought great wealth to the city from the 16th to 18th centuries.

Page 44/45:
Depending on how you count them the Churfirsten Range in the Appenzell Alps consists of six to thirteen mountains, their distinctive crest jagged and uneven. The range once formed the boundary to the territory of Chur; the name "Churfirst" (literally: "crest of Chur") is thus a reference to the city and not to the seven "Kurfürsten" or electoral princes of the Holy Roman Empire, as is often claimed by various advertising slogans.

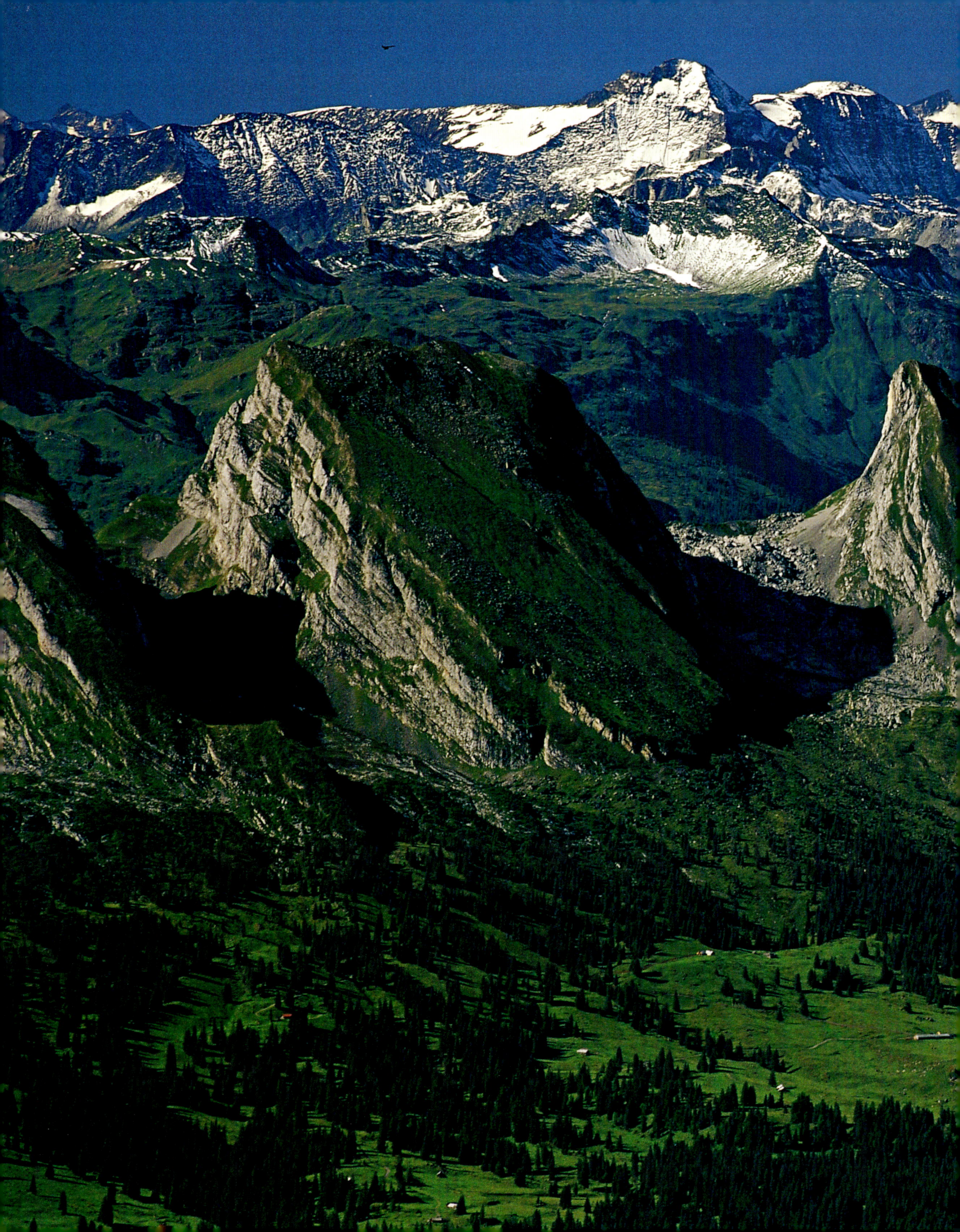

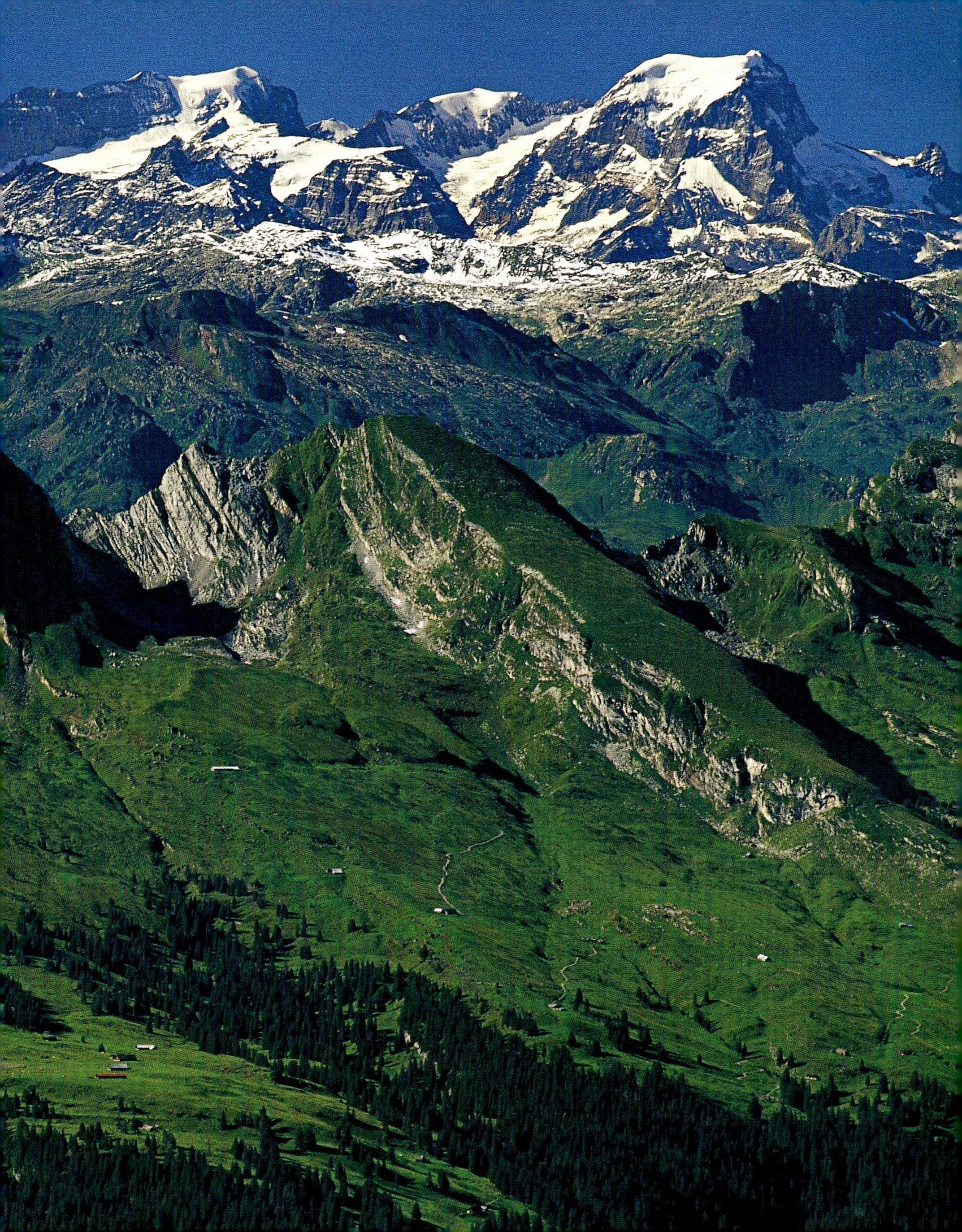

It's hard to believe that idyllic Toggenburg was once the scene of bloody fighting. Until 1803 and the founding of the canton of St Gallen the area belonged to the royal abbey of St Gallen but was reformed. This conflict of interests sparked off the Toggenburg War. Today Toggenburg is roughly half Catholic and half Protestant.

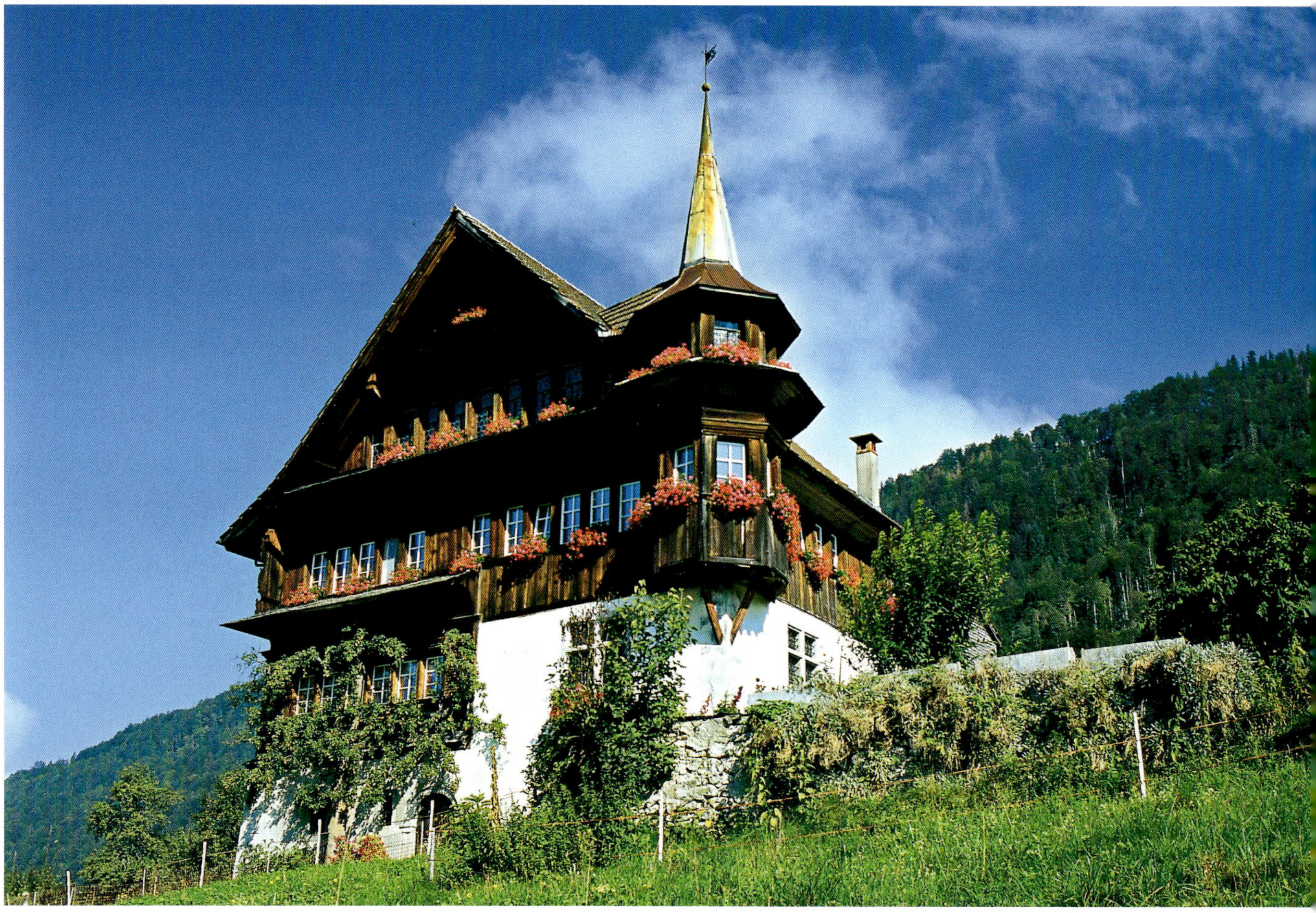

Like Toggenburg the neighbouring Appenzeller Land is also largely agricultural, with cattle markets still very much part of life.

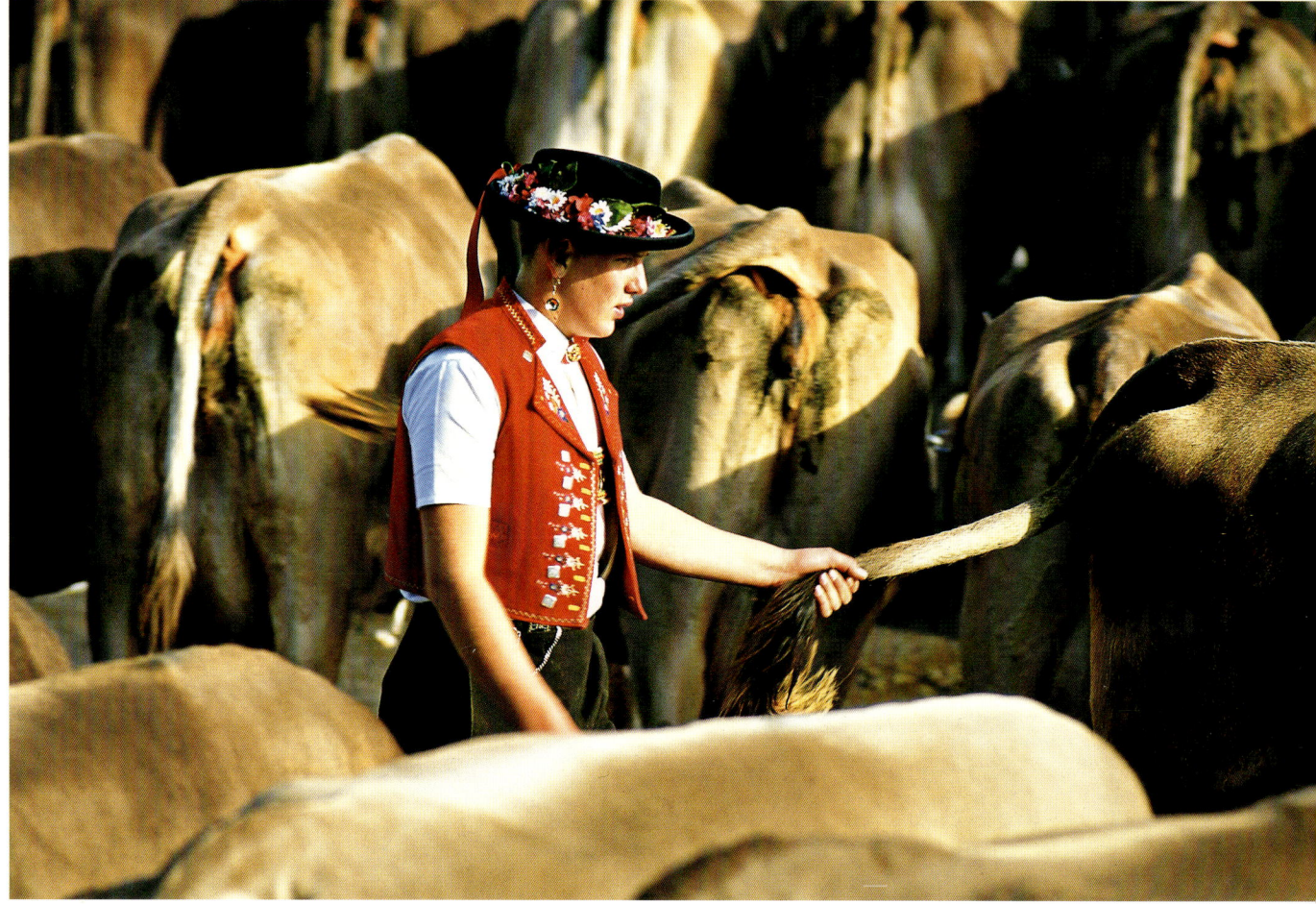

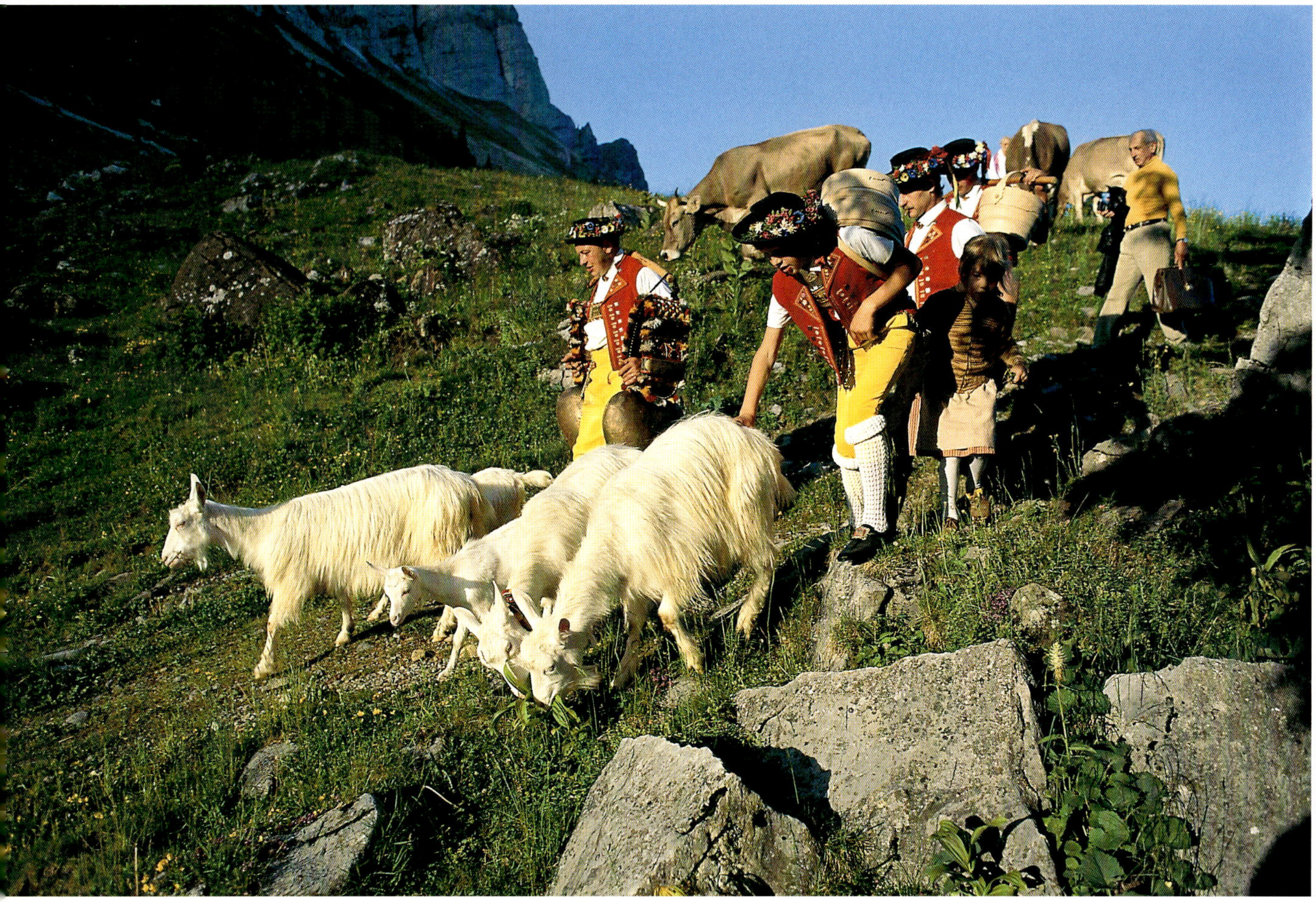

Driving the animals up to their summer pastures on the Schwägalp in the Appenzeller Land is a merry and colourful occasion, if on a more modest scale than the grand autumn festivities staged in honour of their return.

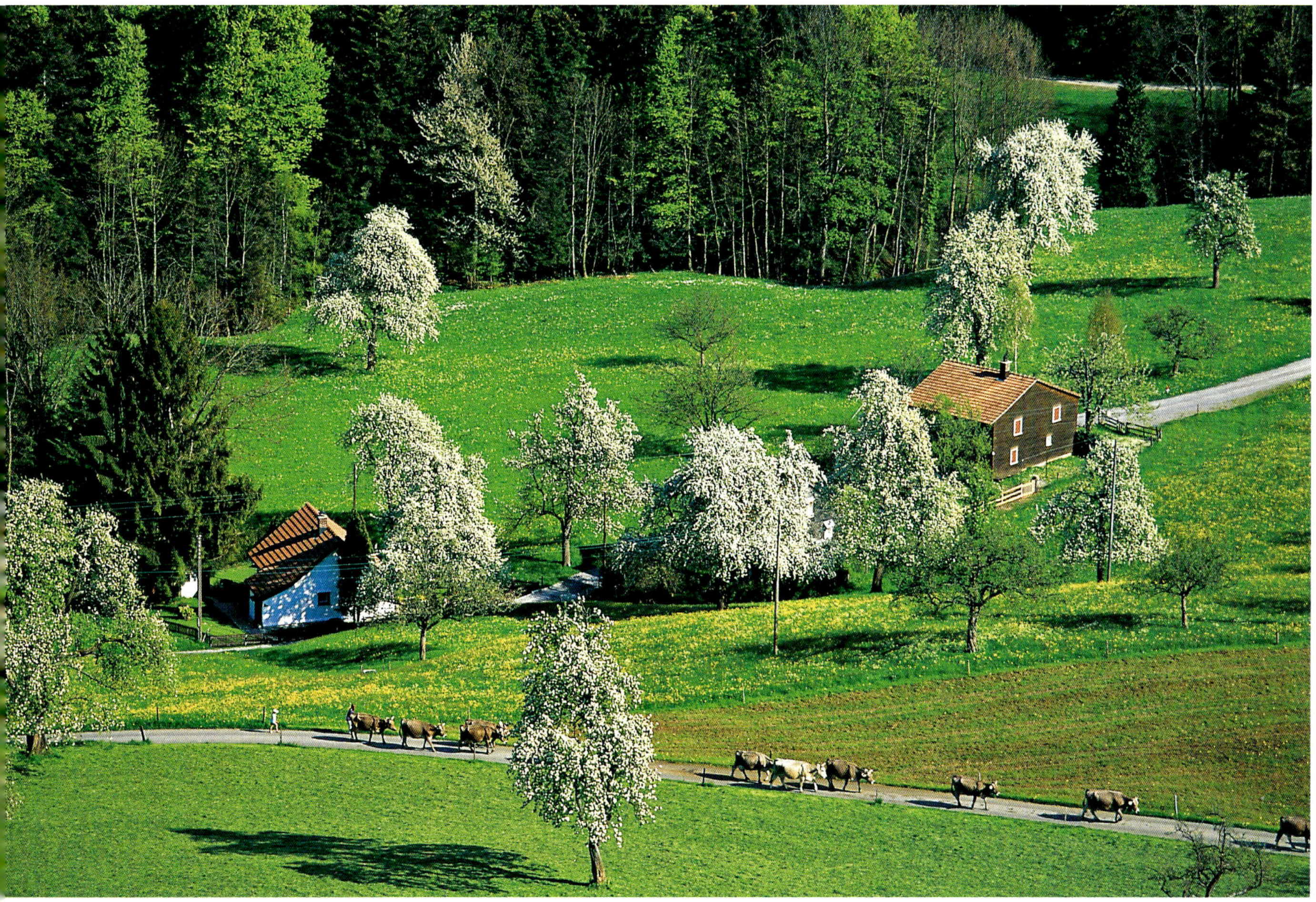

The Appenzeller Land is the only Swiss canton to be completely encircled by another (St Gallen).

*Page 48/49:
The sun bathing the Altmann in a golden orange glow. Seen from the Säntis the second highest mountain in the Alpstein Range on the border to the canton of Appenzell-Innerrhoden is a magnificent sight.*

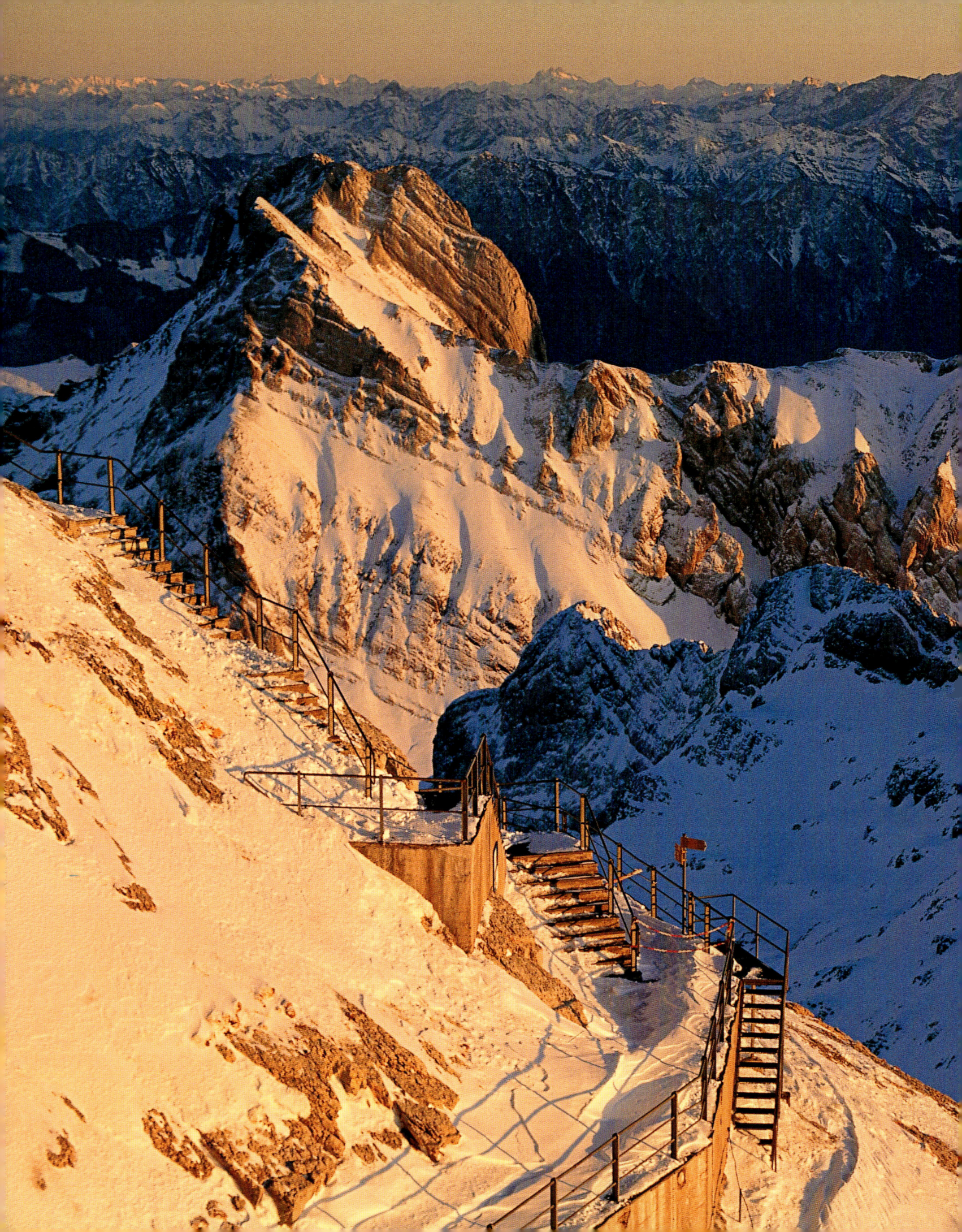

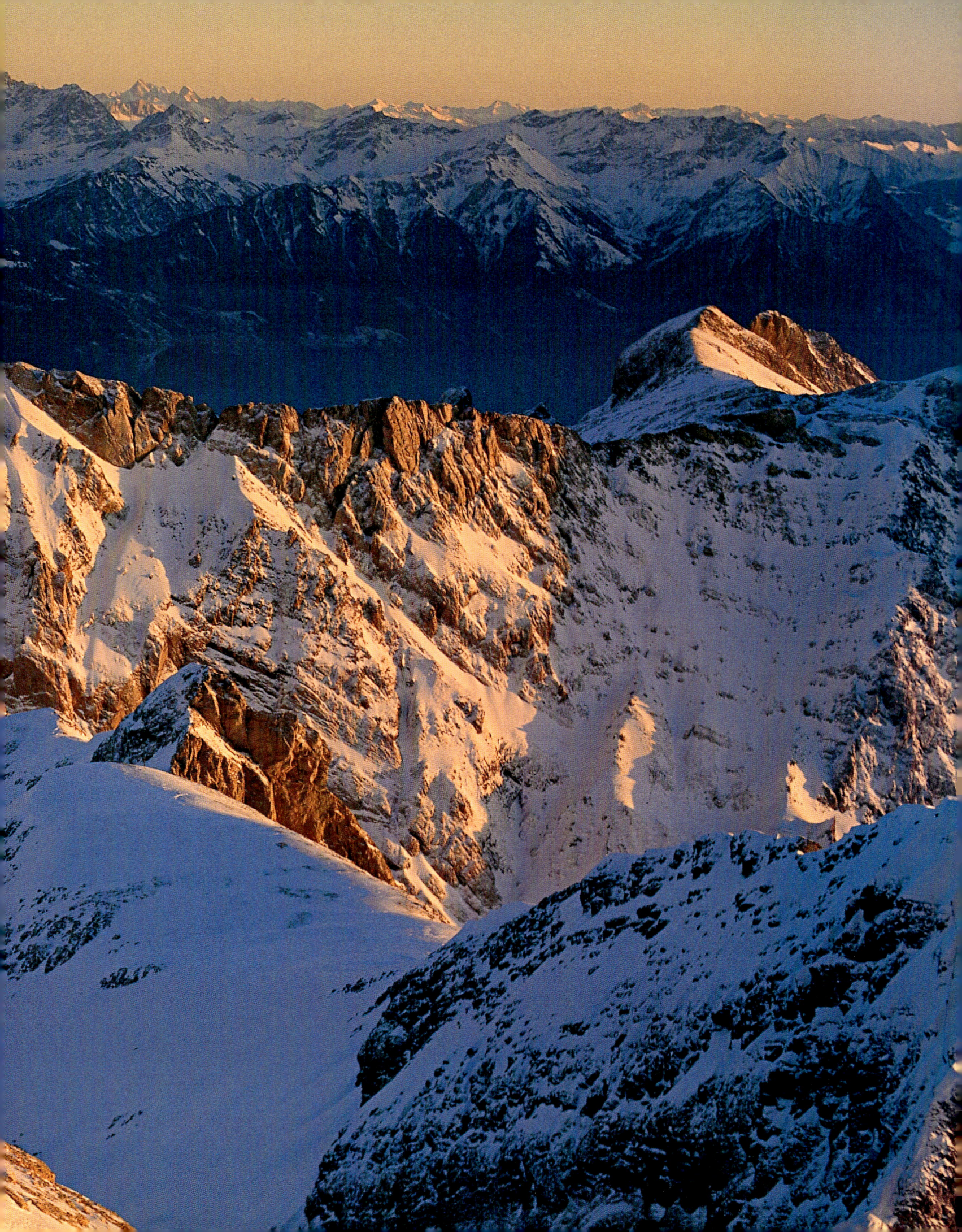

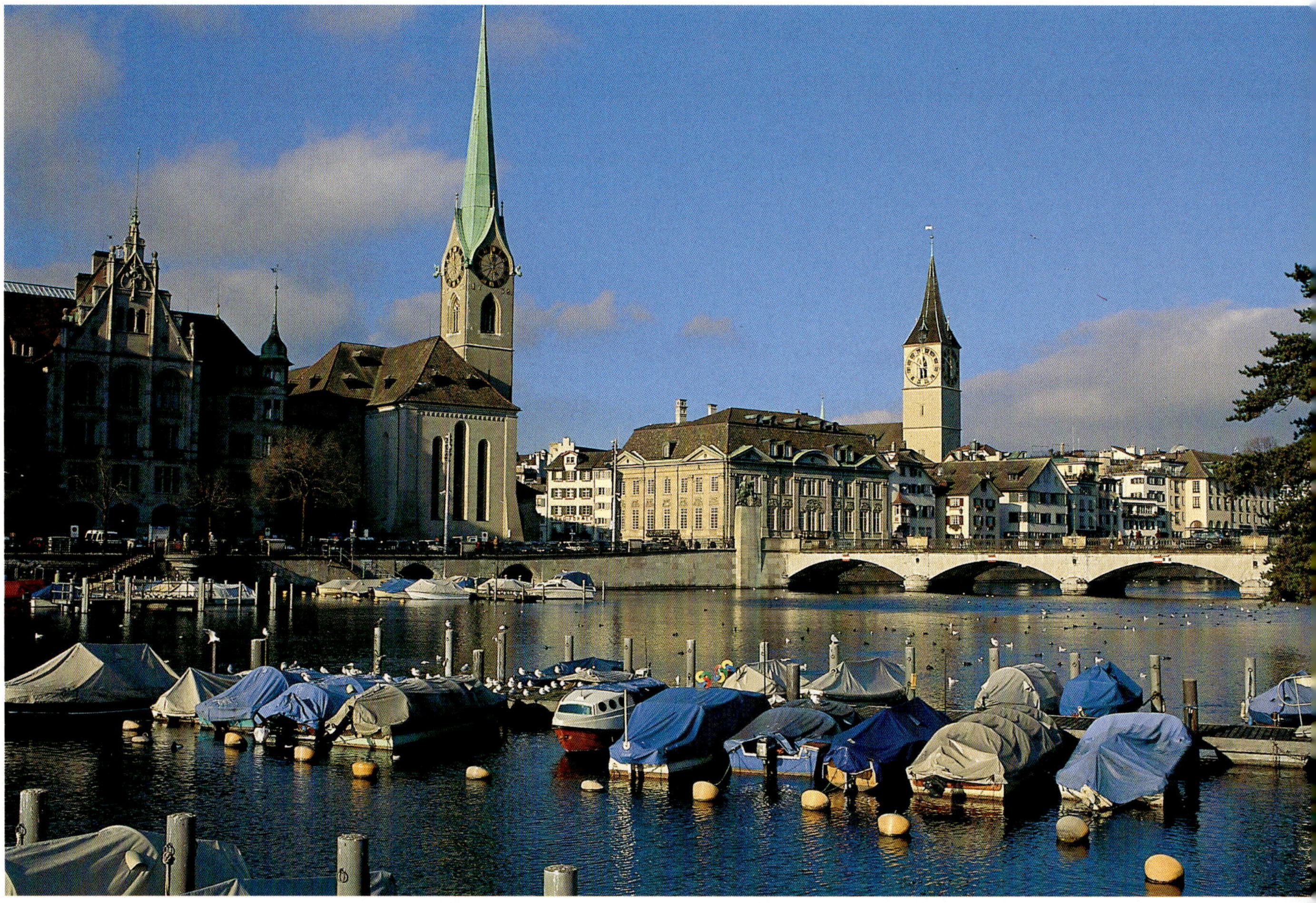

The bridge across the River Limmat in the centre of Old Zürich. Despite Bern being the political hub of the country Zürich has long been considered the secret capital of Switzerland – which is perhaps not an unjust assertion if you consider that it was the liberal powers in this city which were instrumental in founding the country's modern and democratic state.

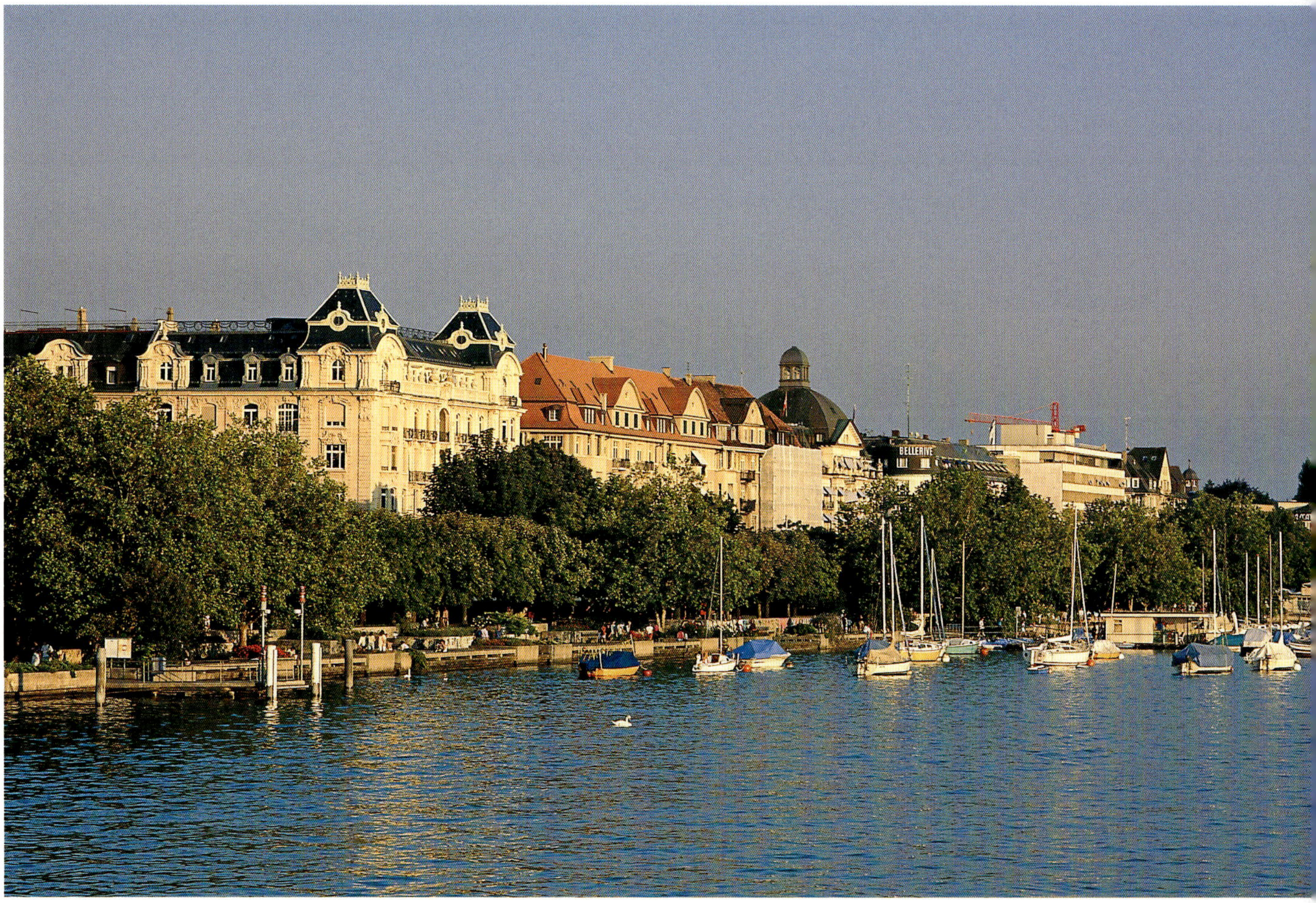

Lake Zürich to the southeast of the city laps the shores of three cantons: Zürich, St Gallen and Schwyz. Its waters are clean enough to drink and fed by the River Linth which exits the lake as the Limmat.

Right page:
Zürich is the largest city serviced by the River Limmat. Small boats can sail the river up to the first weir regulating the amount of water drained from Lake Zürich. In former times the Limmat was navigable all the way downstream from Zürich; traders could start their journey on the River Linth and skipper along the Limmat and Aare to the Rhine where they then sold their wares at the rivers' confluence. This is no longer possible now that a number of hydroelectric power stations have been built near Zürich.

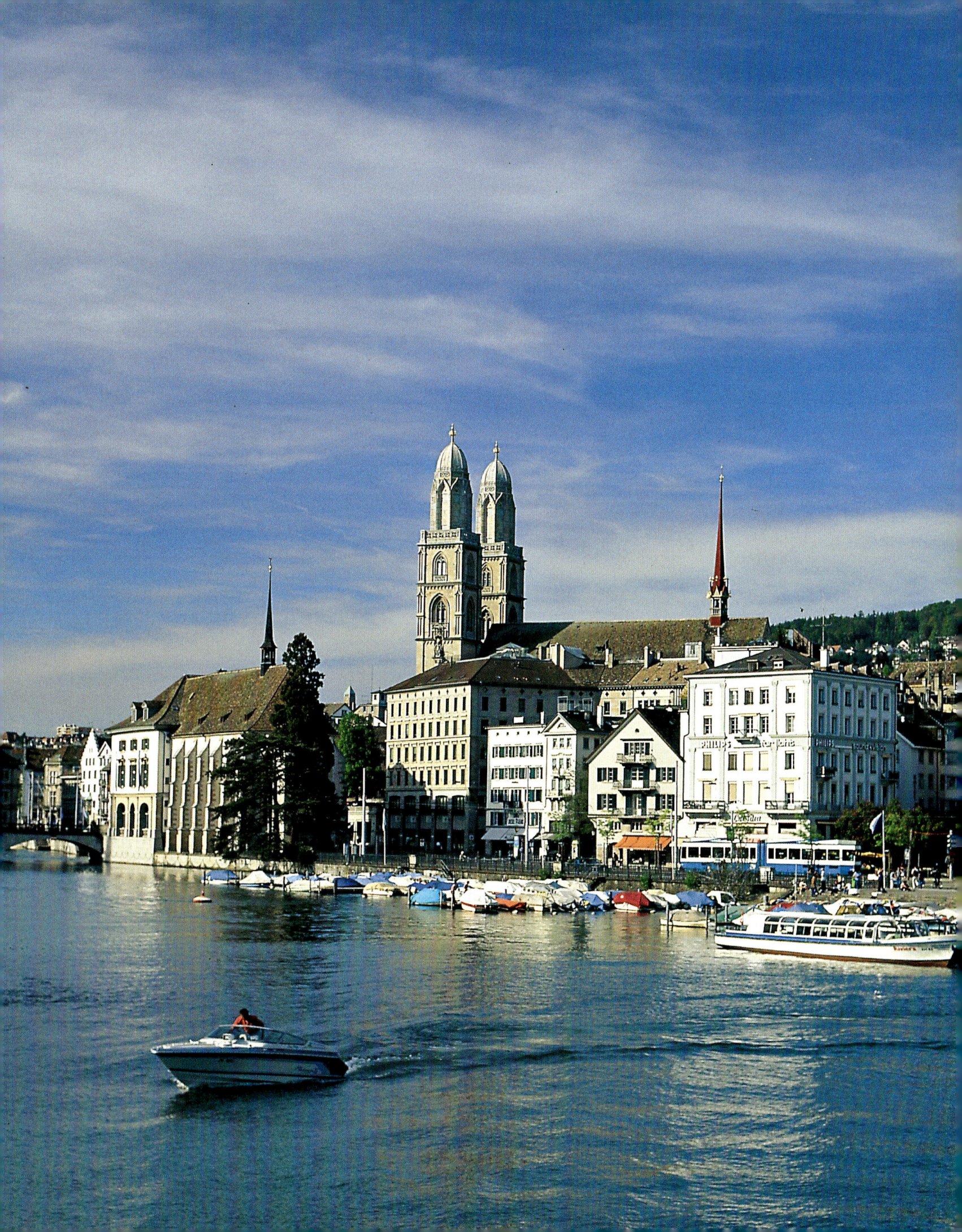

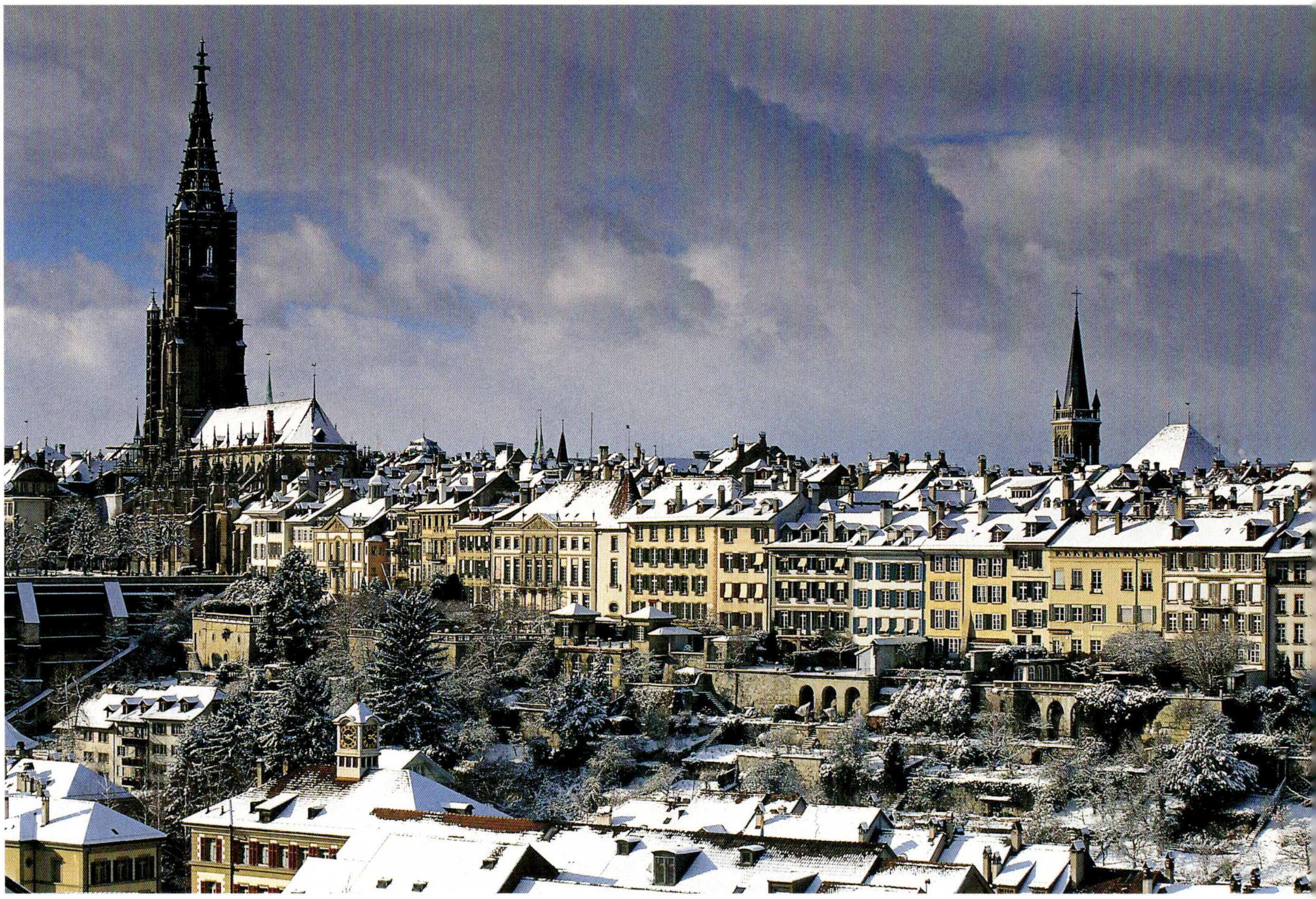

The 'capital' of Bern is a typically Swiss compromise. As the Swiss Constitution doesn't actually allow for a capital city Bern is known as the country's "national city": a capital by name since 1848 – but not by nature.

In Bern the fourth Monday in November is reserved for the onion market where the pungent vegetable and much more can be purchased. Visitors from all over Switzerland and the neighbouring countries turn up early to begin perusing the stalls when they open at 3 o'clock in the morning. The end of the market is marked by a huge confetti fight at 4 pm.

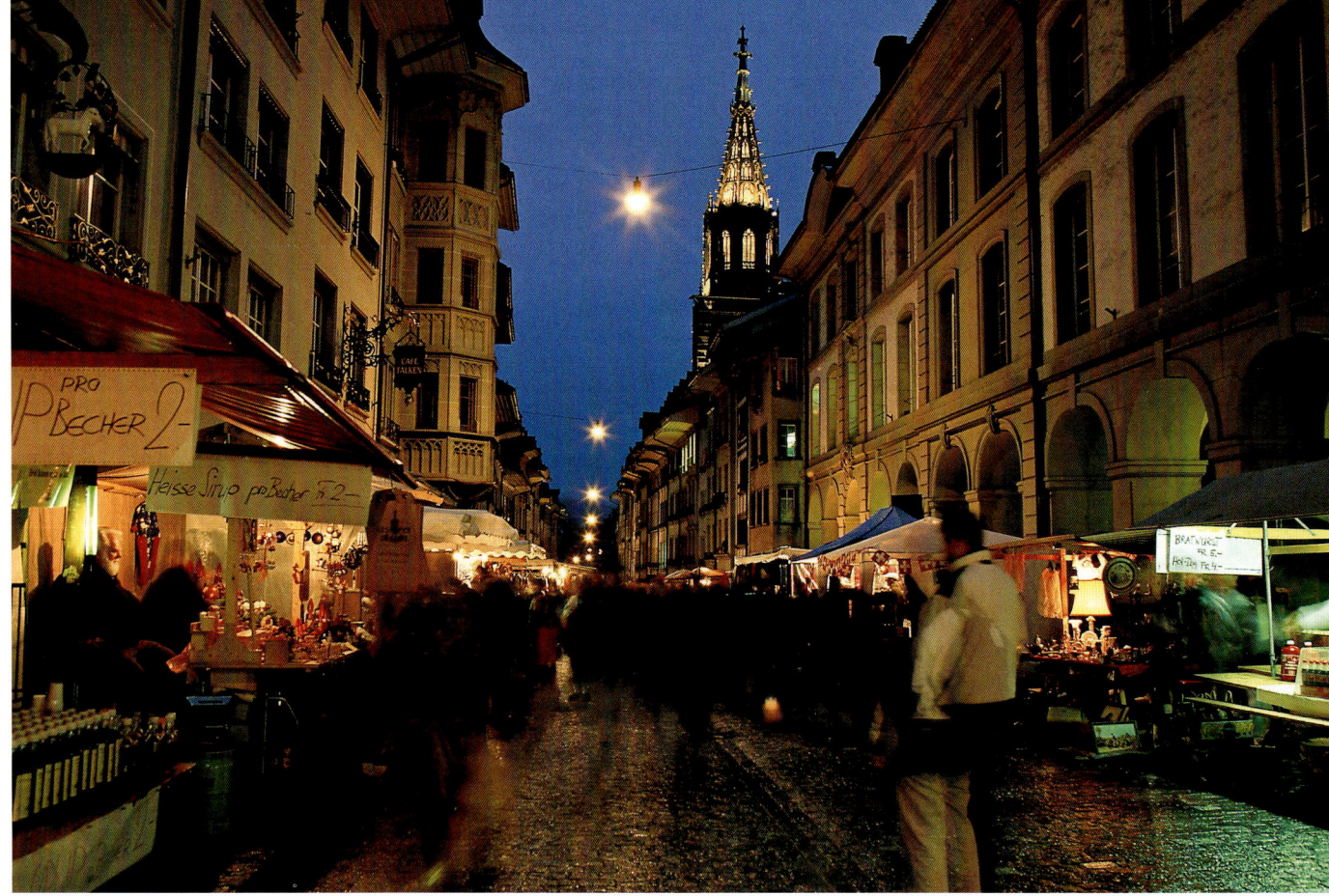

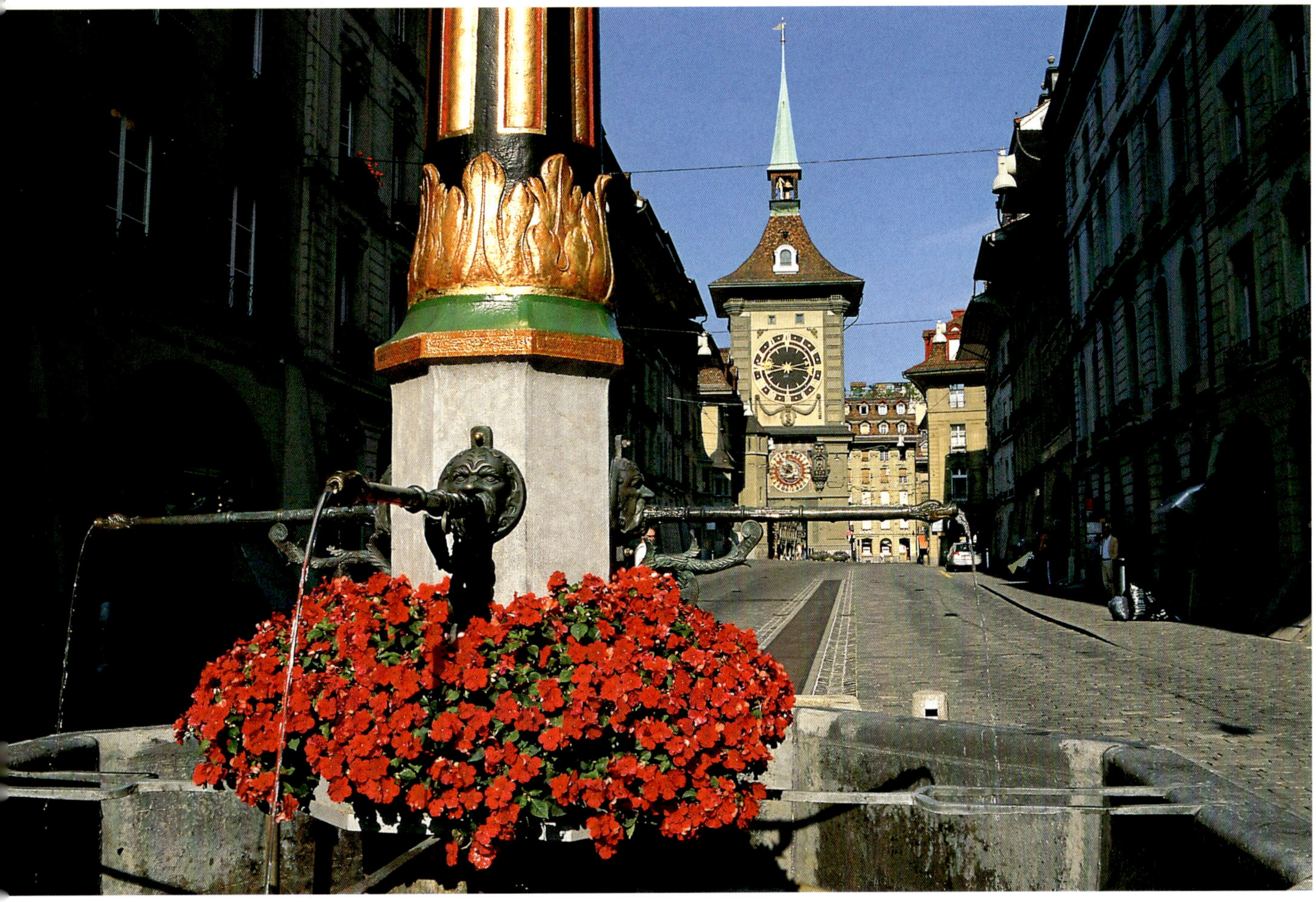

The Zytgloggeturm, built in 1191, is the old western gate of the city once used as a women's prison. Following the great fire of Bern in 1405 a peal of bells was installed. The tower is now adorned by the ornamental figures of the carillon and an astronomical clock from the 16th century.

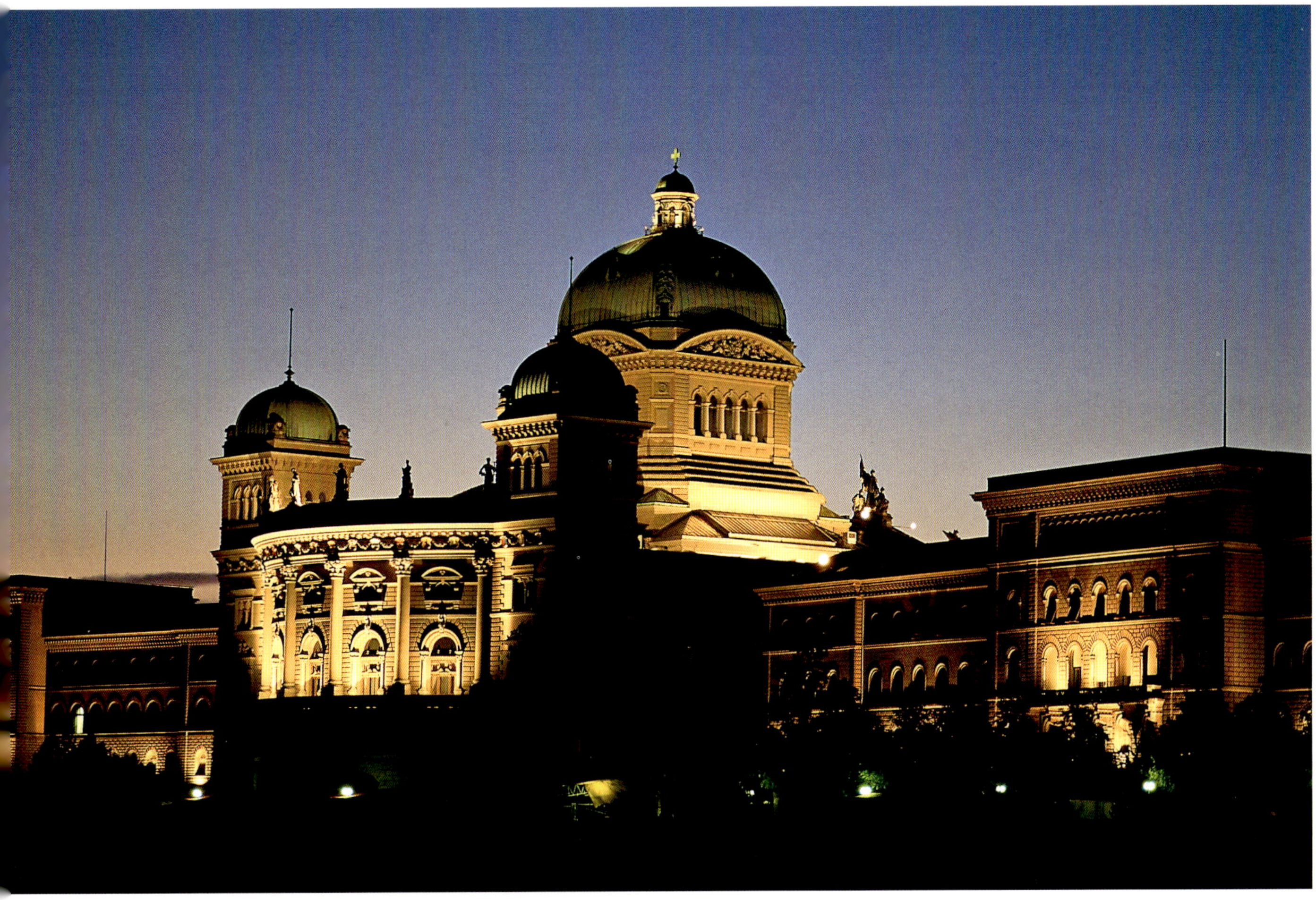

The parliamentary building with its mighty dome was erected in 1902 from Swiss building materials and now houses the main chambers of the Federal Assembly.

Lush pastures and idyllic farmsteads: near Sumiswald in the Emmental life seems to be a peaceful affair.

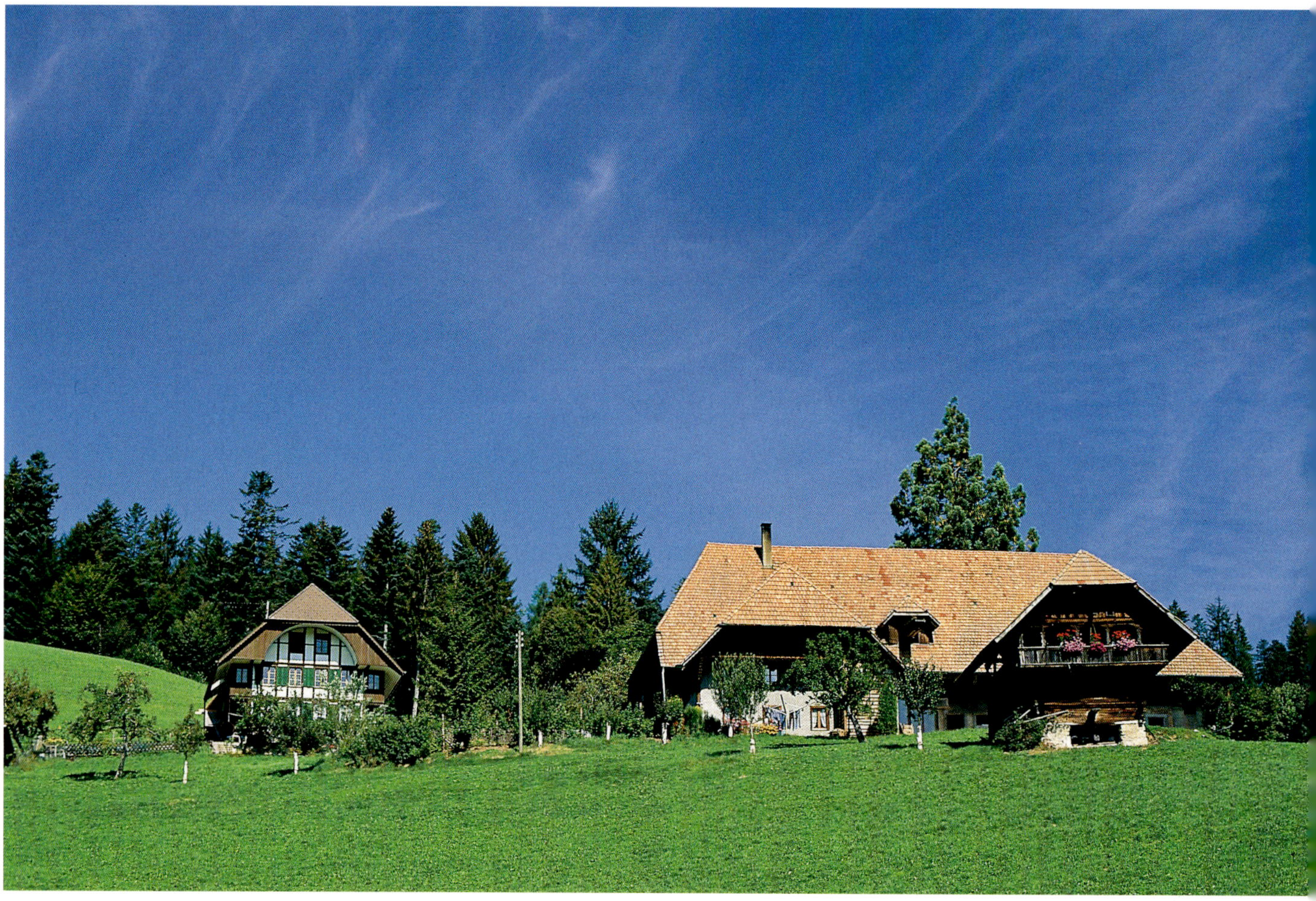

After the last ice age Lake Sarn was part of what is now Lake Lucerne. In time its inlets the Grosse and Kleine Schliere and the Grosse Melchaa washed up scree and debris, creating a natural dam and a new lake 35 metres (115 feet) above the water level of Lake Zürich.

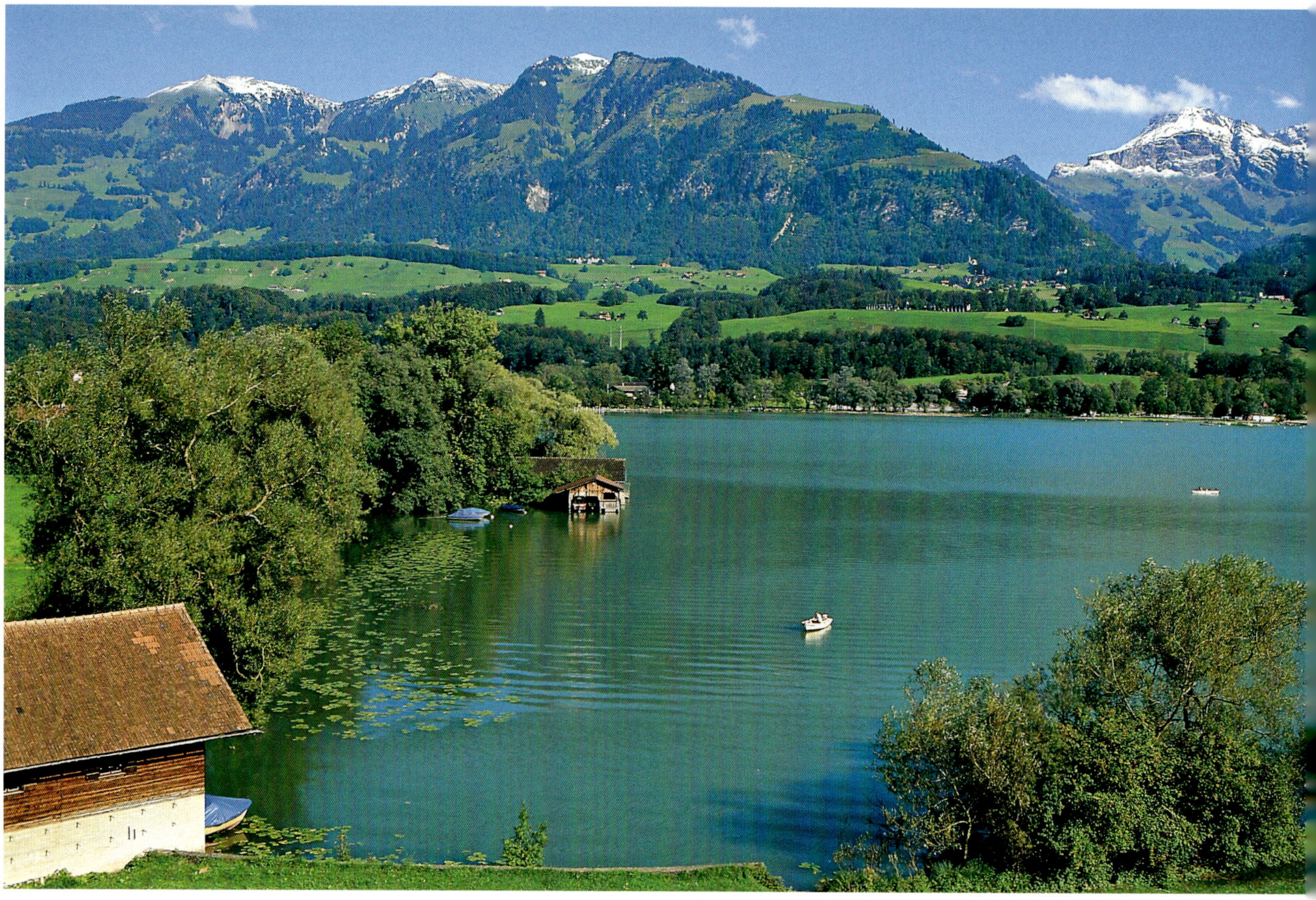

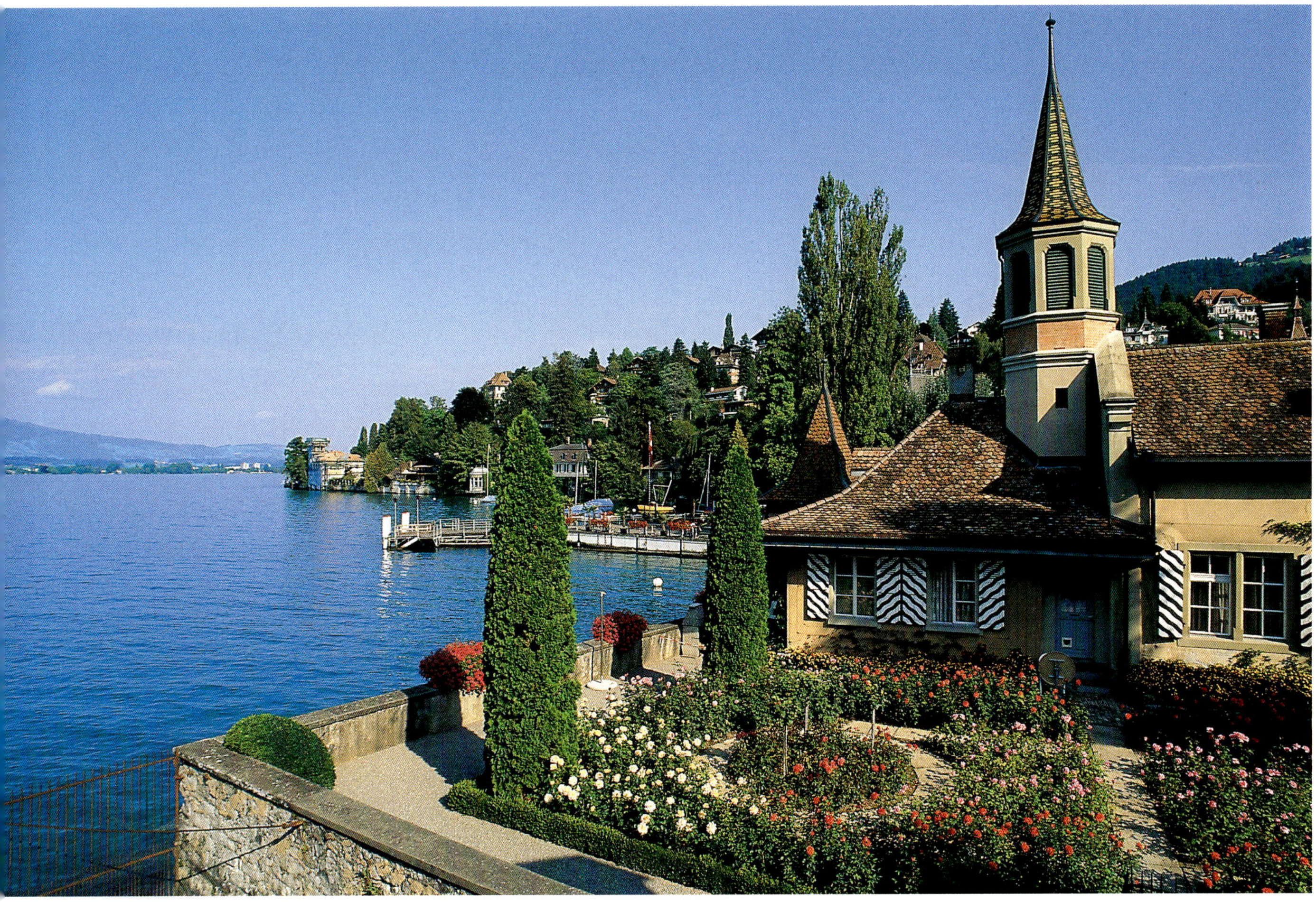

The palace gardens of Oberhofen on Lake Thun. The old castle has been a division of the Historisches Museum in Bern since 1954.

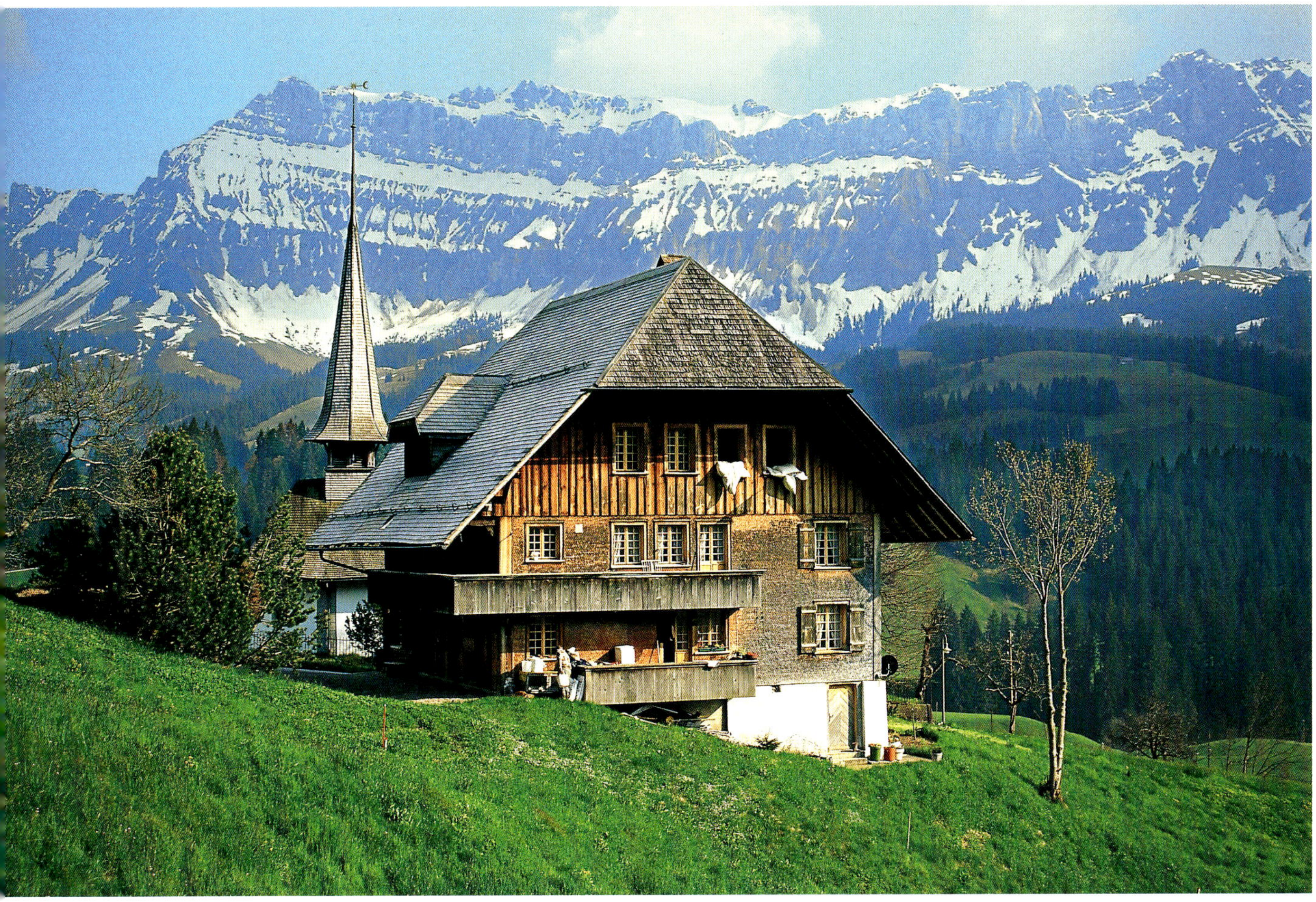

Large farmhouses with long hipped roofs are typical of the Emmental. The gable on this one is half hipped.

Right page:
On the left side of the Lauterbrunnental the Staubbachfall crashes 300 metres (984 feet) down into the depths. The falls inspired Johann Wolfgang von Goethe to write "Gesang der Geister über den Wassern" (Song of the Spirits of the Water).

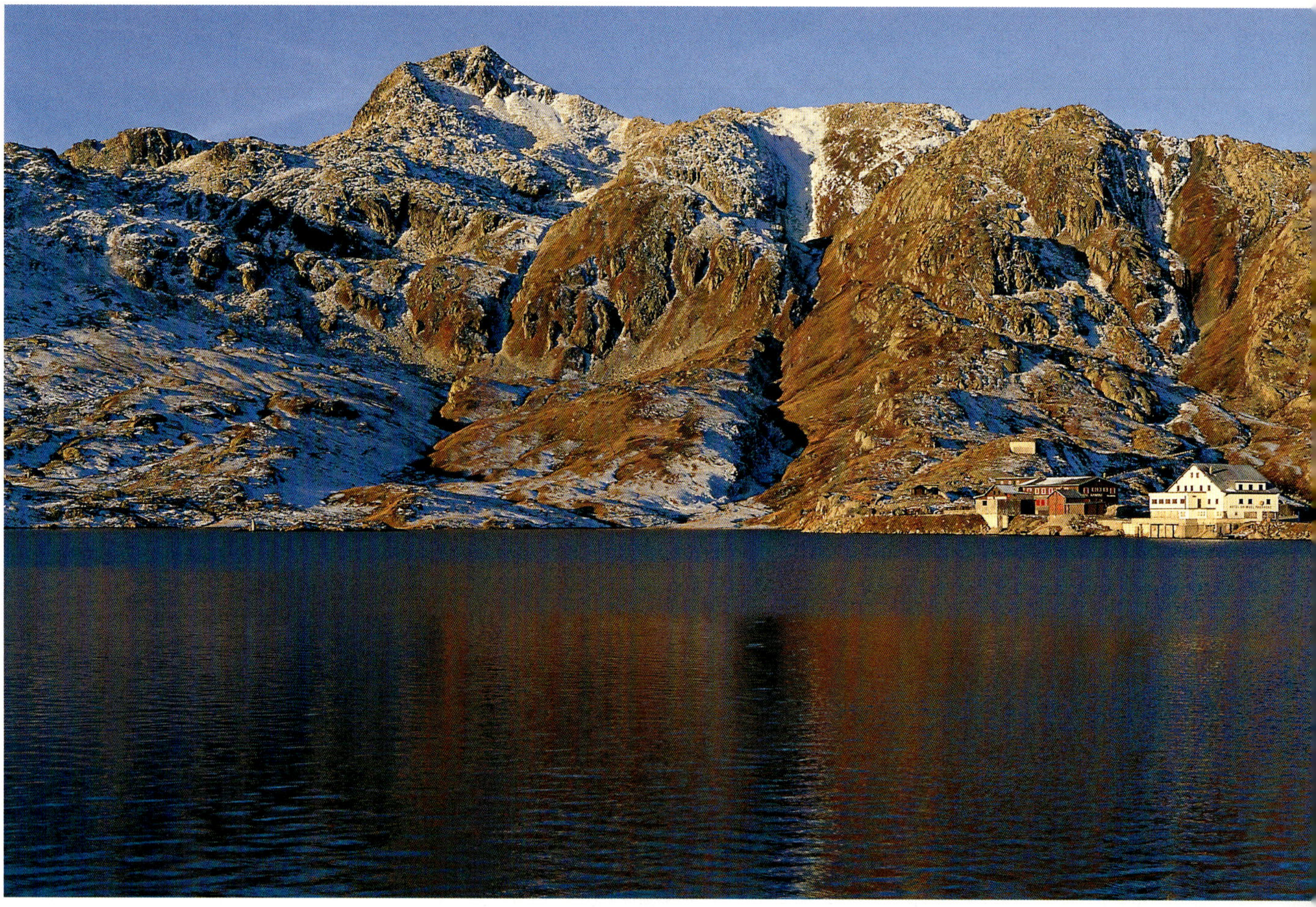

The Grimsel Pass in the canton of Bern is situated on the European watershed 2,165 metres (7,103 feet) above sea level. Along the north approach are a number of reservoirs serving the power station at Oberhasli. Water has been dammed to create Lake Grimsel 1,909 metres (6,263 feet) up.

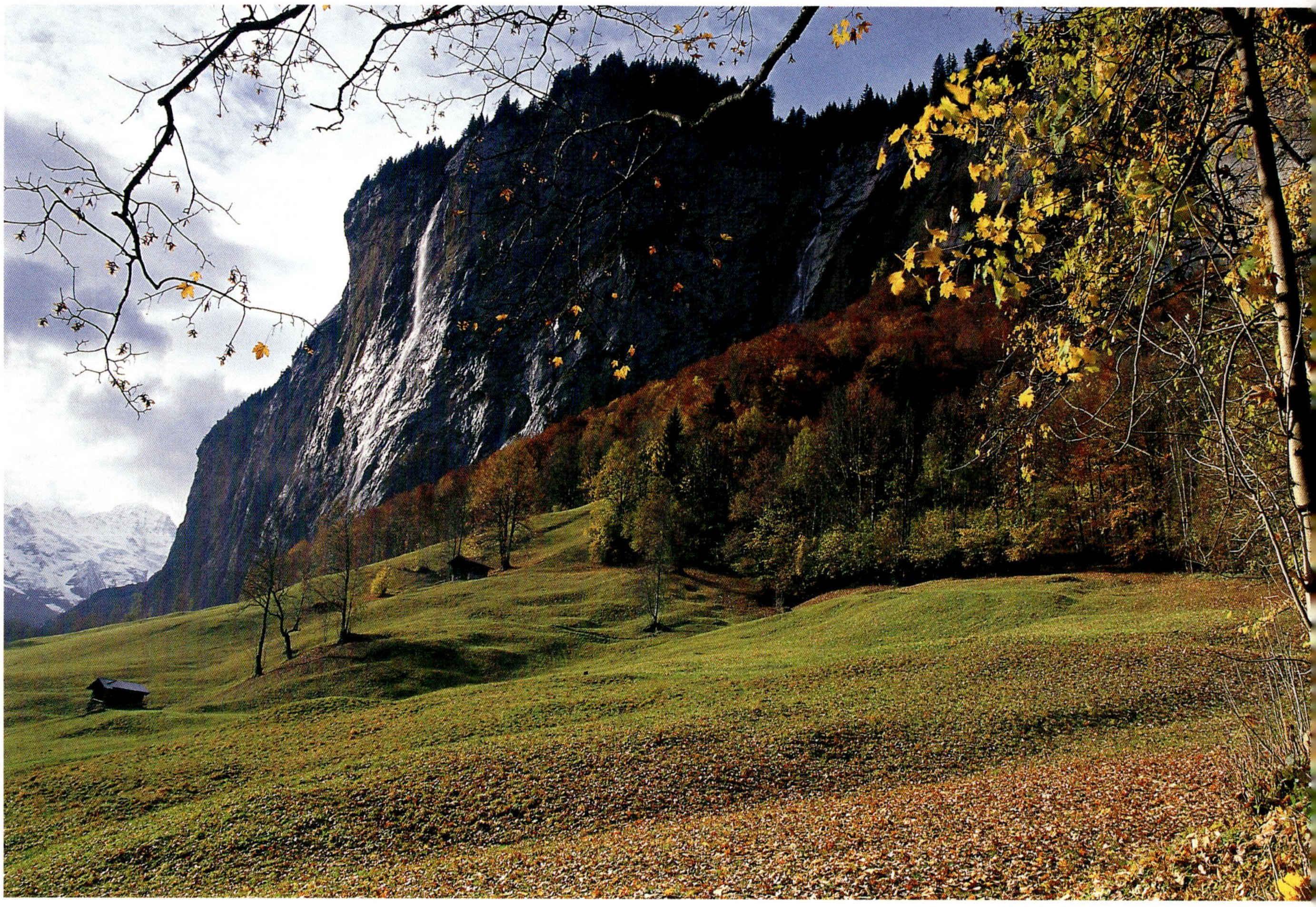

The Lauterbrunnental gets its name from "lauter", which means "clear" here, and "Brunnen" or well. The glaciated valley has many high waterfalls cascading down steep walls of rock.

Page 58/59:
The three distinctive peaks of the Eiger, Mönch and Jungfrau positively dominate the Bernese Oberland. The north face of the Eiger is infamous and has sadly cost many experienced mountaineers their lives.

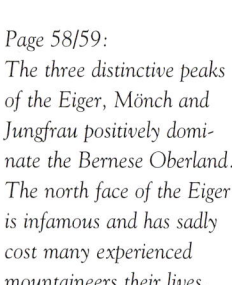

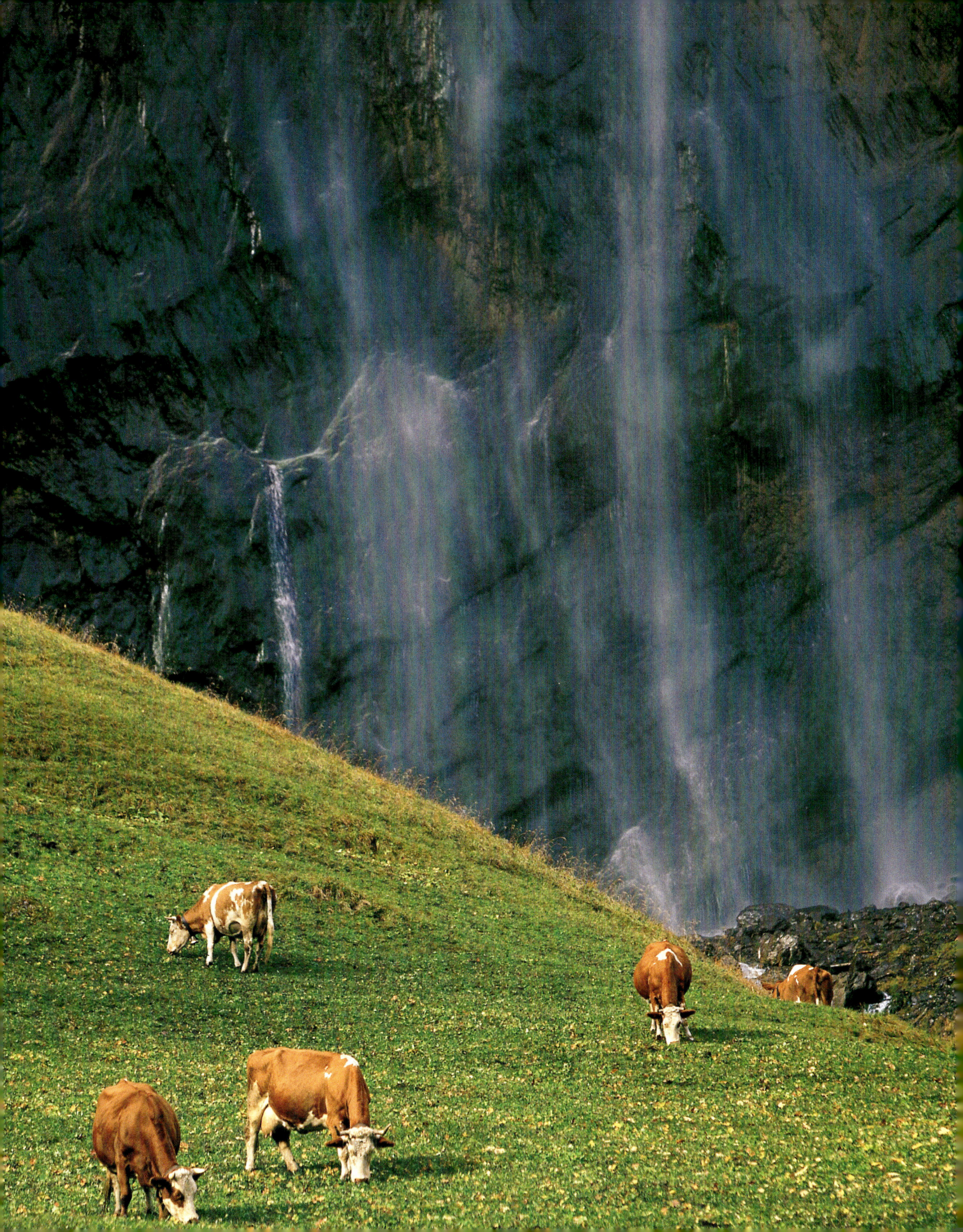

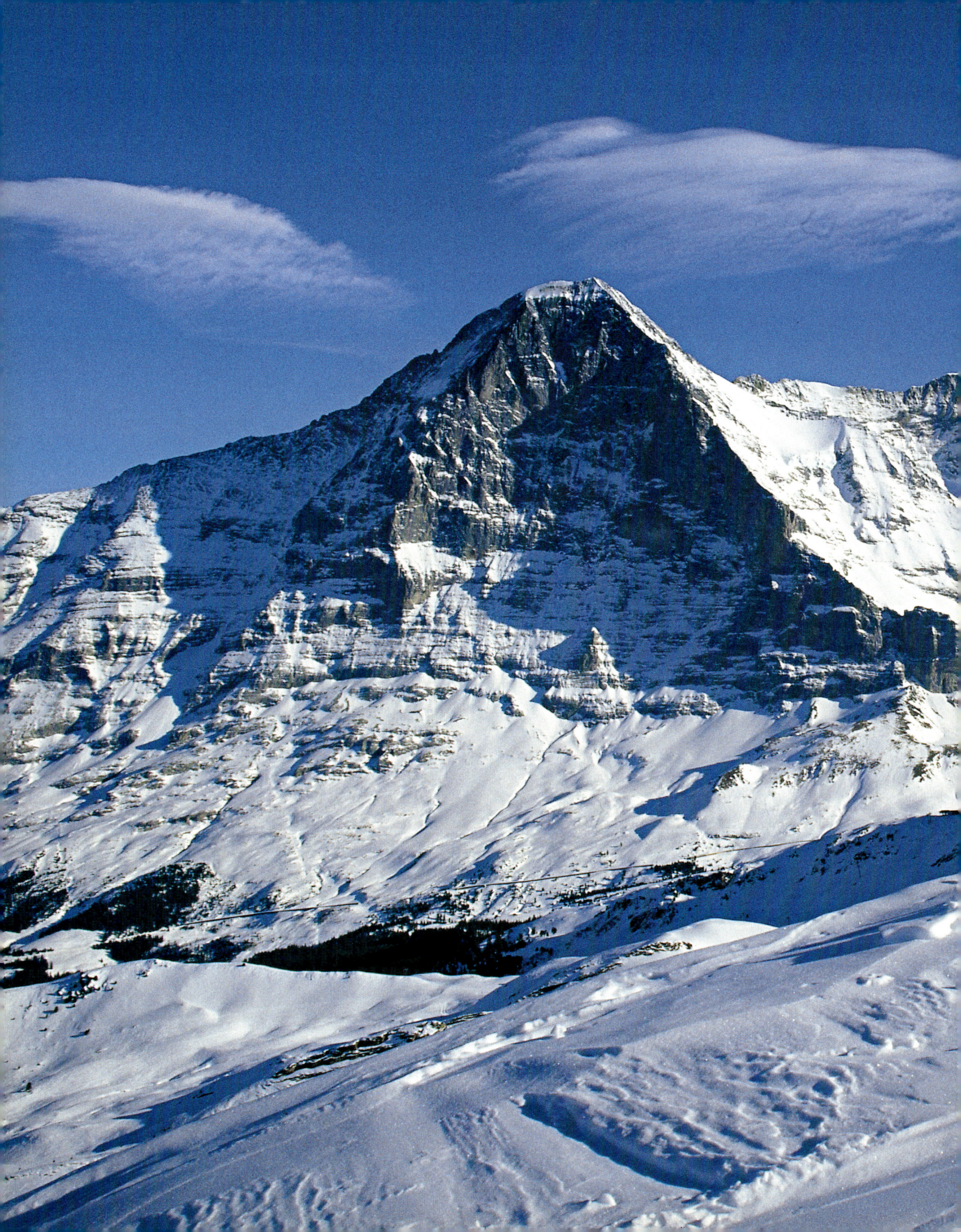

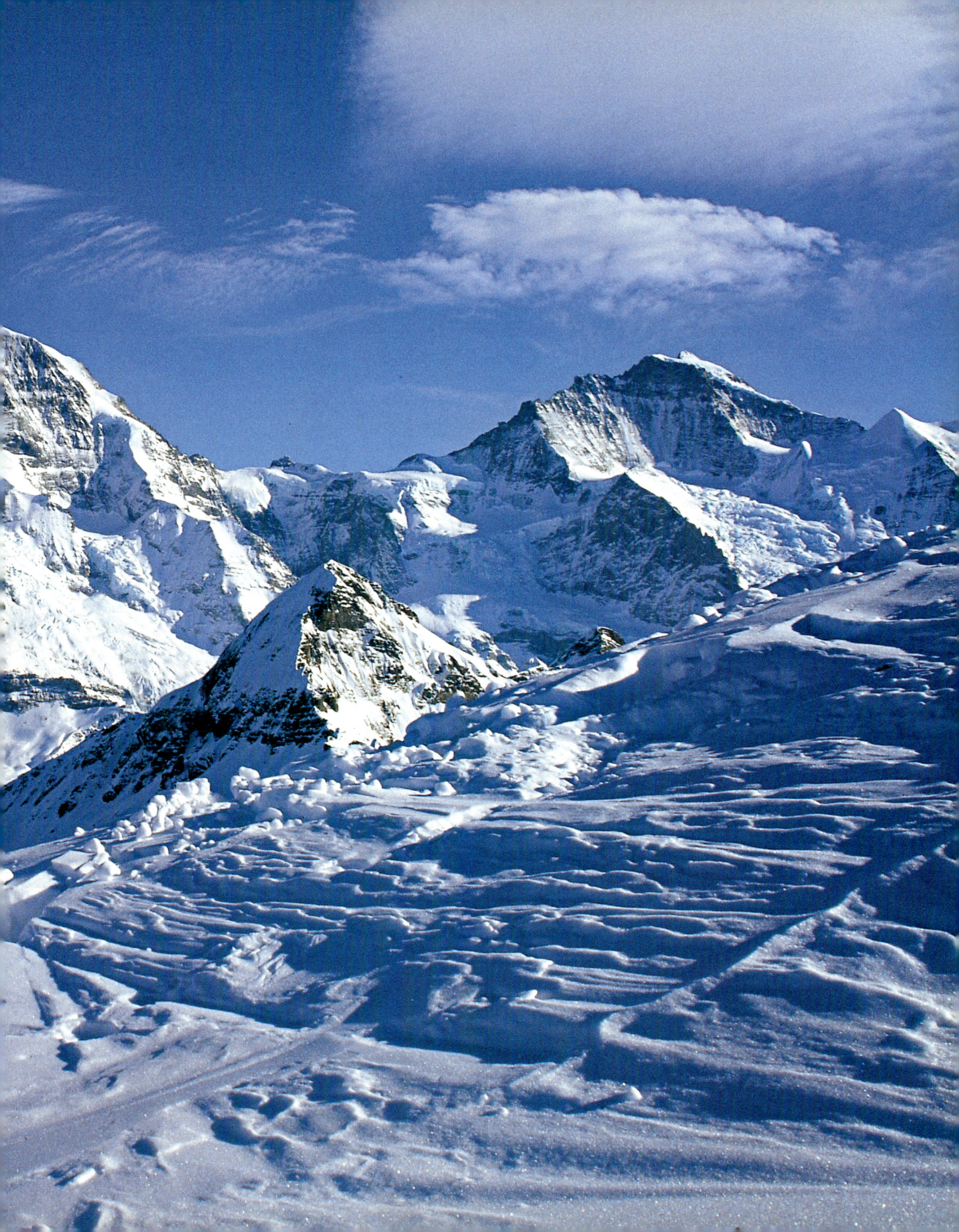

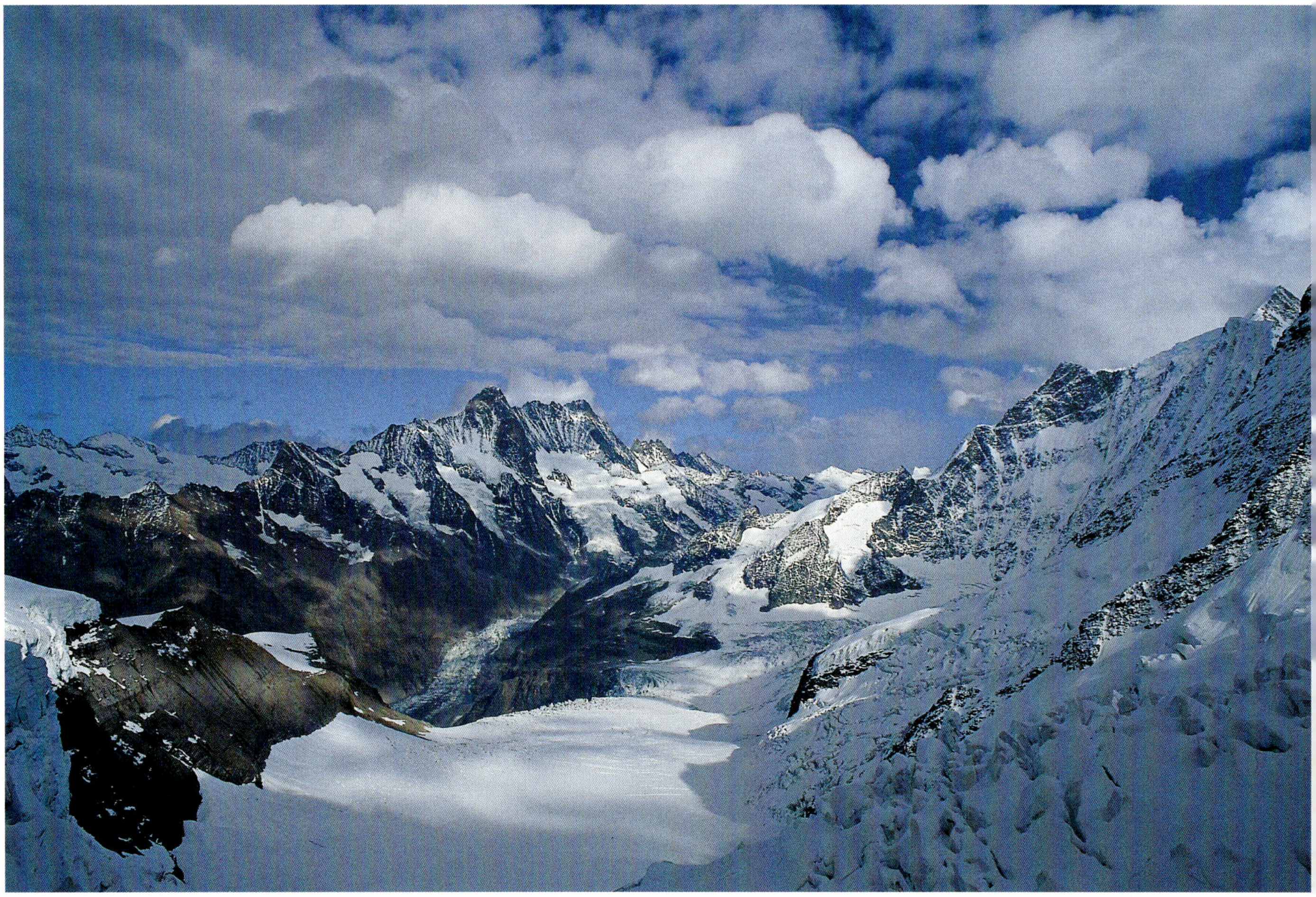

If you're brave enough to tackle the assault on the north face of the Eiger, magnificent views are your reward.

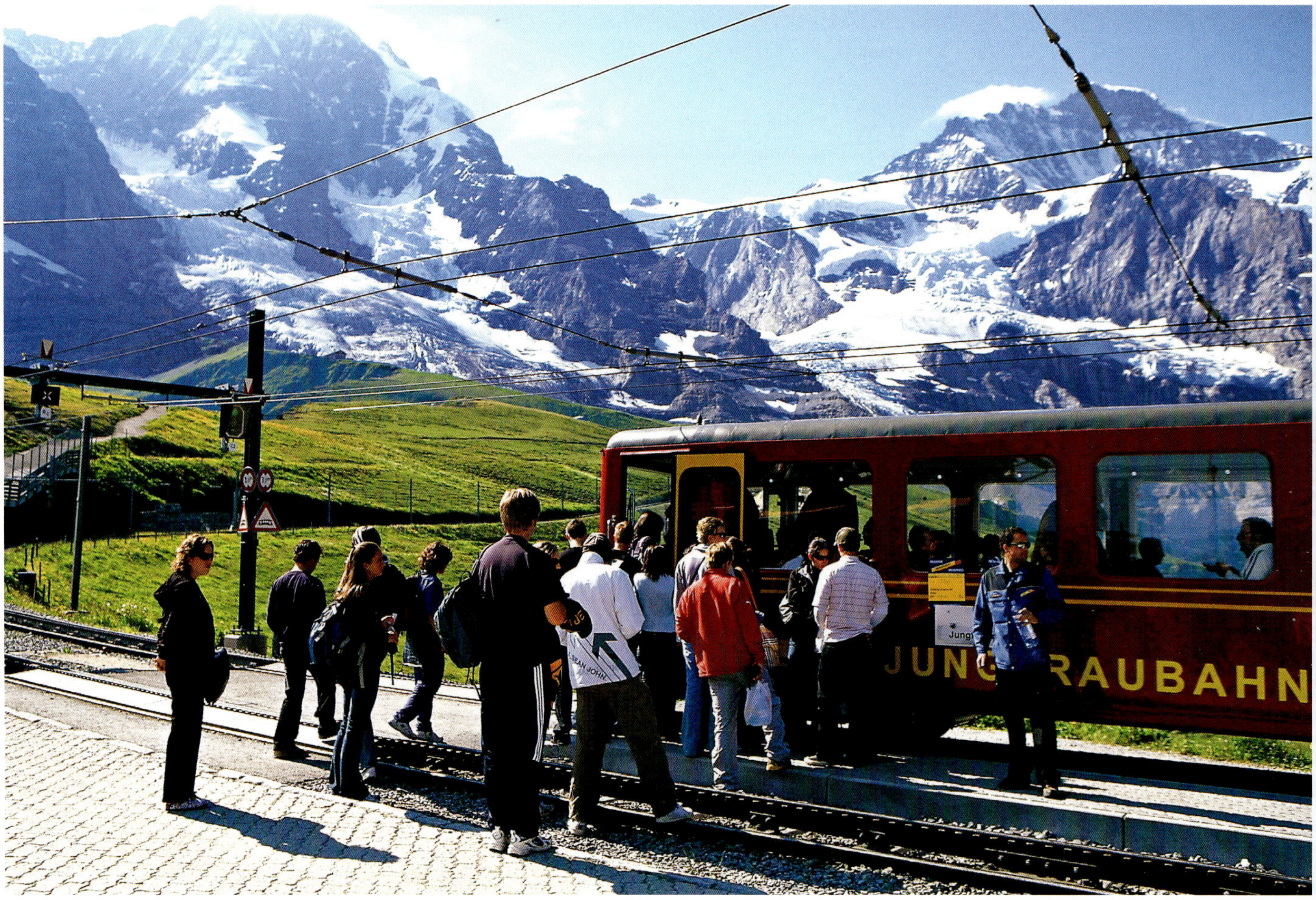

Hotels and stations for the Jungfrau and Wengernalp rack railways are sited at the top of the Kleine Scheidegg Pass between the Eiger and the Lauberhorn. In winter the area is good for skiing.

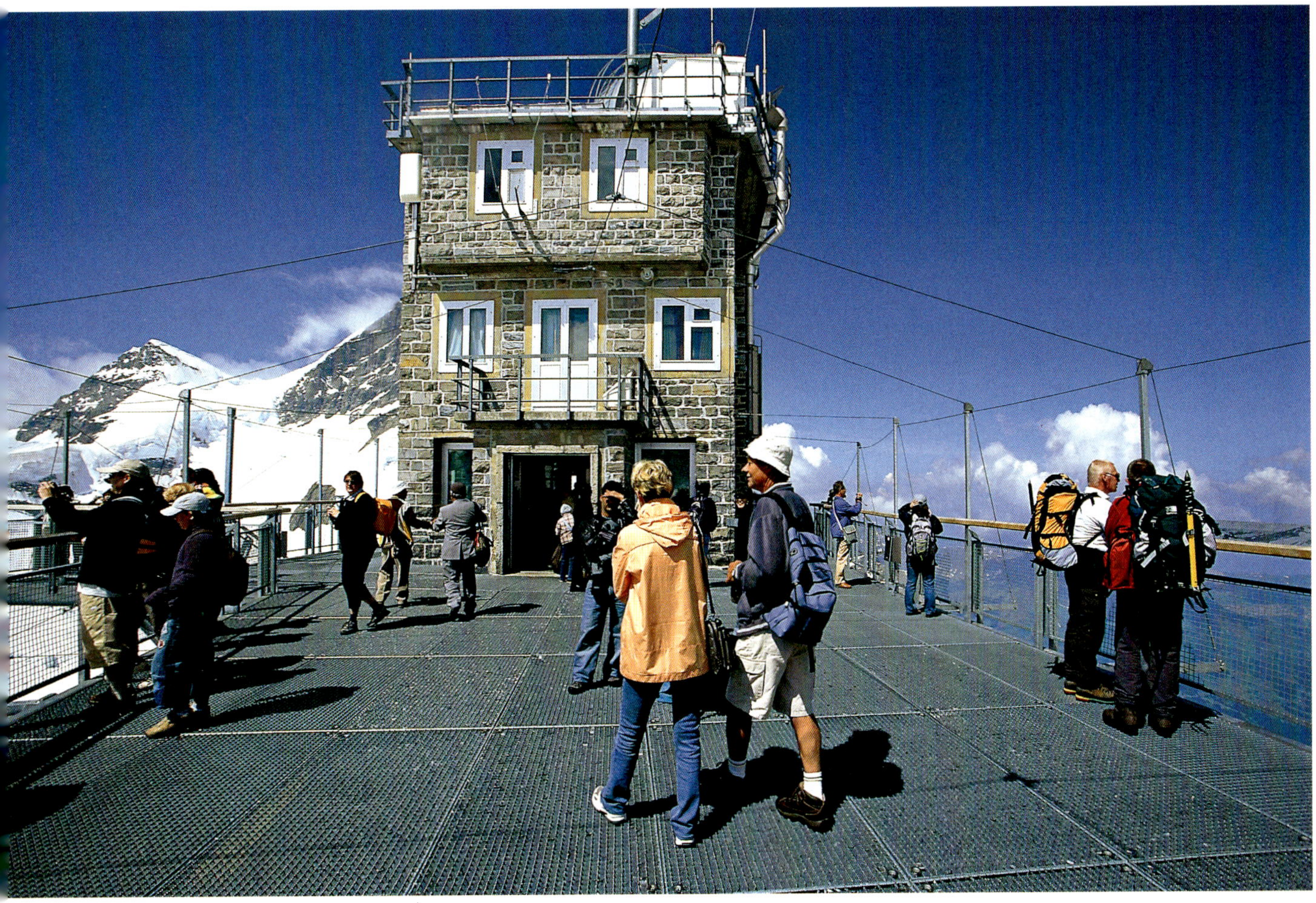

The Jungfraujoch, 3,454 metres (11,332 feet) high, is the final stop on the Jungfraubahn railway and the lowest point on the crest linking the Jungfrau (4,158 metres/13,642 feet) and Mönch (4,107 metres/ 13,475 feet). The Sphinx observatory is named after the mountain top to the east of the ridge.

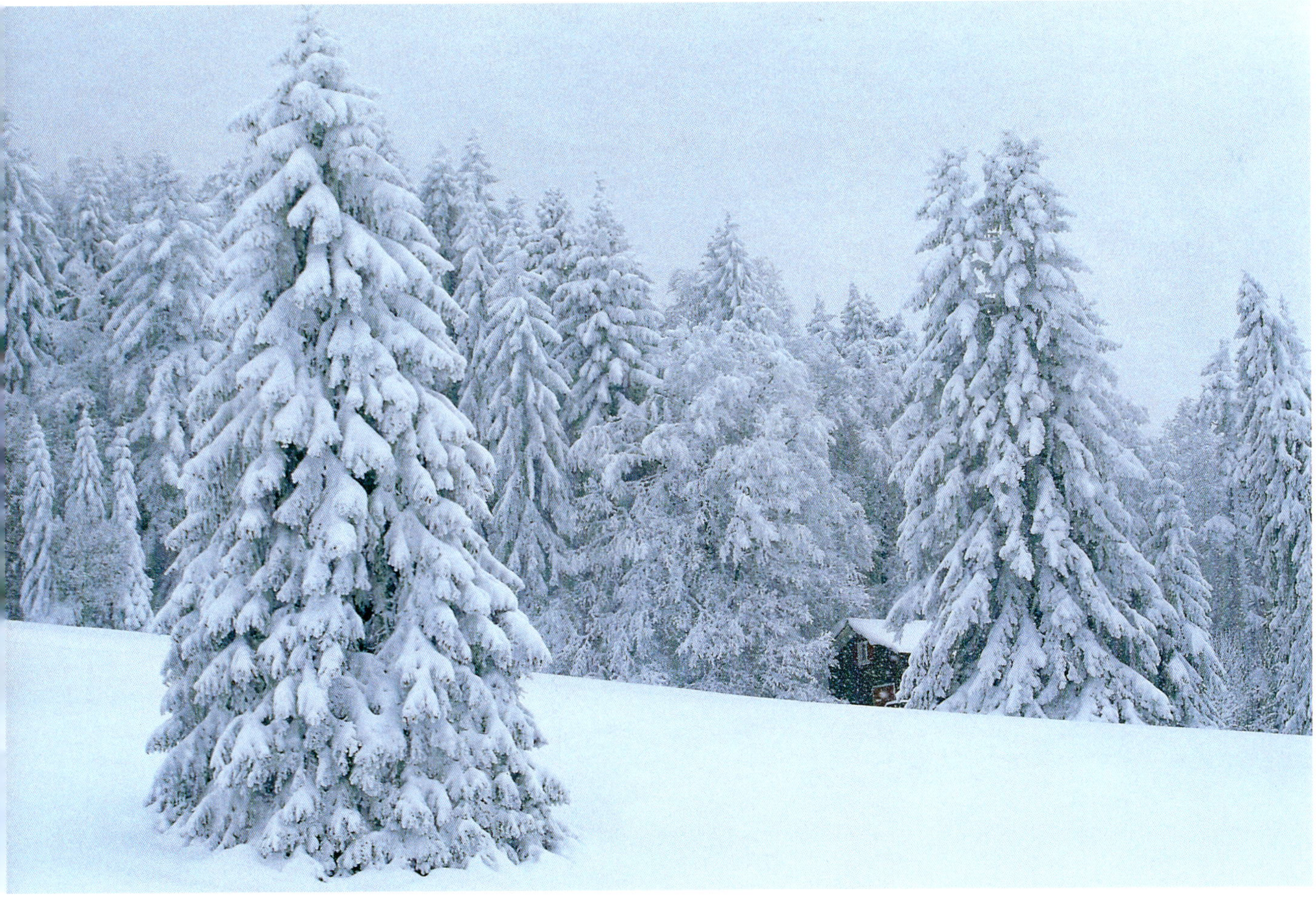

Deep snow on Mont Crosin between St Imier and Tramelan has transformed these fir trees into magical figures.

The Kleiner and Grosser Mythen are pretty characteristic and logical choices as landmarks of the canton's capital Schwyz. The summit boasts a restaurant and also an honorary table for regulars; those eligible to join the 100er-Club have to have climbed the mountain a hundred times in a year – every year. A safe track leading up the mountain renders professional mountaineering gear redundant in the summer months…

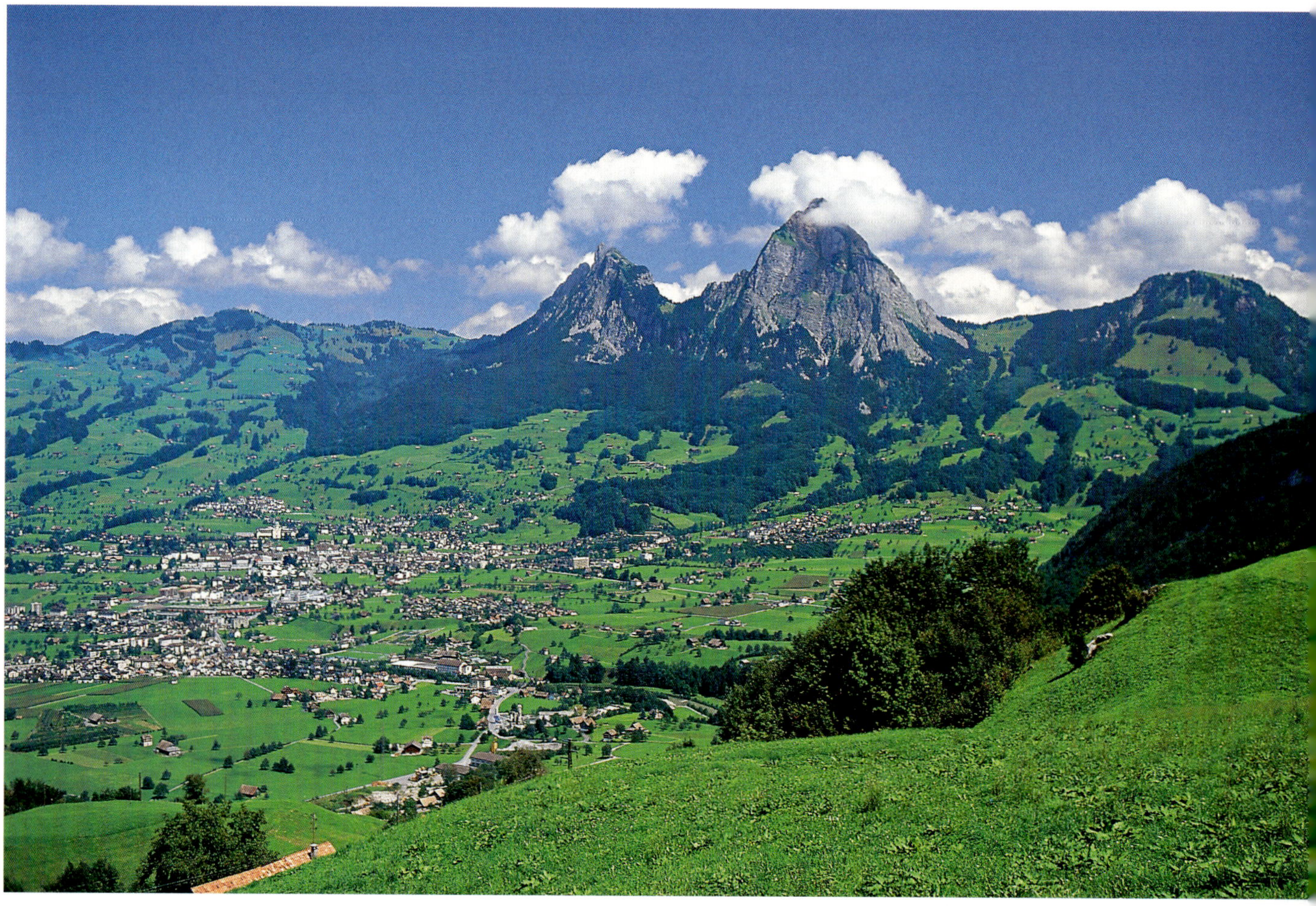

Lucerne lies tucked away at the northwest end of Lake Lucerne at the point where the River Reuss drains the lake. The four forest cantons of Lucerne, Uri, Unterwalden and Schwyz border it – the same four which gave Switzerland the Rütli Oath and the foundations of the Confederation.

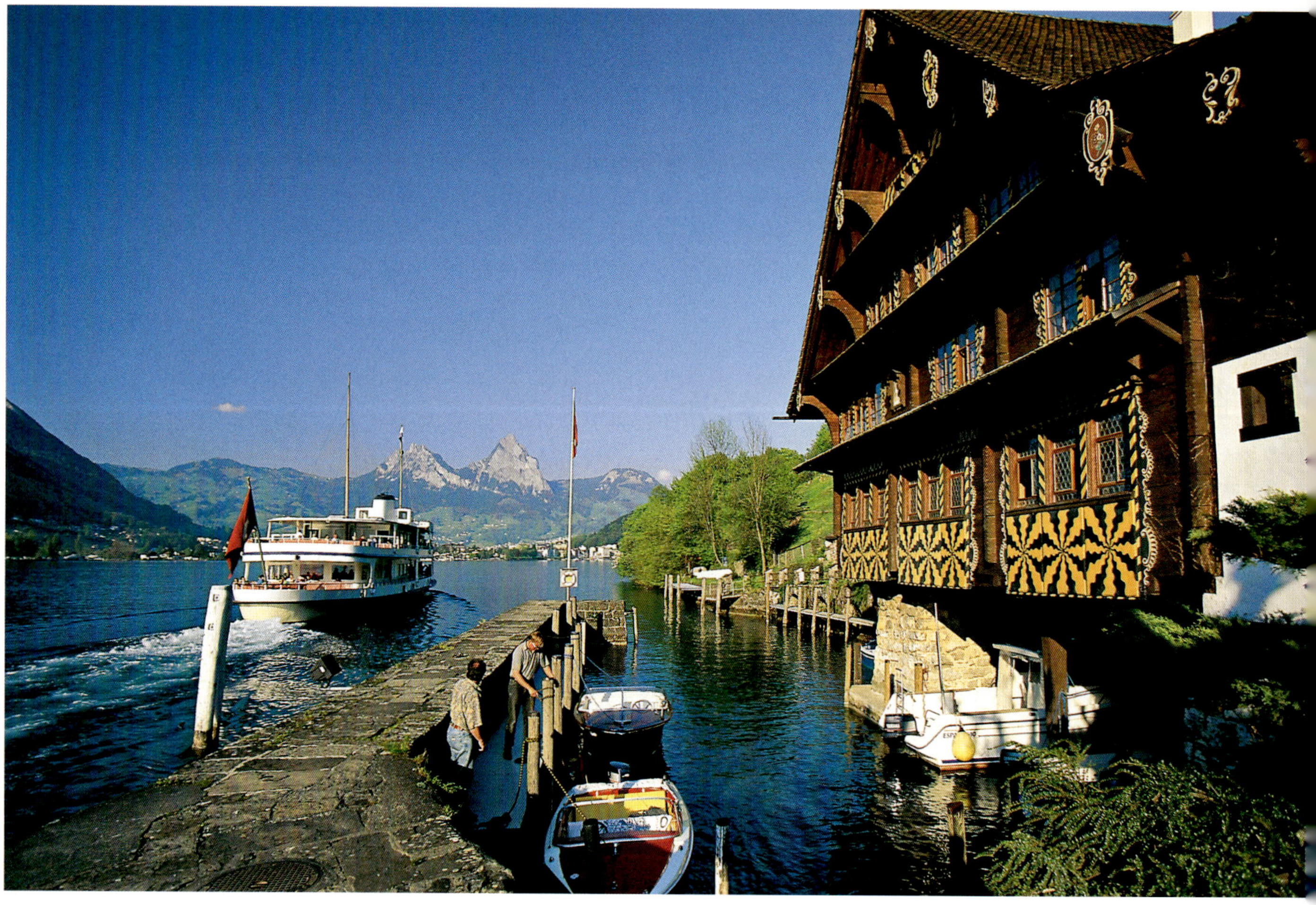

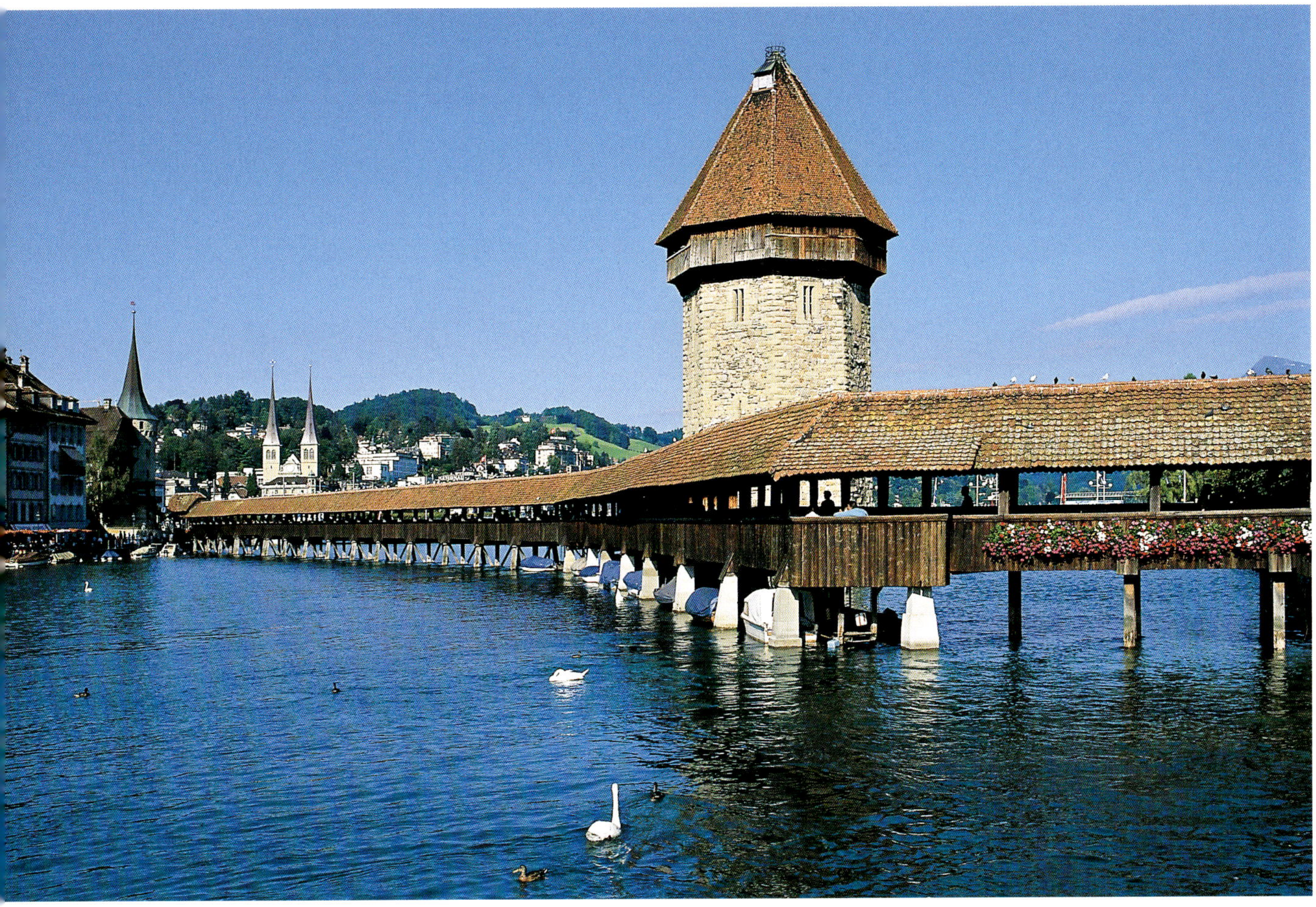

Two of the major sights in Lucerne are the Kapellbrücke and water tower, its local landmark. The bridge links the old and new towns and much of it has had to be rebuilt. A fire in 1993 almost totally destroyed the ancient structure. Using plans drawn up in the 1960s the bridge was carefully restored to its original state – in as far as this was possible.

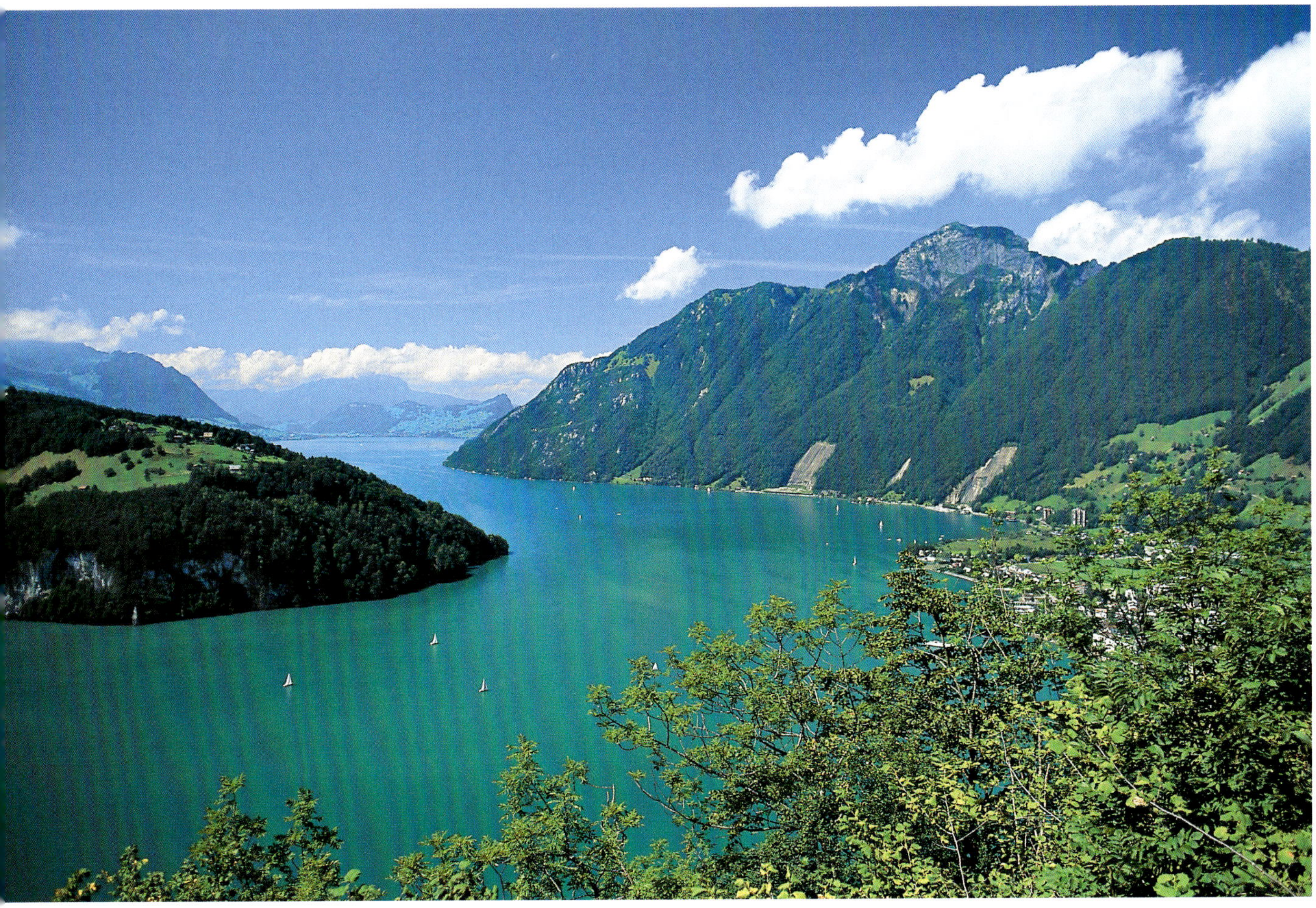

The rugged shape of Lake Lucerne makes it impossible to see from one end to the other. The landscape, the mild climate and the almost Mediterranean vegetation draw many visitors; Japanese couples come here to get married and Indian directors make their Bollywood films here now that the situation in the mountains of Kashmir has become too volatile.

Page 64/65:
Lucerne is the economic and cultural nucleus of Central Switzerland. Its wonderful lakeside setting, surrounded by majestic peaks, made it popular with visitors relatively early on in the history of tourism.

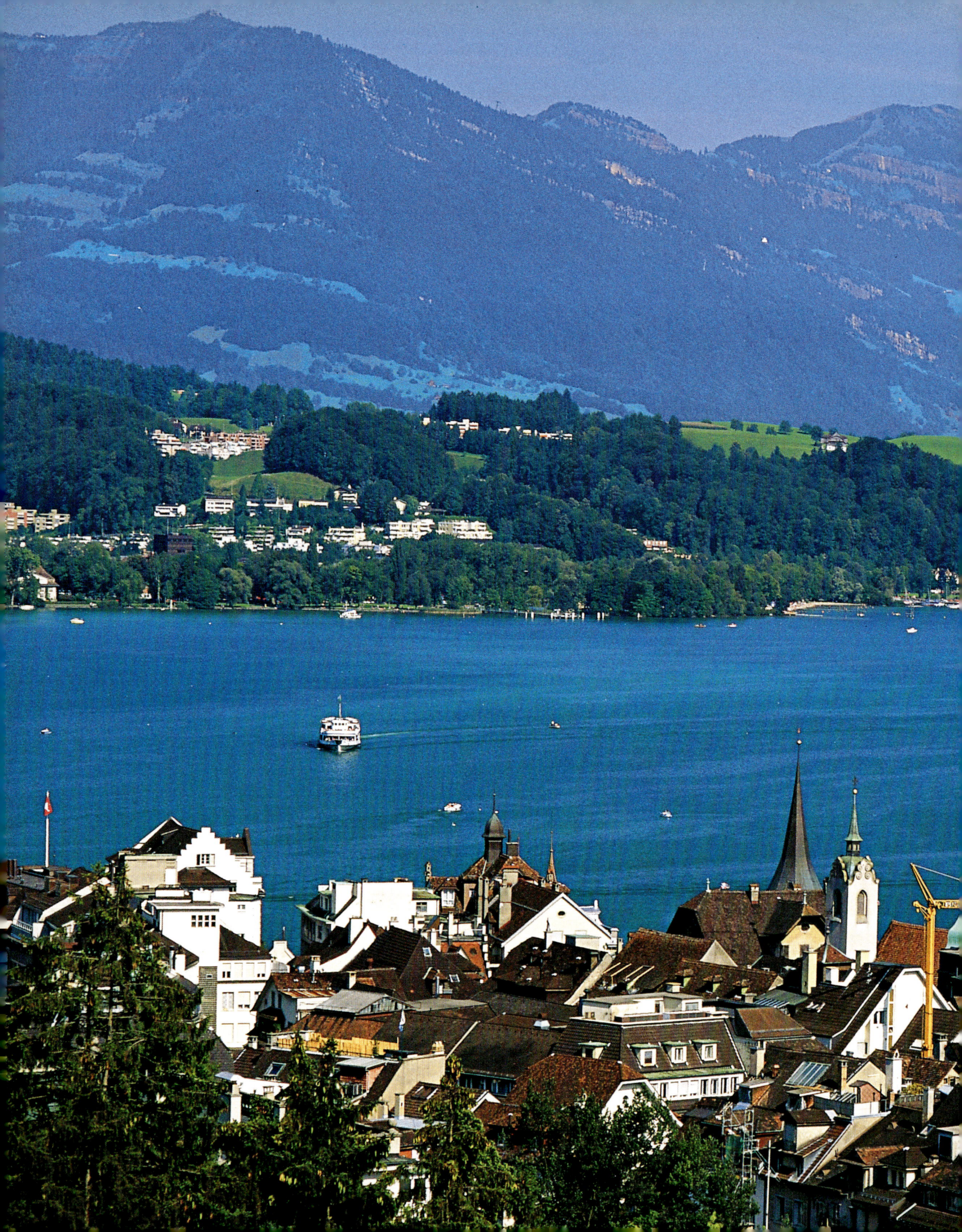

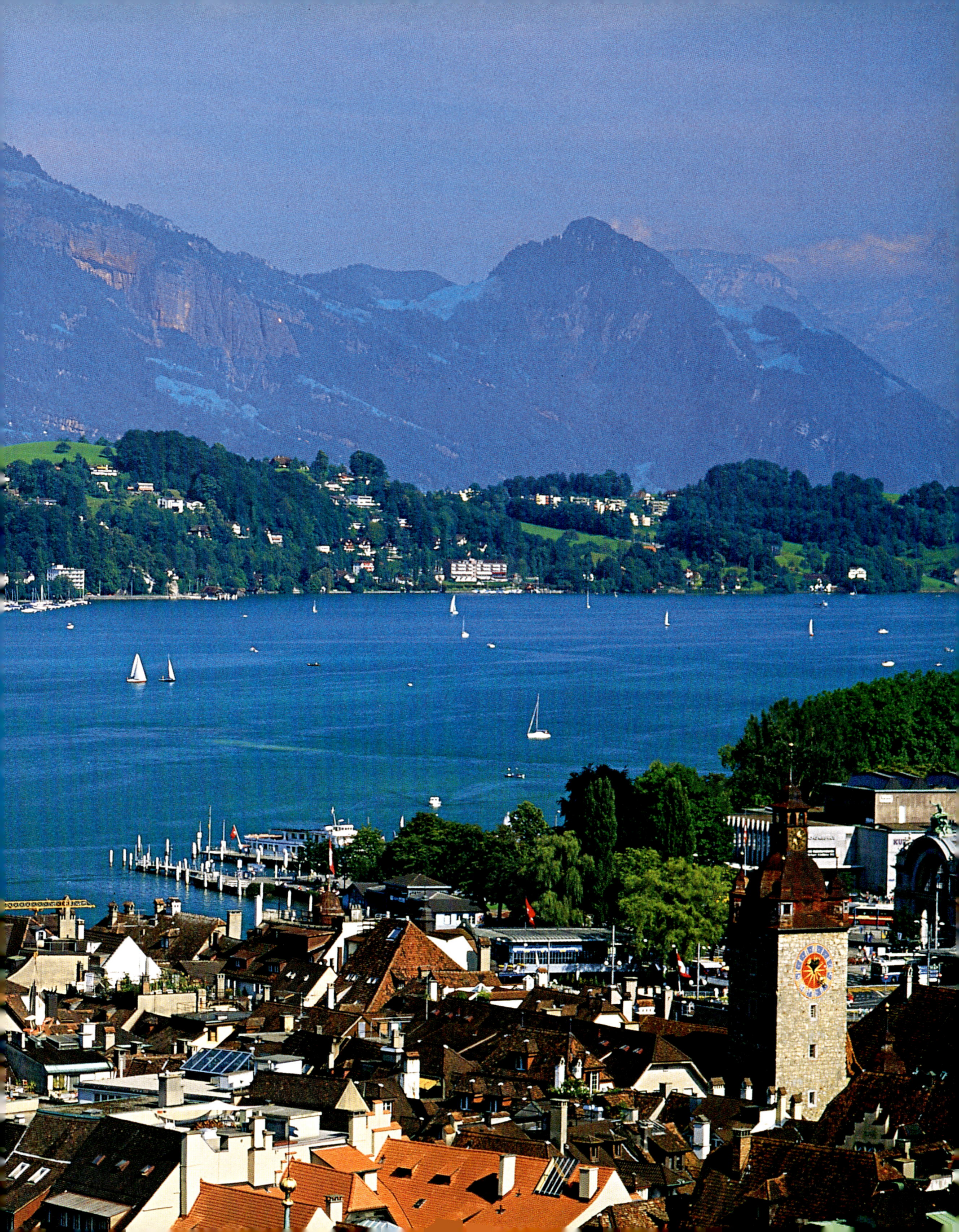

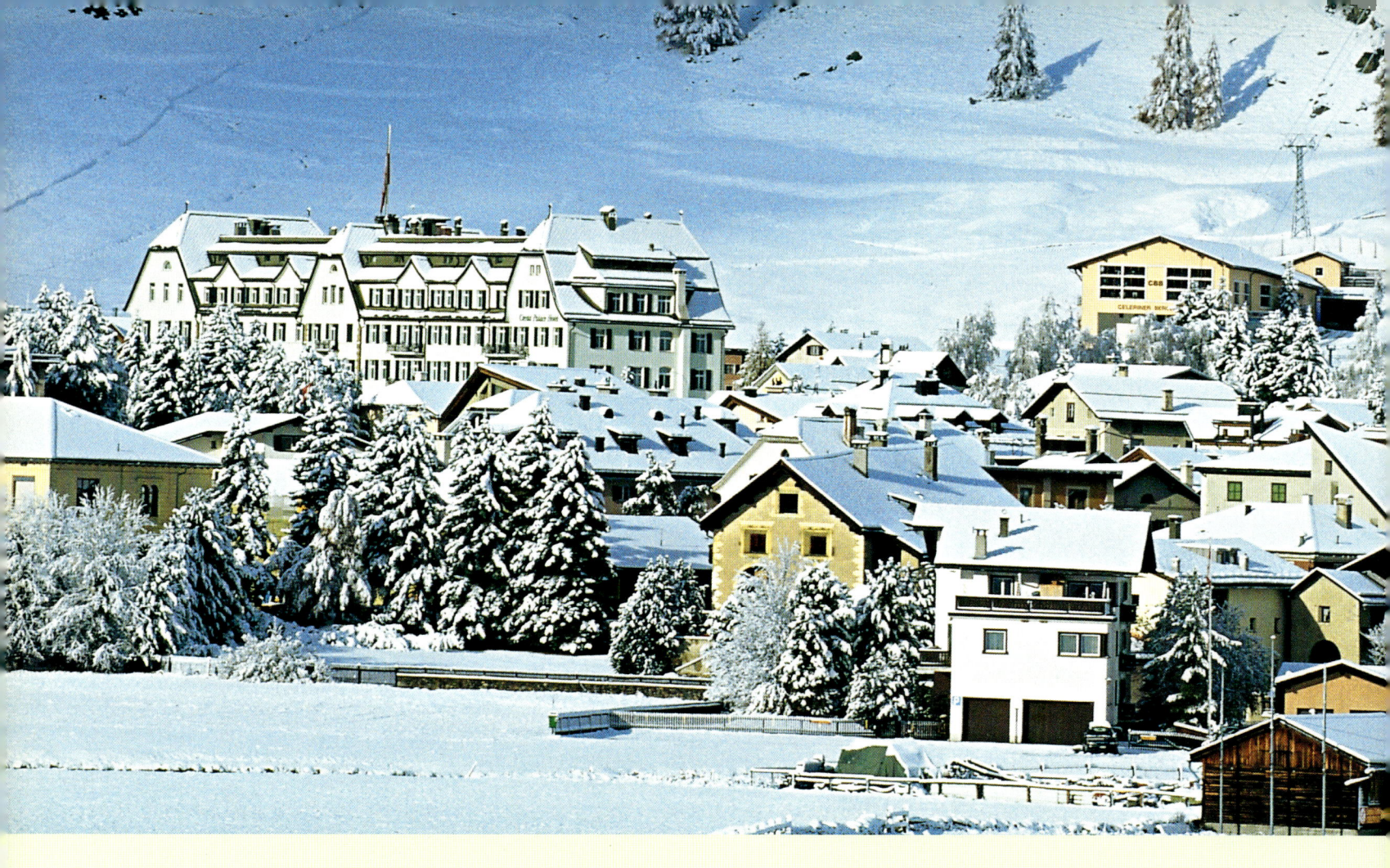

Svizzera Italiana – where the Confederation goes Mediterranean

If you travel to Ticino, be prepared to try out your Italian. For many years the lands and estates of the present canton belonged to the duchy of Milan. Not just the language of the canon is rooted firmly in Italy; its architecture, too, is positively Mediterranean. Time and again hikers traverse elegantly arched stone bridges. Partially derelict mountain villages leave them unsure as to their whereabouts: are they still in Switzerland or already in Italy? Vast expanses of chestnut forest characterise the landscape, their fruit, once a staple of the local diet, still harvested using traditional methods. Many visitors come to Ticino to take in the almost Mediterranean climate and Italian flair, coupled with the scrupulous cleanliness of Switzerland.

Ticino's neighbour, the canton of Graubünden, is Switzerland's largest, famous for its mountains and valleys. It's also the only canton with three official languages: German, Italian and Romansch, the latter an offshoot of the vulgar Latin spoken in the Roman province of Rhaetia. The remoteness of the mountain valleys has ensured the upholding of these linguistic quirks. Tourism is of great importance to the canon of Graubünden which boasts such famous resorts as St Moritz and plenty of spectacular scenery. The canton also has highest density of castles in the country and is serviced by the impressive narrow-gauge Rhätische Bahn or Rhaetian railway. Graubünden's great diversity has often caused it to be nicknamed "the Switzerland within Switzerland".

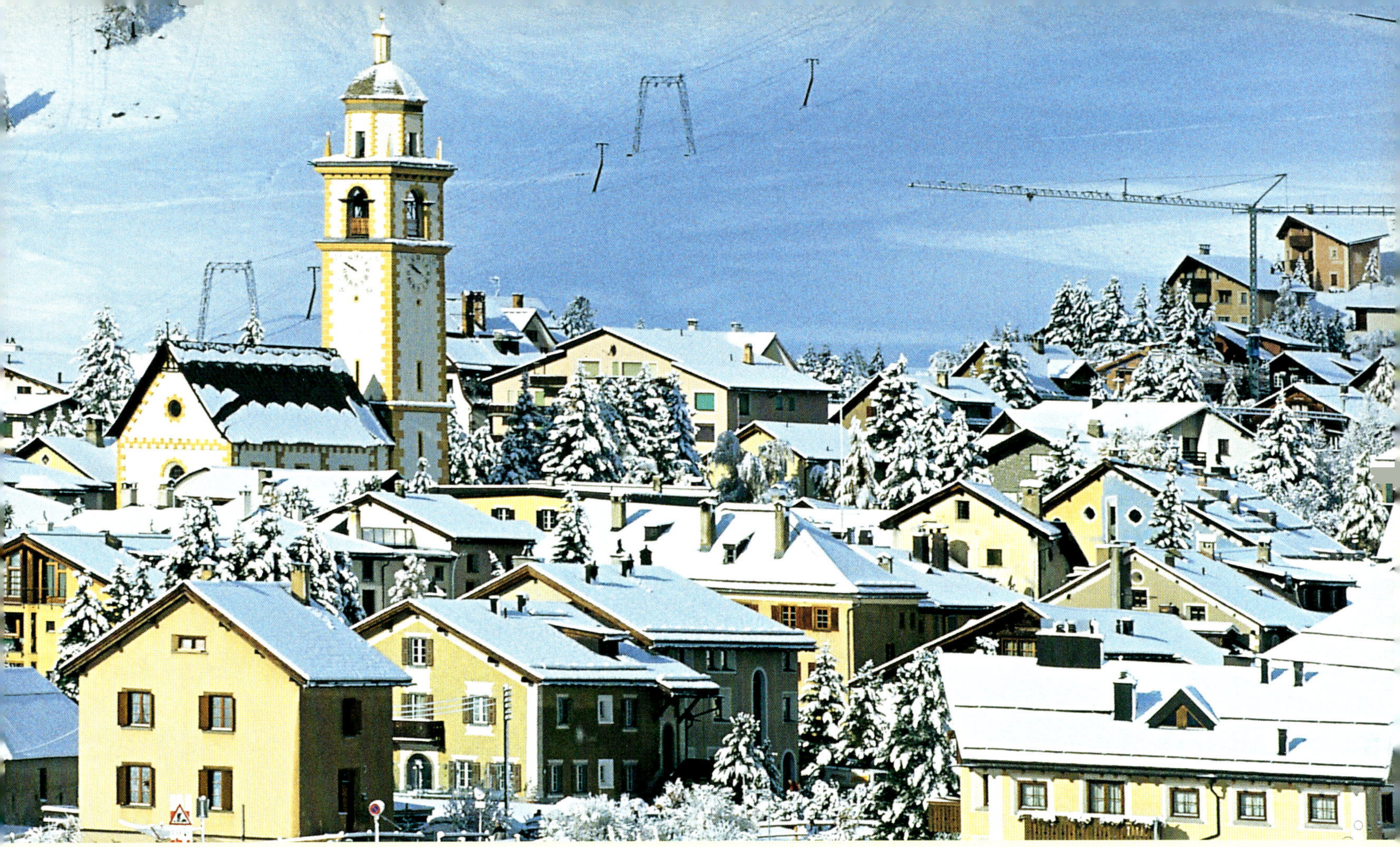

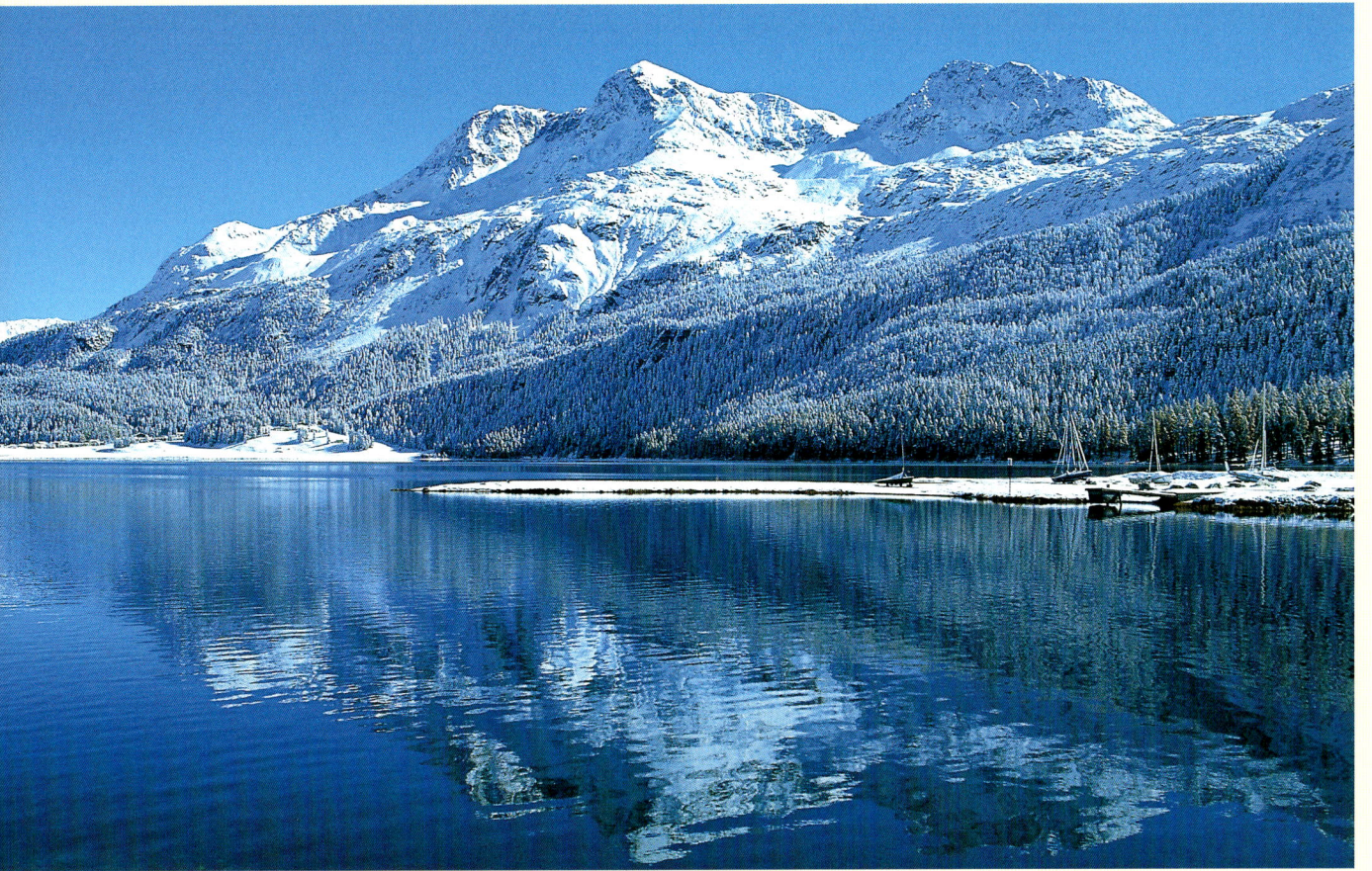

Above:
Not far from St Moritz in the canton of Graubünden is Celerina (Schlarigna in Romansch). Various altercations over its official designation reflect the changing importance of the Romansch language in Switzerland. Up until 1943 the village was known as Celerina. Thereafter it was Schlarigna/Celerina for seven years, only to be renamed Celerina/Schlarigna in 1950.

Left:
Almost every lunchtime Lake Silvaplana in the Upper Engadine is whipped into a frenzy by the reliable Maloja wind, making the lake paradise for kite and wind surfers.

Right:
The latest archaeological research leads us to believe that the area around Chur was inhabited as early as in 11000 BC, making Chur the oldest known settlement in Switzerland. The town's history is mirrored in its name; Chur comes from the Celtic "kora" which means "tribe" or "kin".

Right page:
In 450 Chur was made a bishopric. In 1524 the city accepted the terms of the Reformation – but kept its Catholic bishop. From the 16th century on Romansch gradually disappeared as the people of Chur began increasingly to speak German.

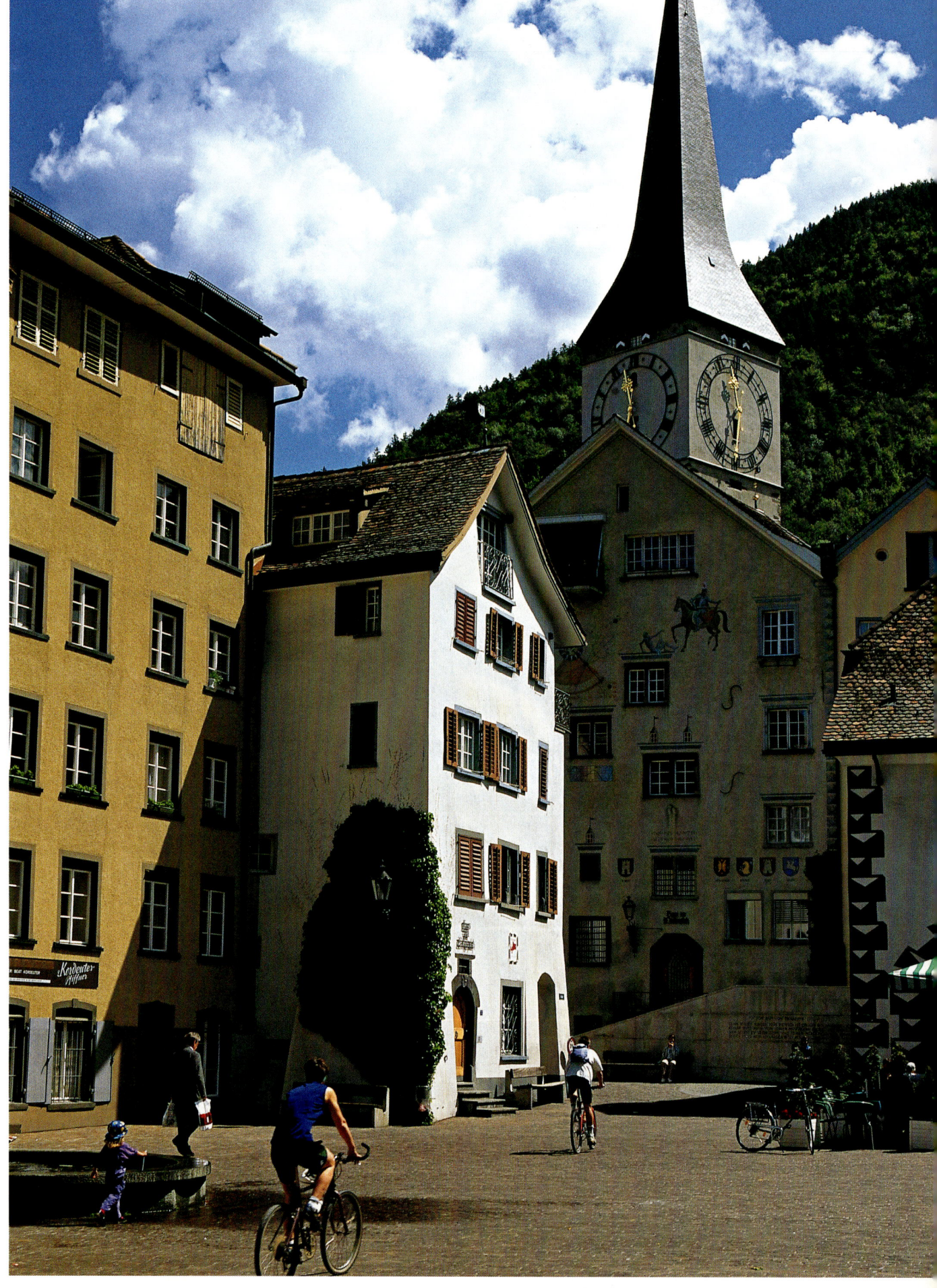

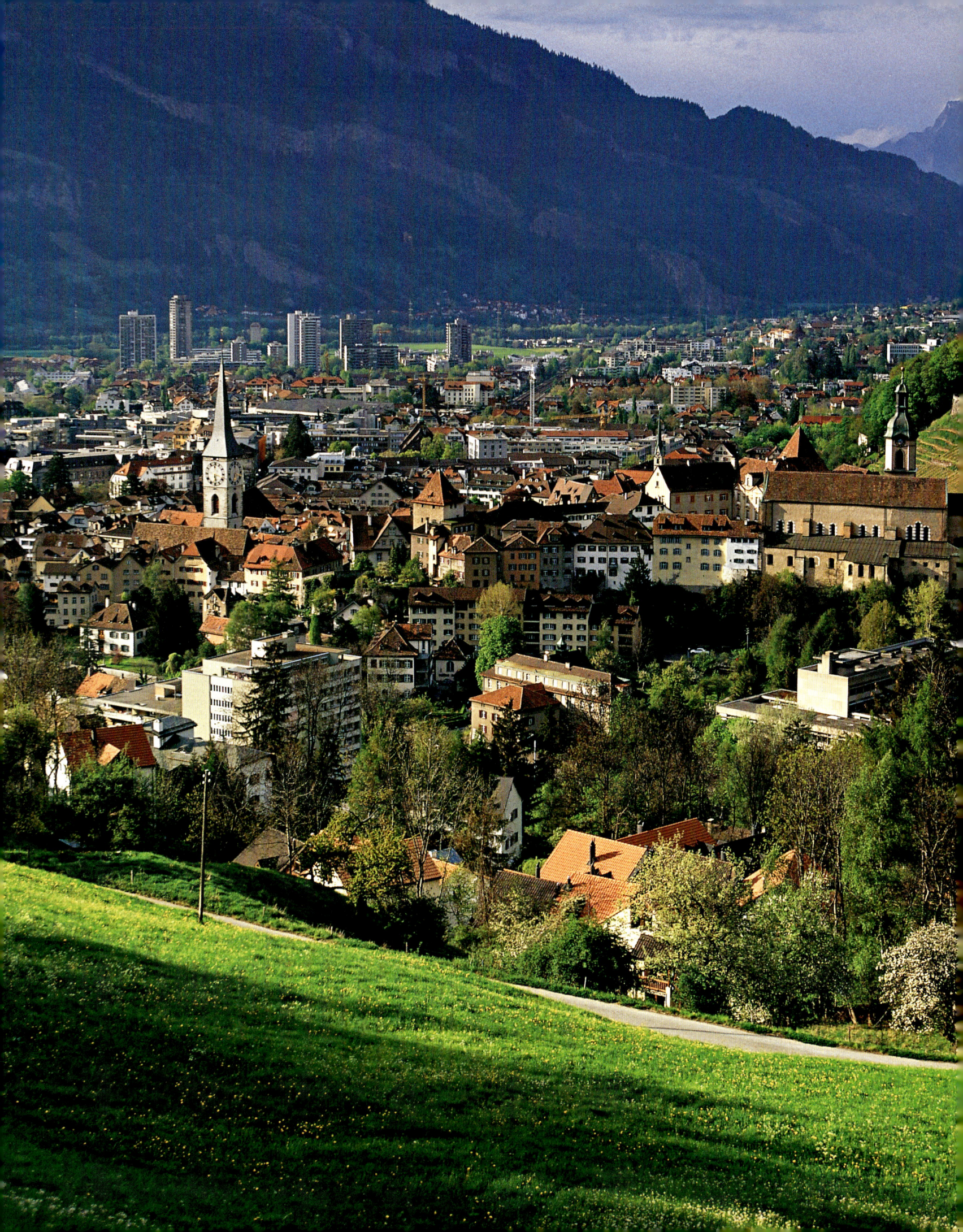

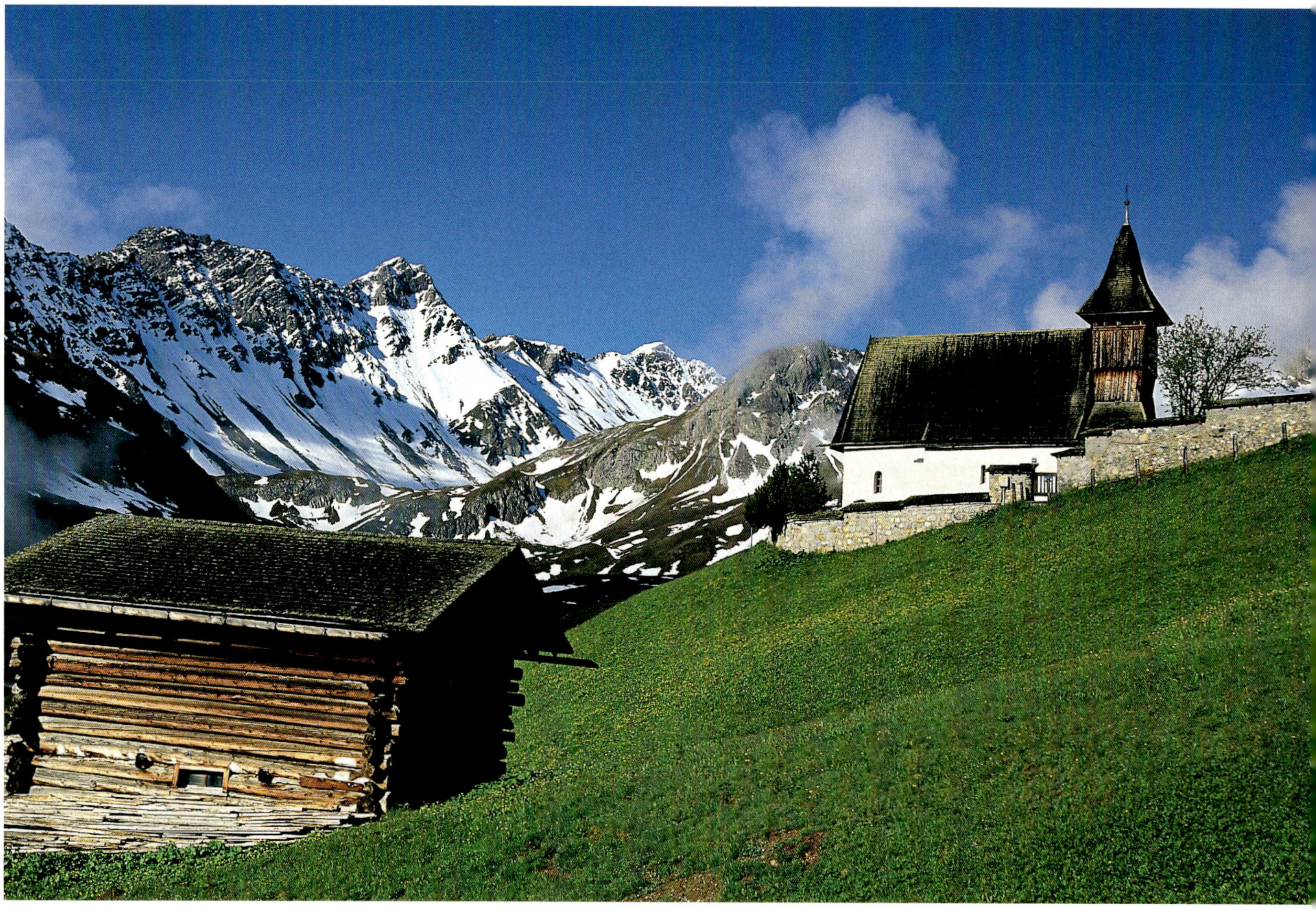

Looking at this serene picture of Arosa it's hard to believe that once a year an open-air opera festival here draws the crowds in their hundreds. Arosa is also the giggling focus of attention during its very own festival of humour, again staged annually.

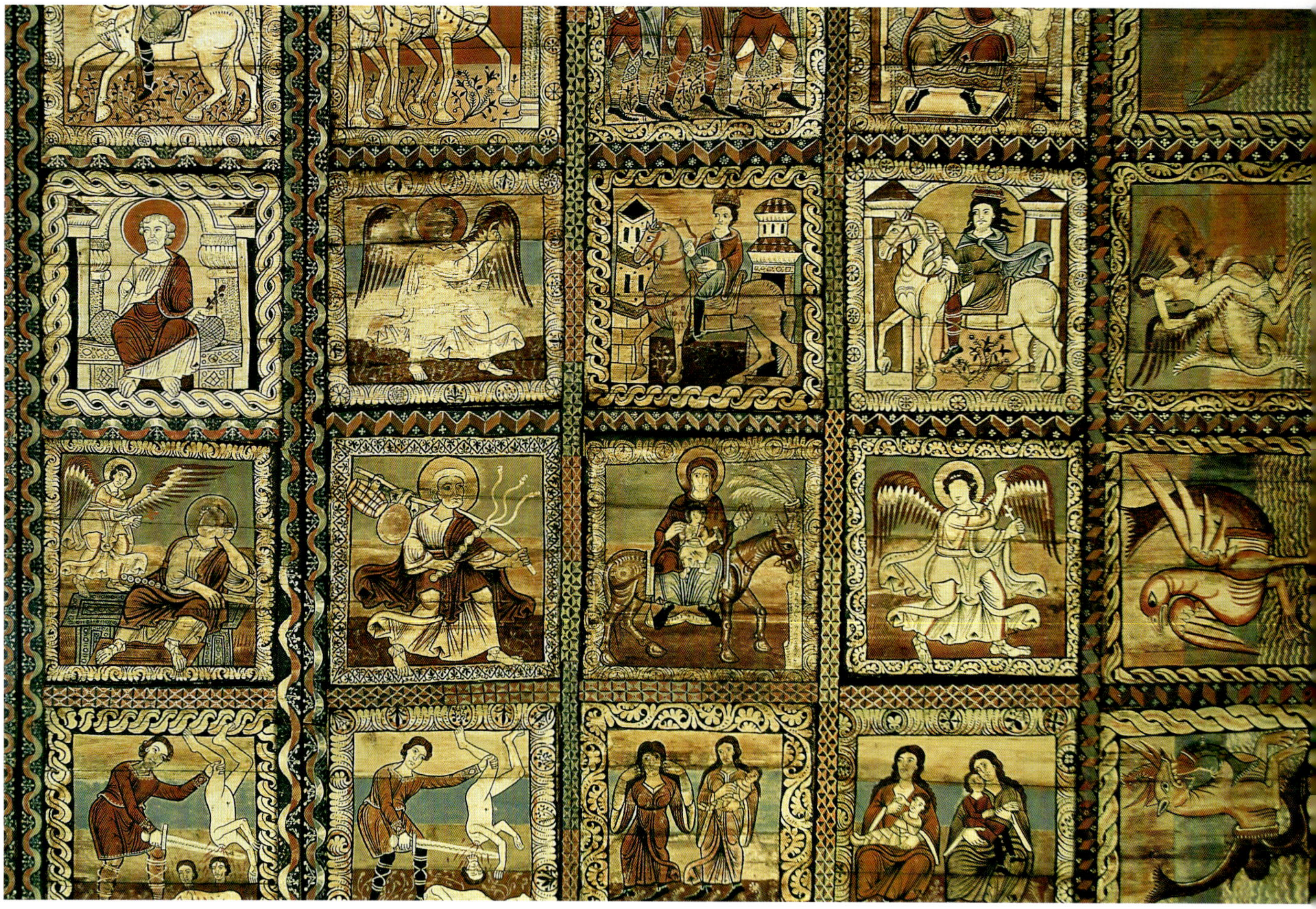

The painted coffered ceiling in the church of St Martin in Zillis is unique the world over. The ceiling, decorated between 1109 and 1114, is adorned with 153 plates which have been preserved almost in their entirety.

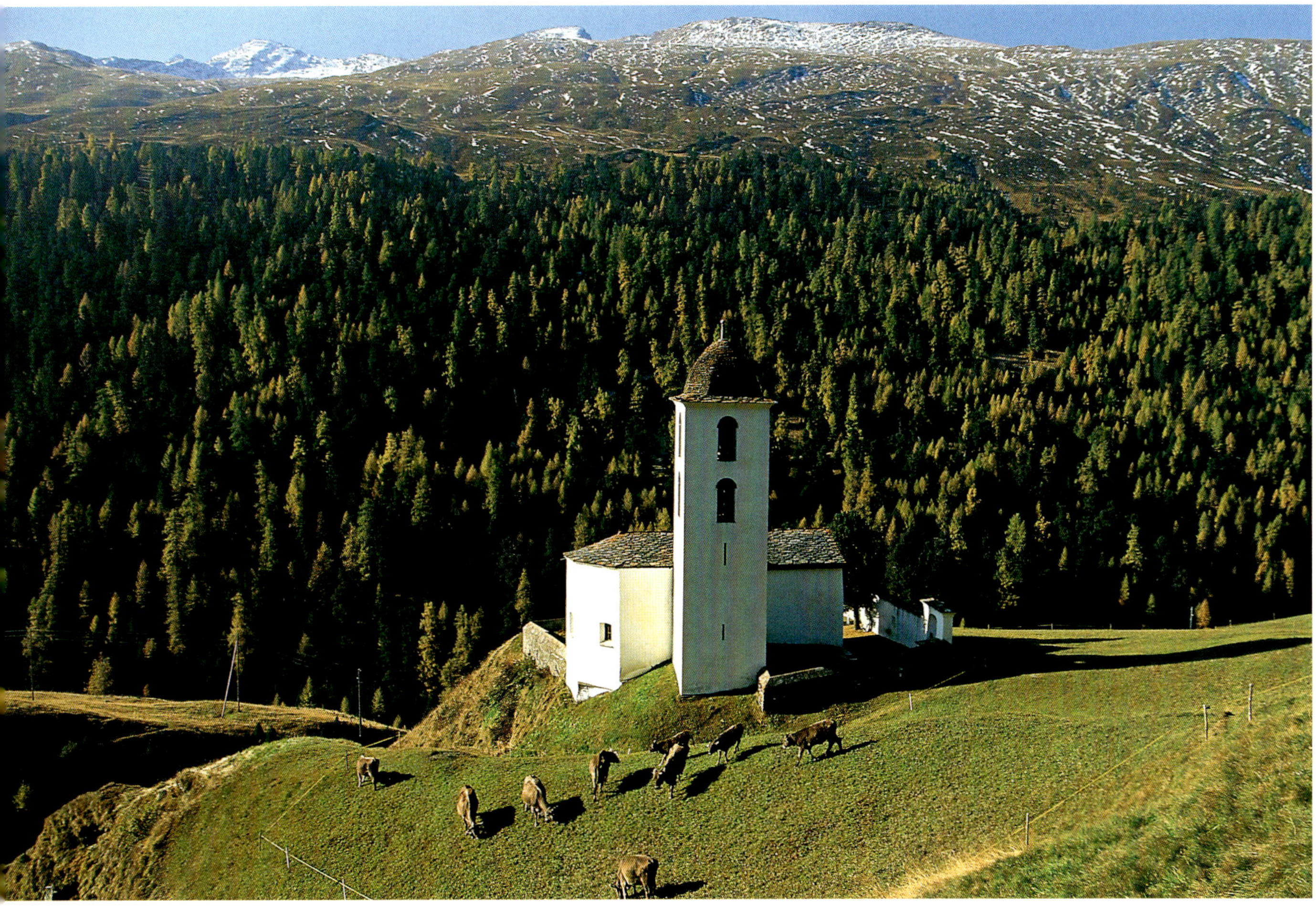

The Averser Tal is a German-speaking oasis in the midst of Romansch country, inhabited by the Wals people who are related to the Alemannians.

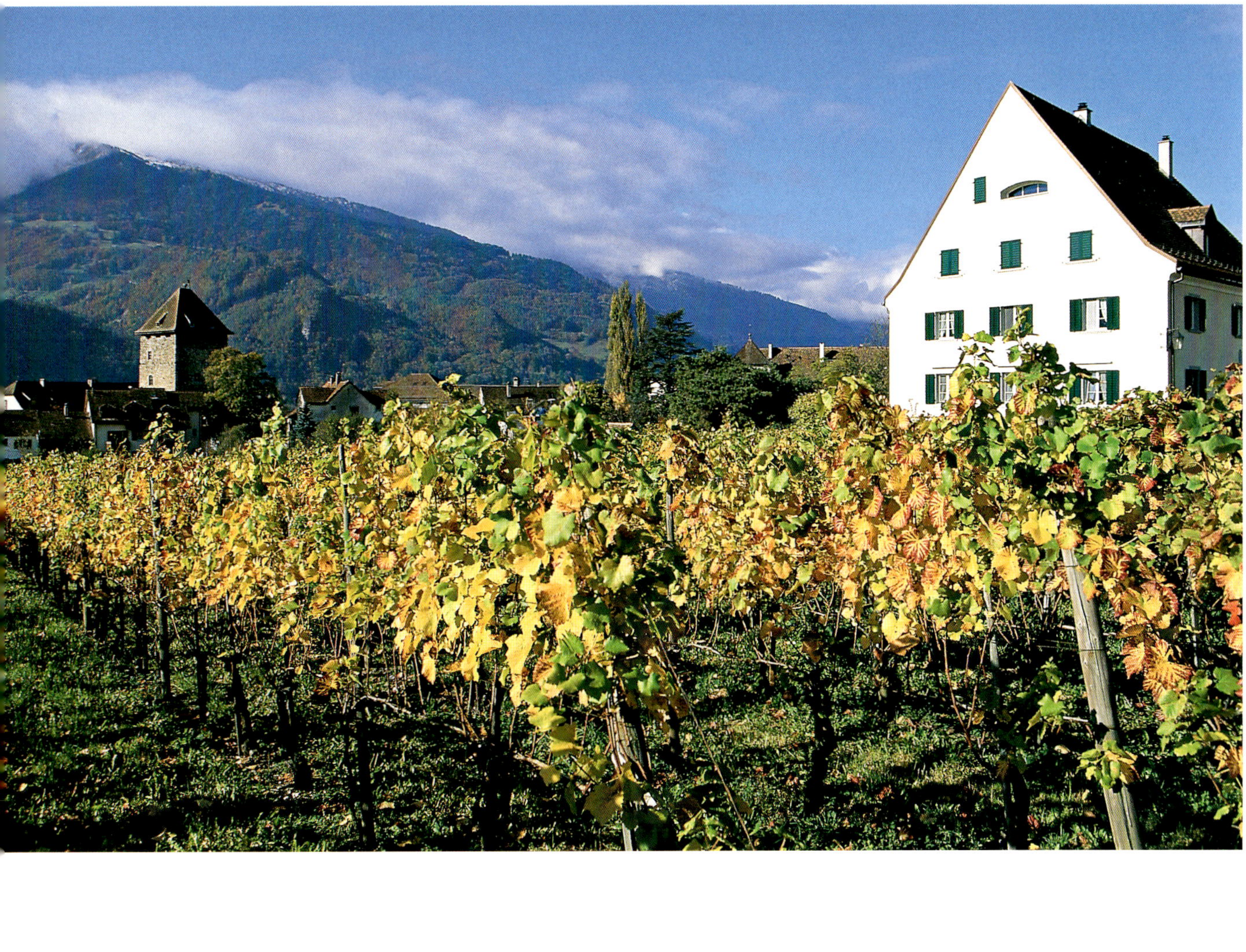

The Pinot noir grape – and the product thereof – is the main source of income for the people of Maienfeld. Since the publication of Johanna Spyri's novel "Heidi" tourism has also played an increasingly important role here, with Maienfeld the fictional birthplace of the little heroine. Many of the more avid admirers are from Japan.

Accessible all year round, the Julier Pass between the valleys of Oberhalbstein and the Engadine is charmingly scenic with peaks reflected in its icy blue lakes at 2,284 metres (7,494 feet) and 1,680 metres (5,512 feet).

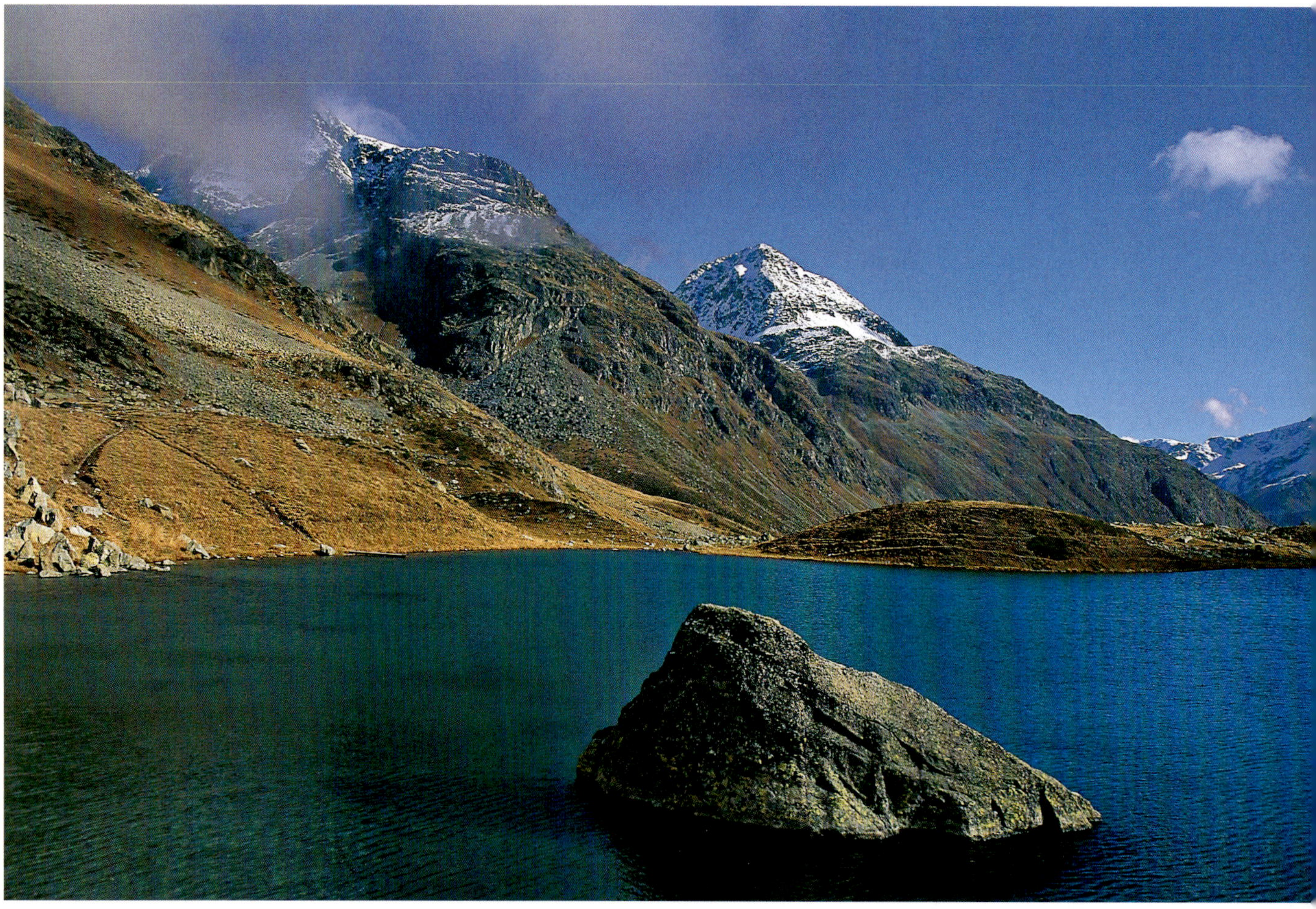

An almost impassable obstacle blocks the 'low road' from Chur to the Alpine passes of Splügen and San Bernardino: a deep ravine. Via Mala ("bad road") is the Romansch name given to this infamous stretch of track along the Lower Rhine between Thusis and Zillis in the canton of Graubünden. The inventive Romans were the first to forge a road through this rough terrain.

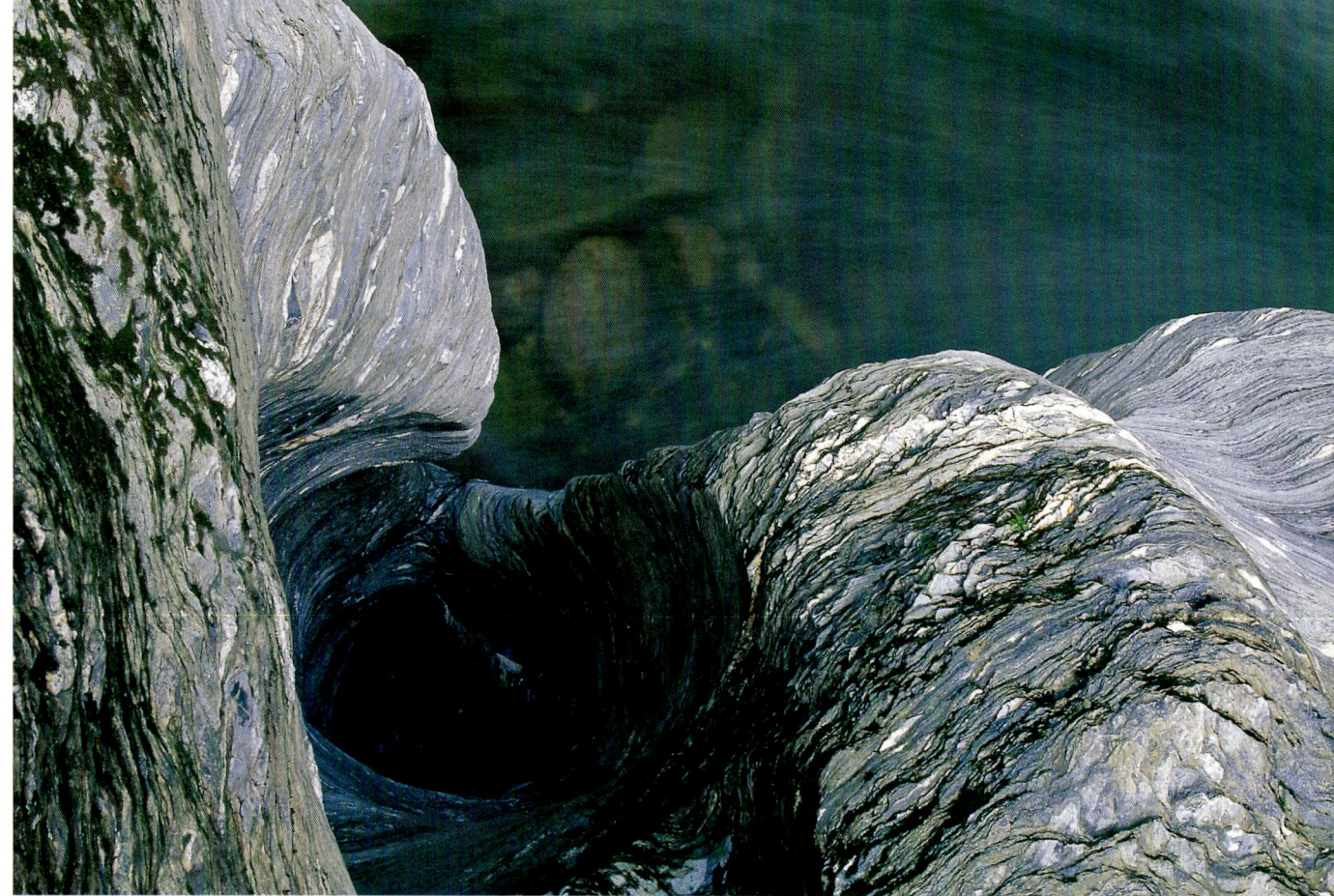

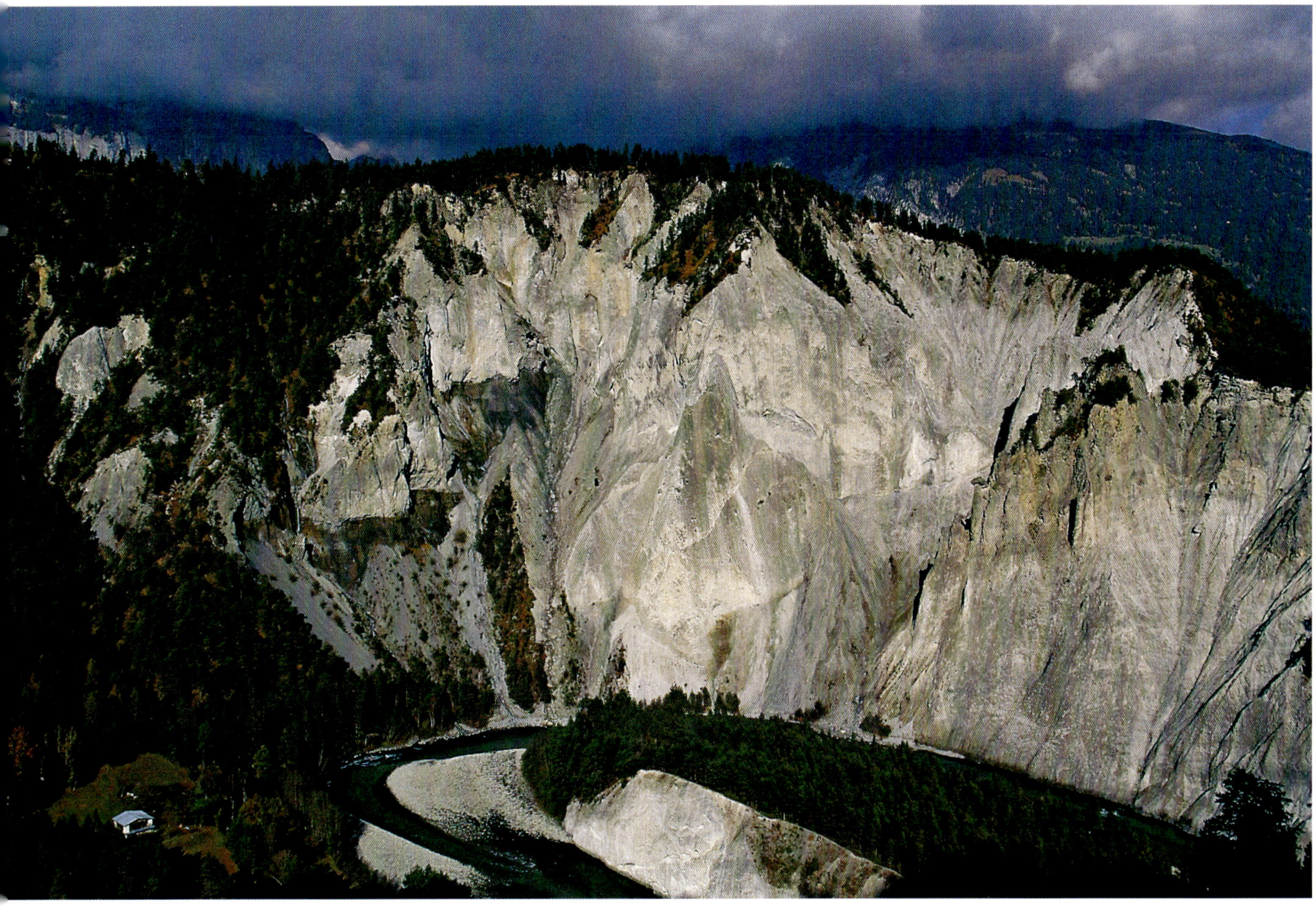

Not far from the Oberalp Pass the three streams of Tumarhein, Maighelsrhein and Nalpser Rhein join together to form the Upper Rhine. The river then flows through a longitudinal Alpine valley to Ilanz before spilling into the Upper Rhine Gorge.

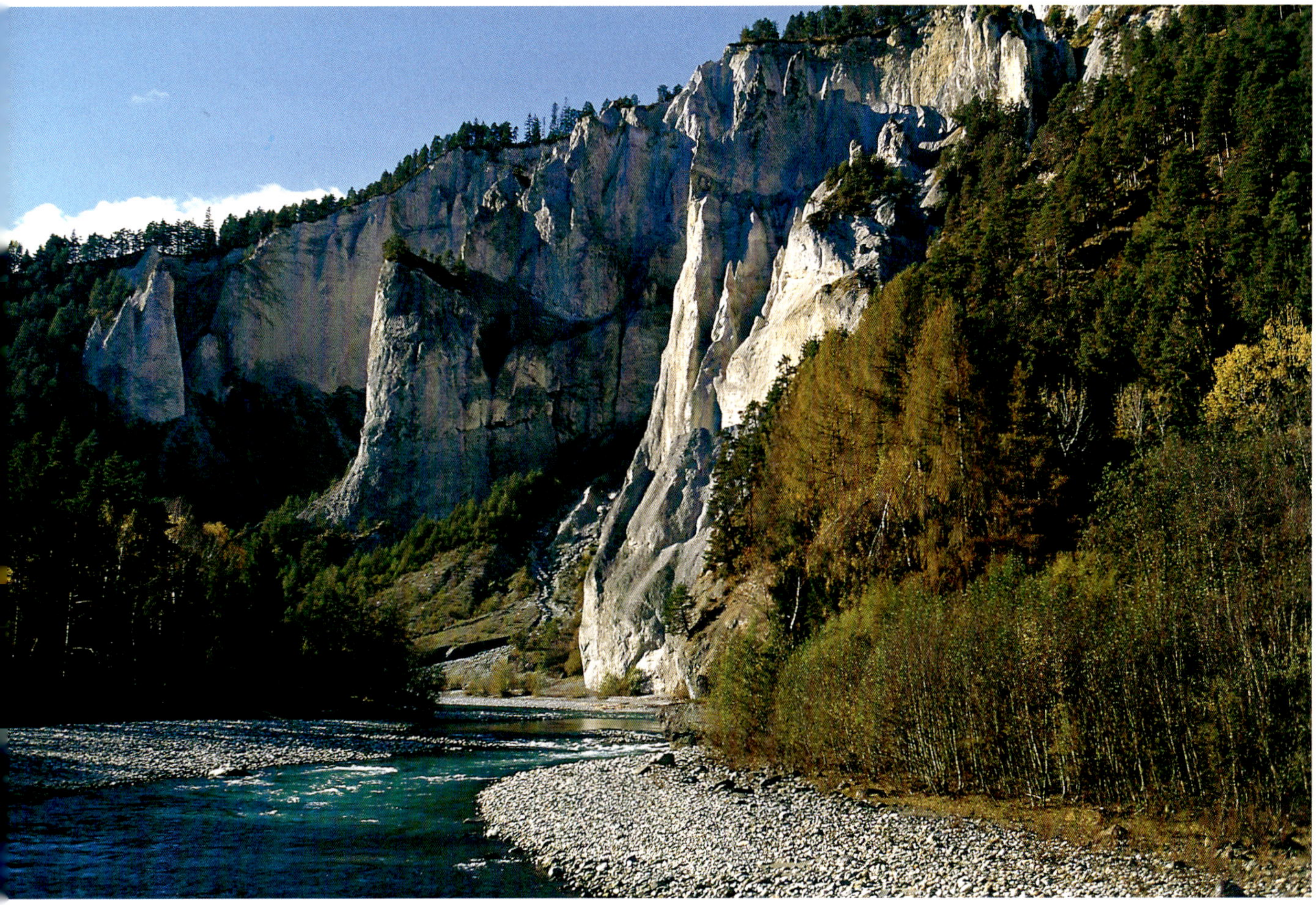

The gorge of the Upper Rhine was created during the last ice age by a landslip around Flims, with the scree damming the Upper Rhine to form a huge reservoir. In time the water spilling out of the lake gouged a deep valley out of the rock. At the end of the gorge at Reichenau the Upper Rhine joins the Lower Rhine as the River Rhine.

Page 74/75:
Despite having just 5,000 inhabitants guests to St Moritz can enjoy all the trimmings and flair of one the great Alpine metropolises. With its luxury hotels and illustrious clientele the name St Moritz has become synonymous with the world's jet set. St Moritz is made up of St Moritz-Bad, St Moritz-Dorf and half the village of Champfèr about a mile down the road.

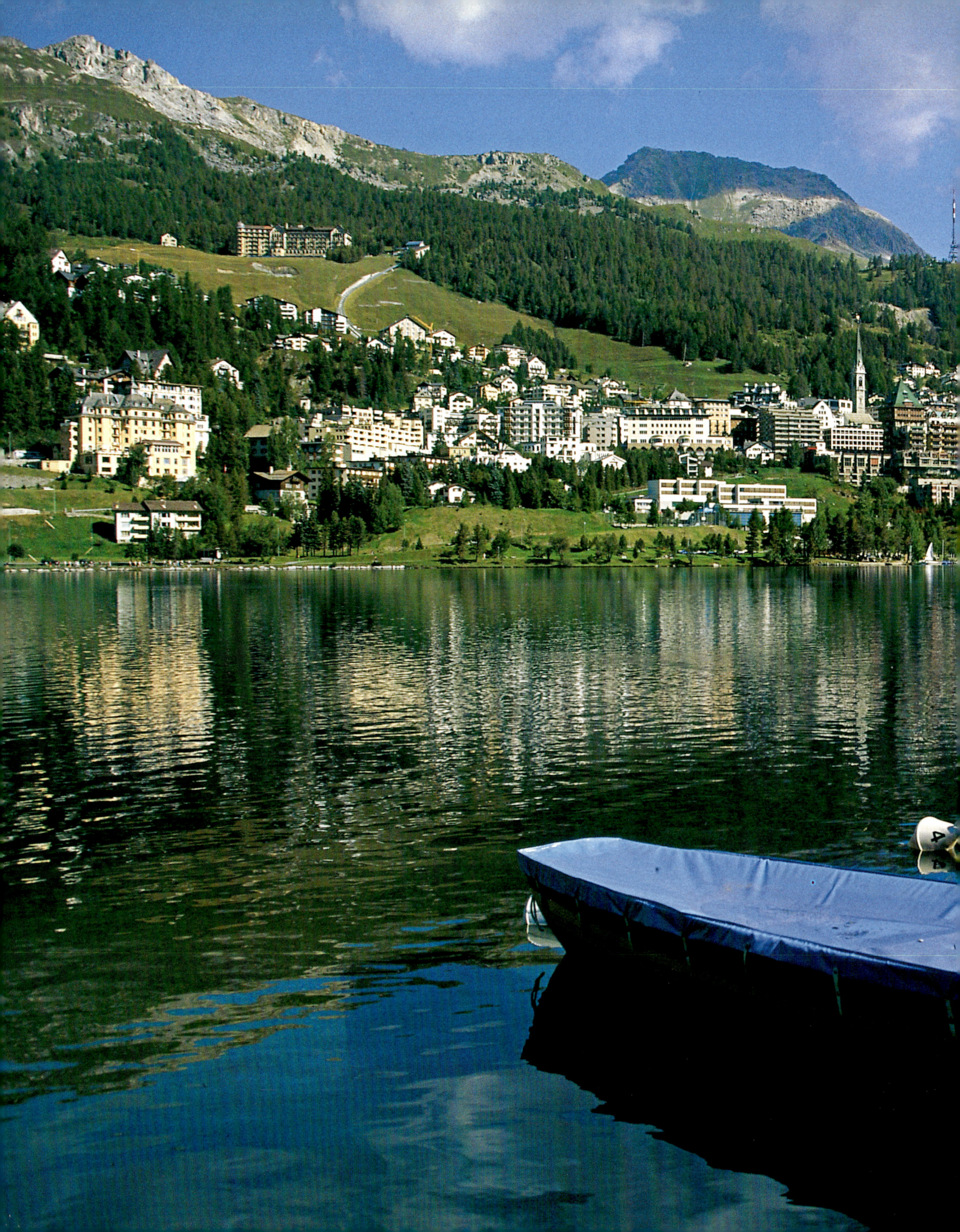

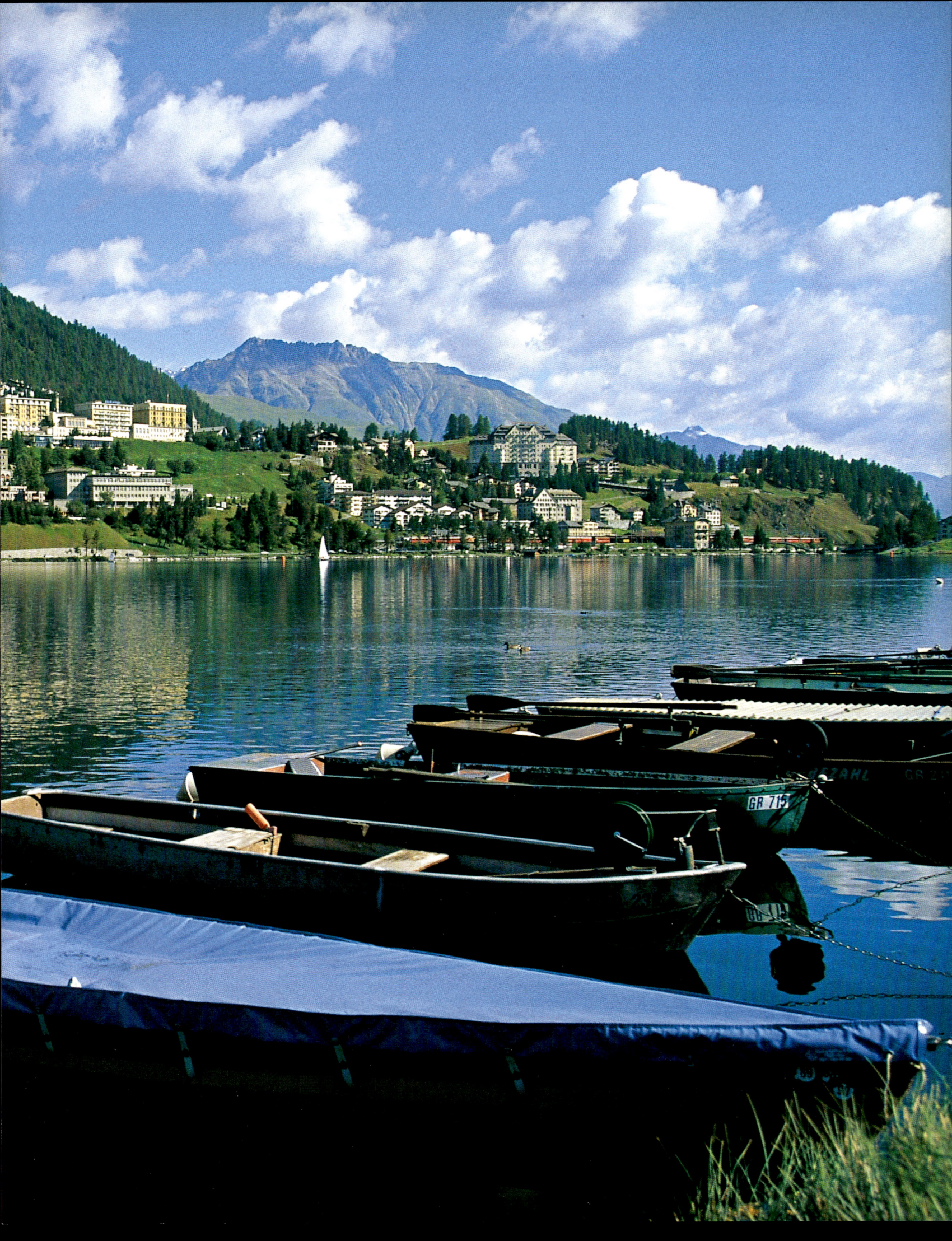

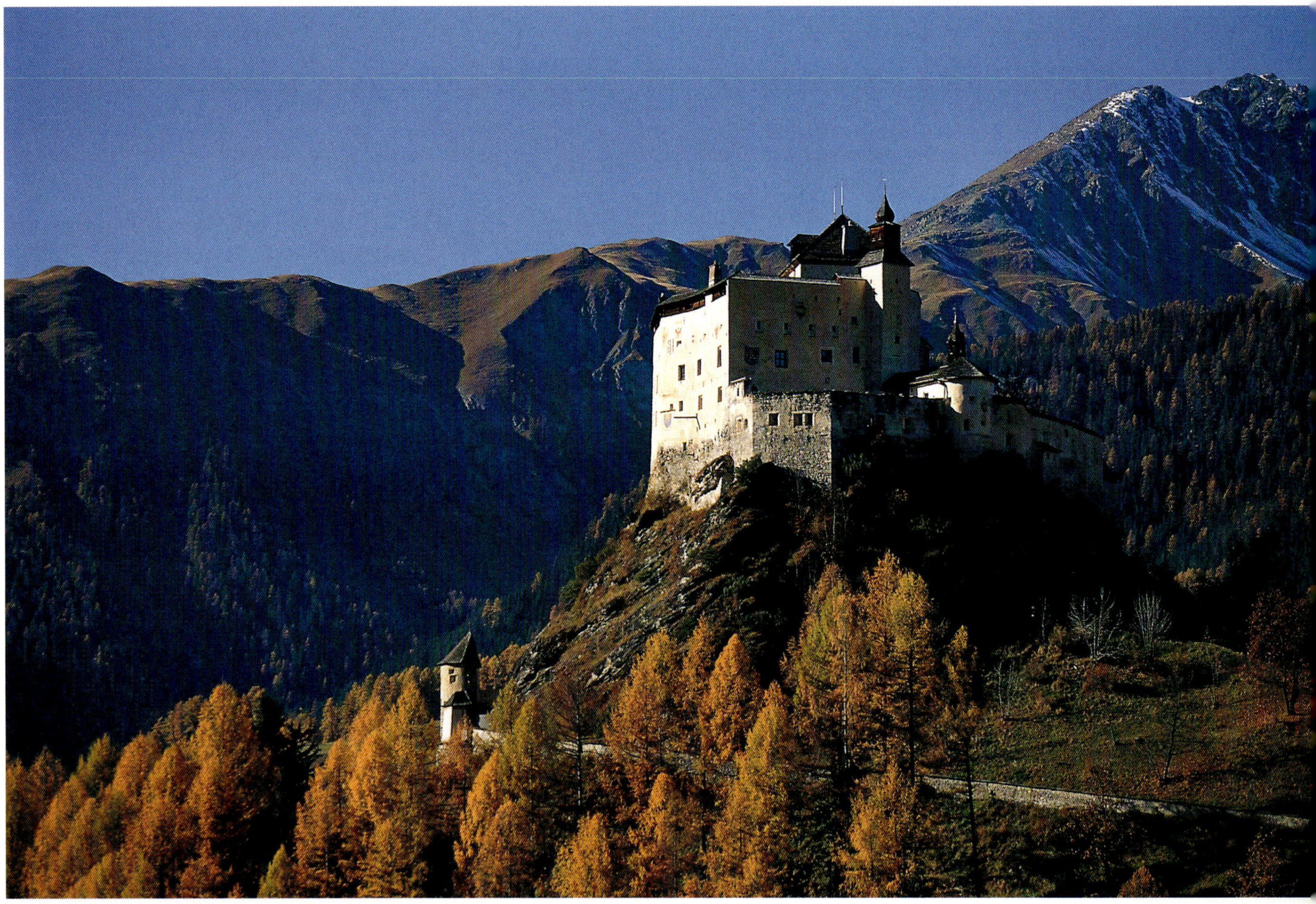

Schloss Tarasp rises up impressively above the little town of the same name on the River Inn. For centuries Tarasp was Austrian with a local populace who spoke Romansch, only becoming part of Switzerland under the Helvetic Republic. The castle now belongs to the descendants of the house of Hesse-Kassel.

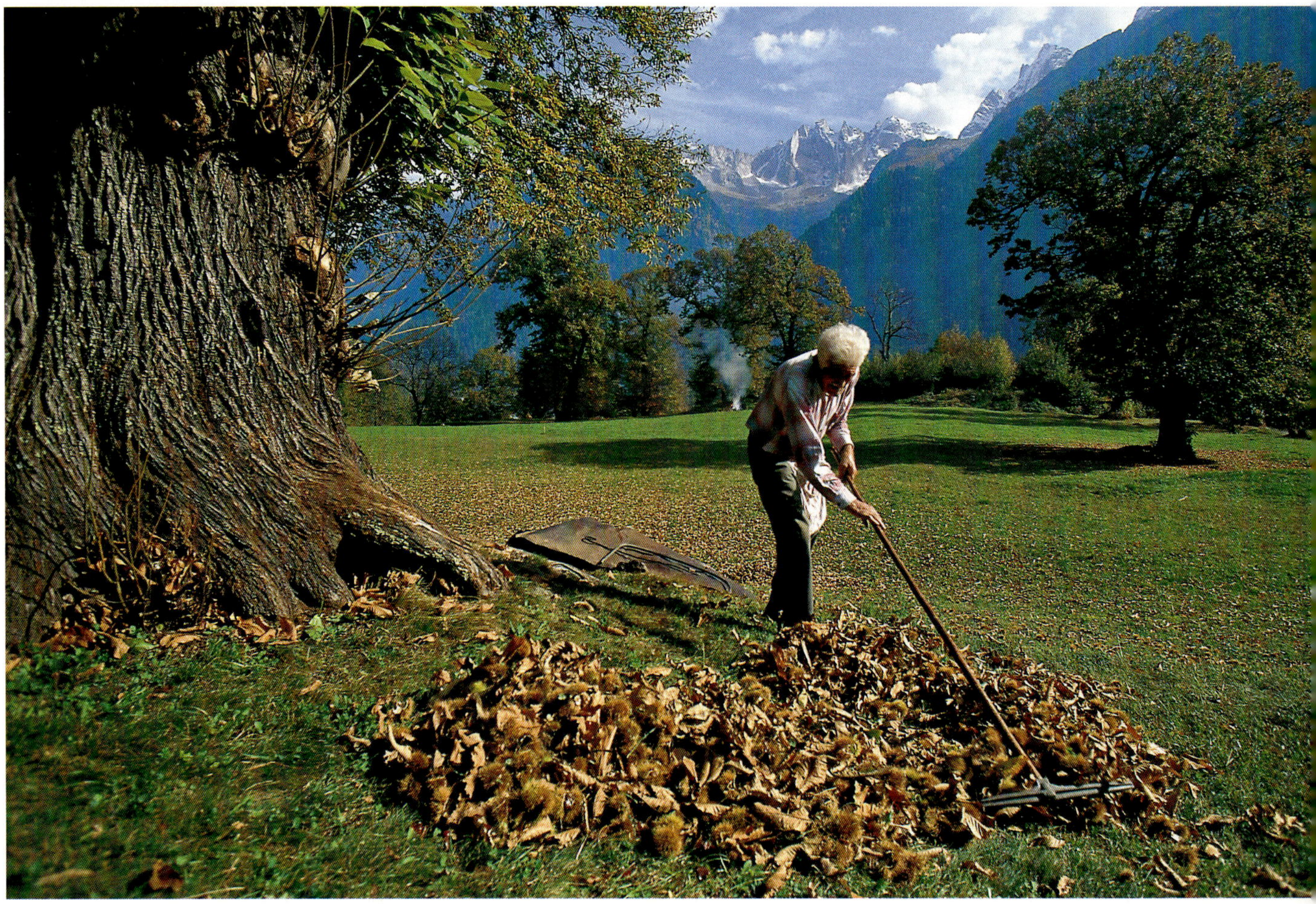

In the past the chestnuts grown in the Alpine valleys of Italian Switzerland were part of the staple diet – especially when the harvest failed. In some communities anybody without a plot of land was allotted a chestnut tree so that they could survive the winter on the fruit rich in starch. Forests of sweet chestnut still exist in parts of Ticino and the south-lying valleys of Graubünden.

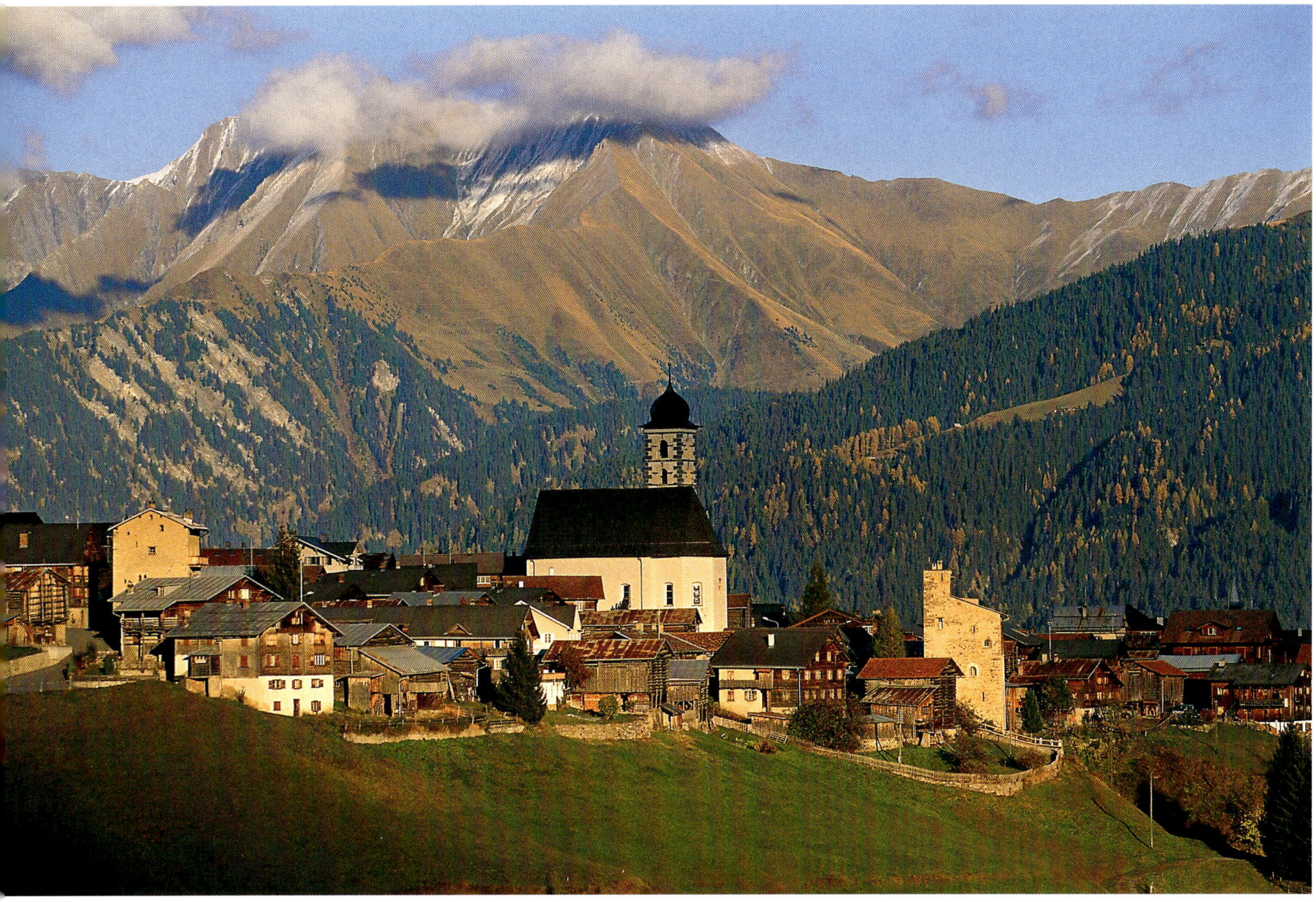

Lumbrein (then Lamarine) was mentioned as being the property of the emperor as early as in 830 AD. The little village in Graubünden is much older, however, dating back to a hilltop settlement founded in c. 1500 BC.

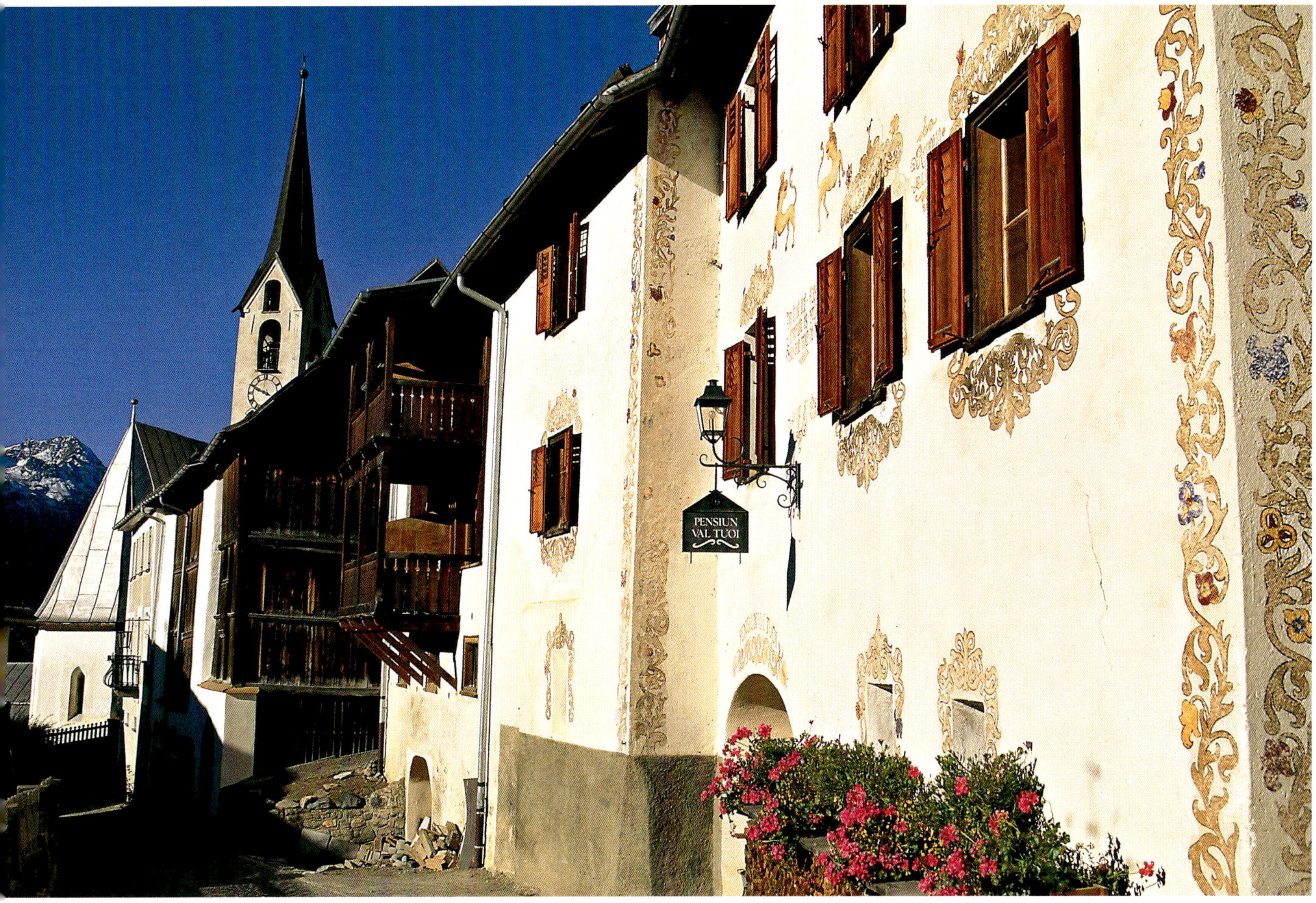

Romansch is spoken in Guarda. Up until 1980 the tiny village had been getting smaller and smaller, with many of the locals seeking their fortune in the bigger industrial towns and tourist centres. Since then the number of inhabitants has been on the increase; at just 180, however, it's lower than it was in 1850. Guarda is one of the best preserved villages in the Engadine and almost exclusively made up of typical Engadine buildings.

Marvellous view of Lake Sils in the lakes of the Engadine, 1,797 metres (5,896 feet) above sea level.

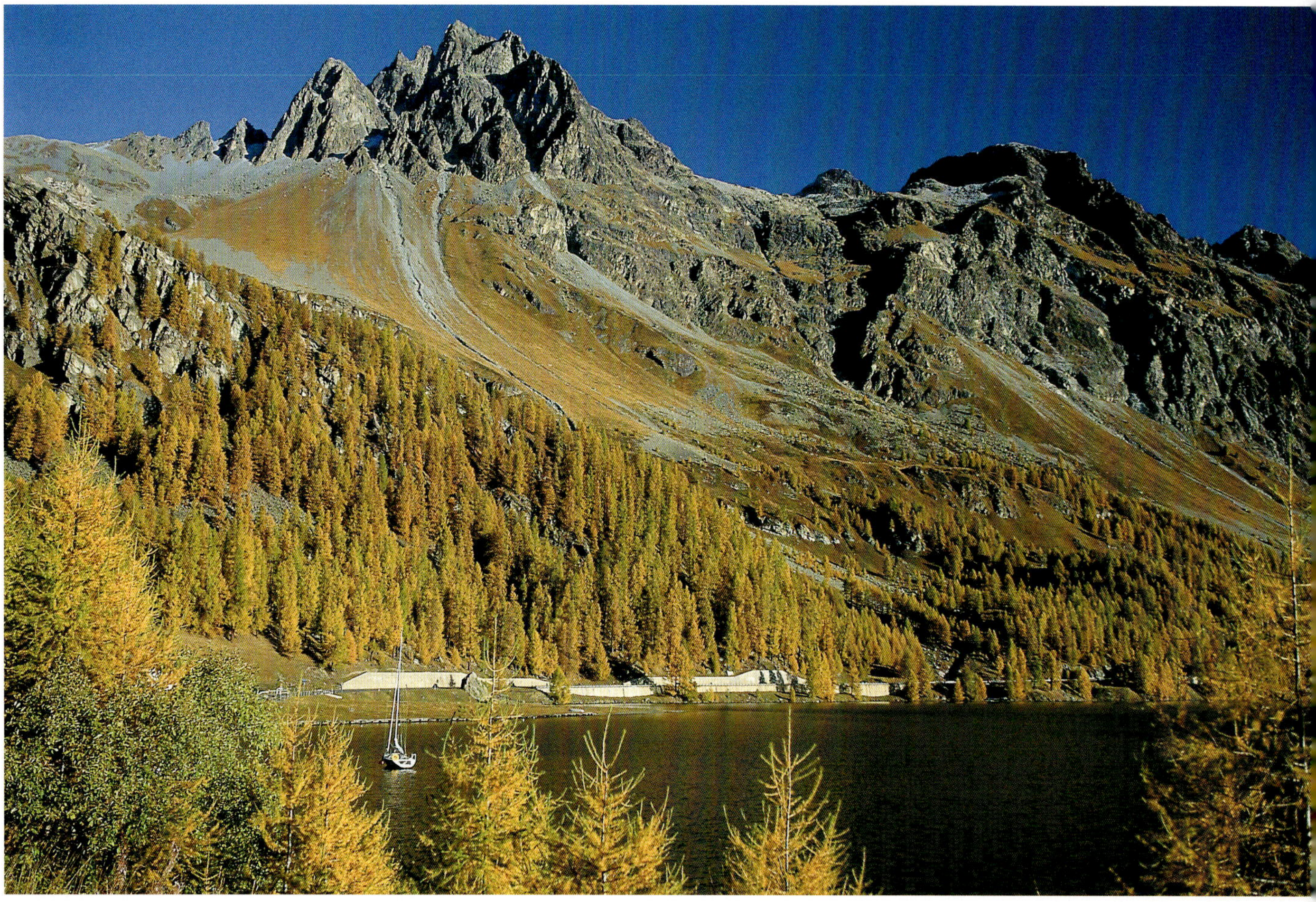

A flash of red against a blue Alpine sky denotes the passing of the Bernina Express. The fast tourist train operated by the Rhätische Bahn connects Chur with Tirano in Italy, taking four hours and 17 minutes from one end to the other. The Brusio viaduct – where the train turns a complete circle – is a popular motif for railway enthusiasts all over the world.

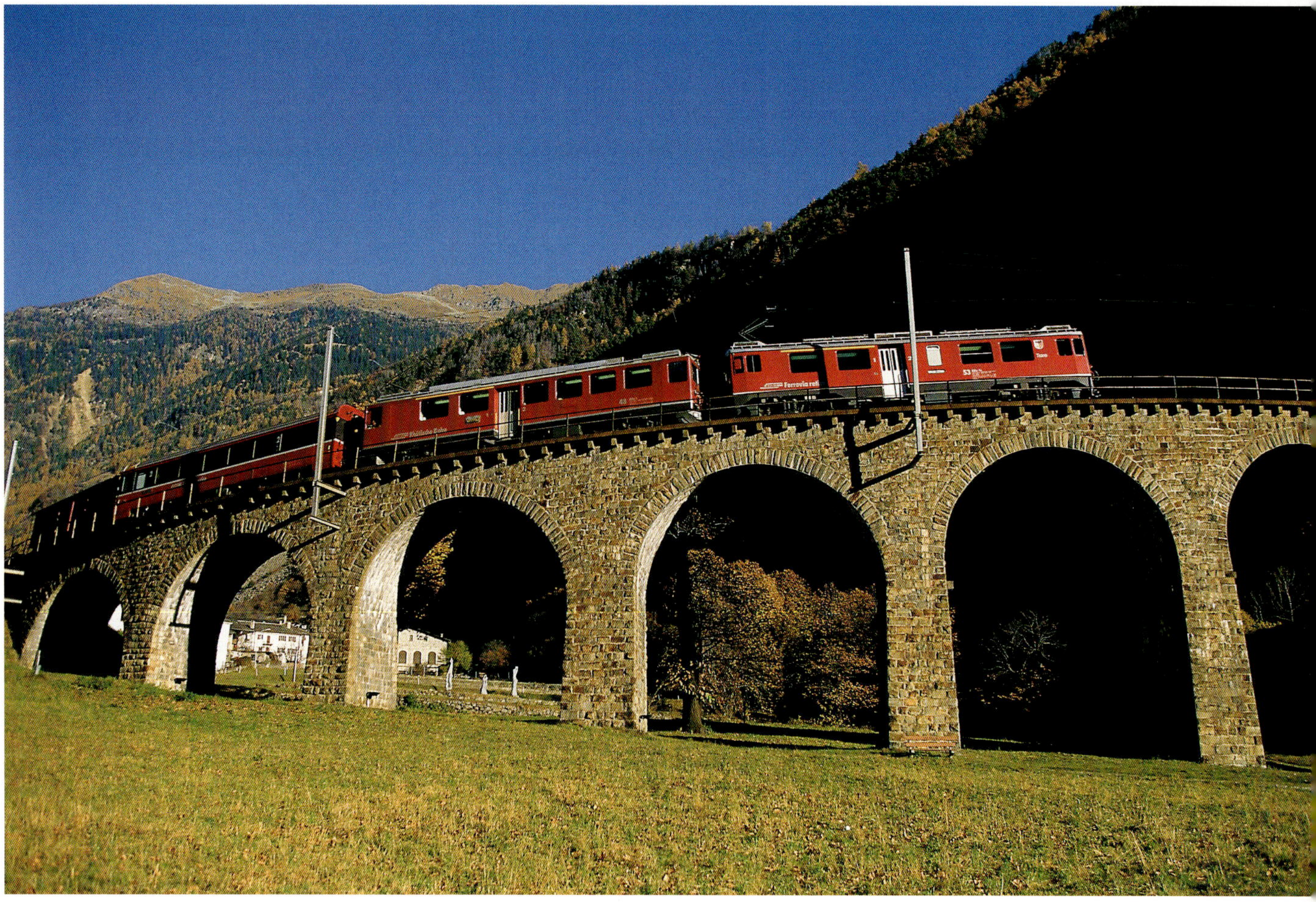

Right page:
Glittering snow on the Corvatsch Glacier near Silvaplana in the Engadine. July 2004 saw the opening of the artificial Corvatsch Gletscherworld cave which tunnels 140 metres (460 feet) into the ice – complete with polar bear.

78

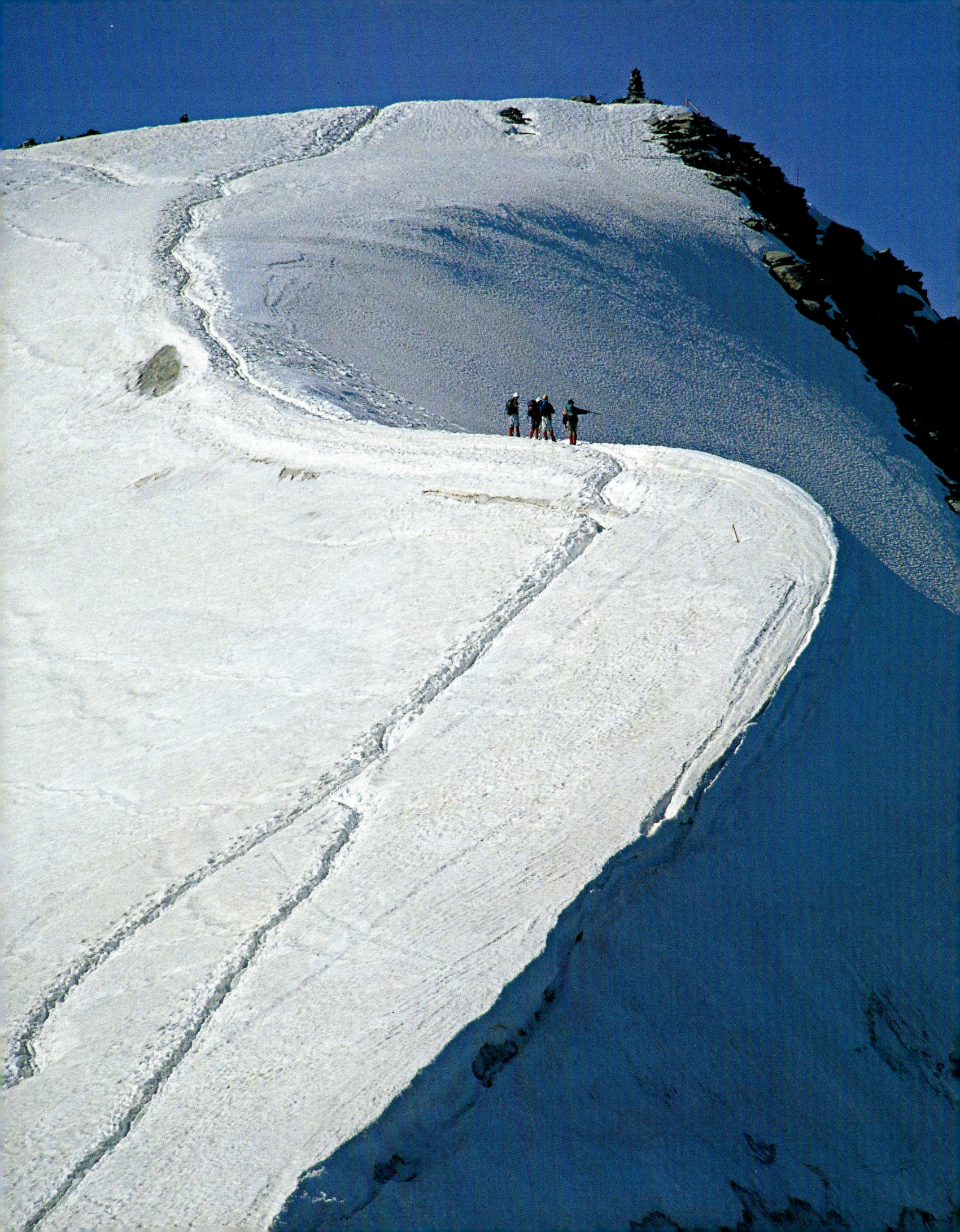

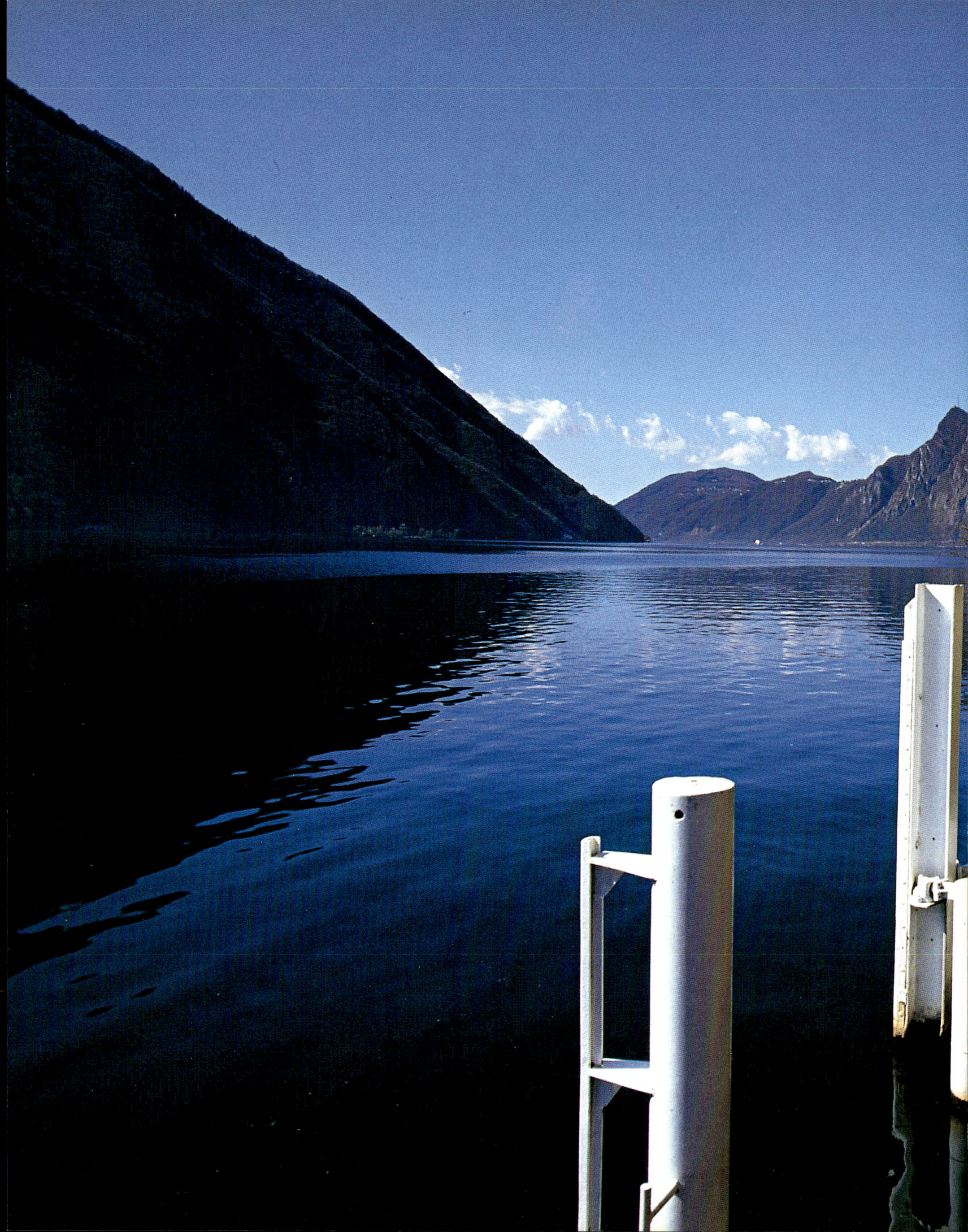

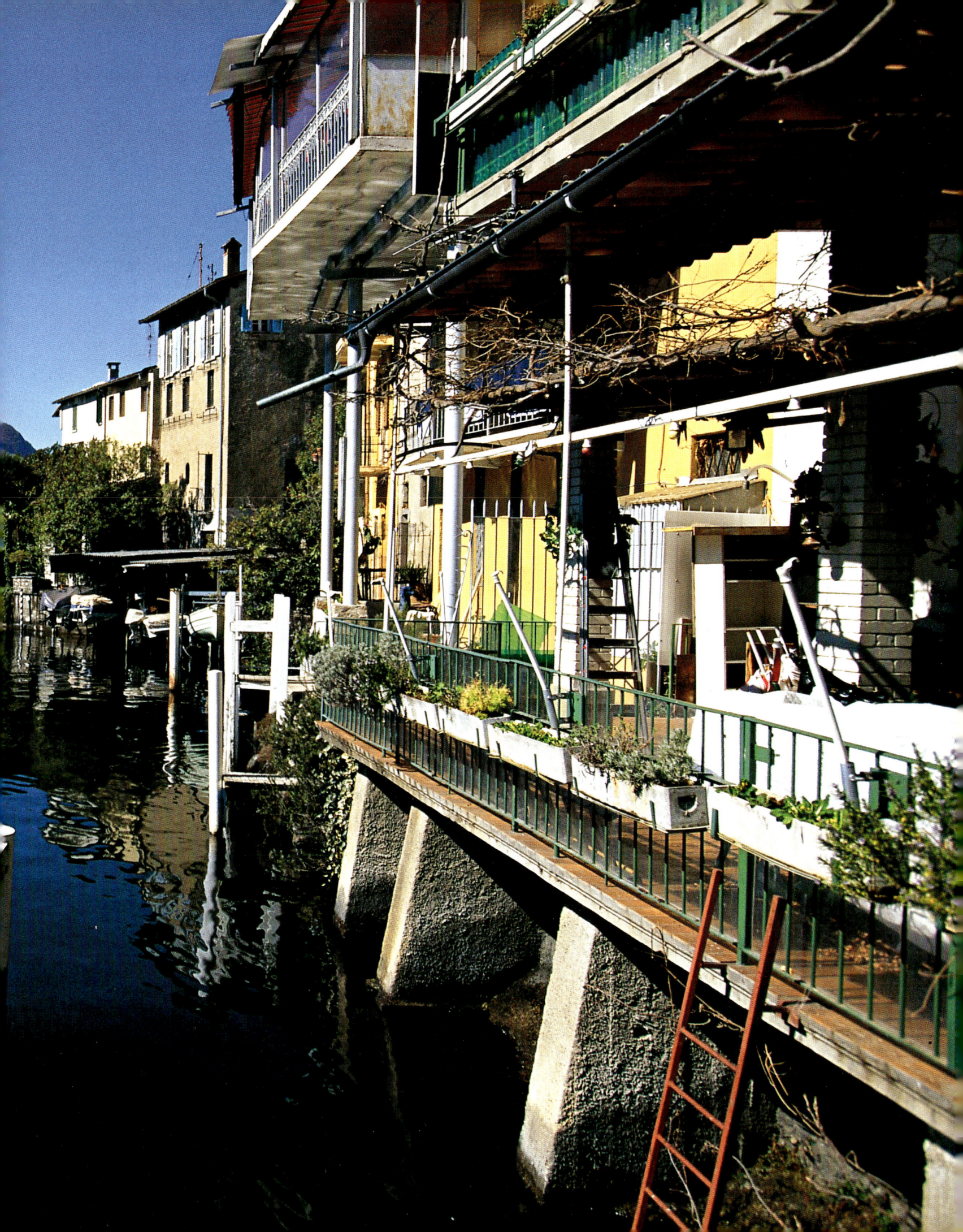

Page 80/81:
Gandria clings to the shores of Lake Lugano in the canton of Ticino. Despite having just 200 inhabitants the pretty hamlet has no less than nine restaurants! In the past home to fishermen and border guards, the village museum (Schweizerisches Zollmuseum) is aptly dedicated to tolls, border crossings and customs posts.

In two elegant arches the medieval Ponte dei Salti bridges the river at Lavertezzo. The village is a good place to embark on tours of the Piccascia, Carecchio, d'Agro and Orgnana valleys.

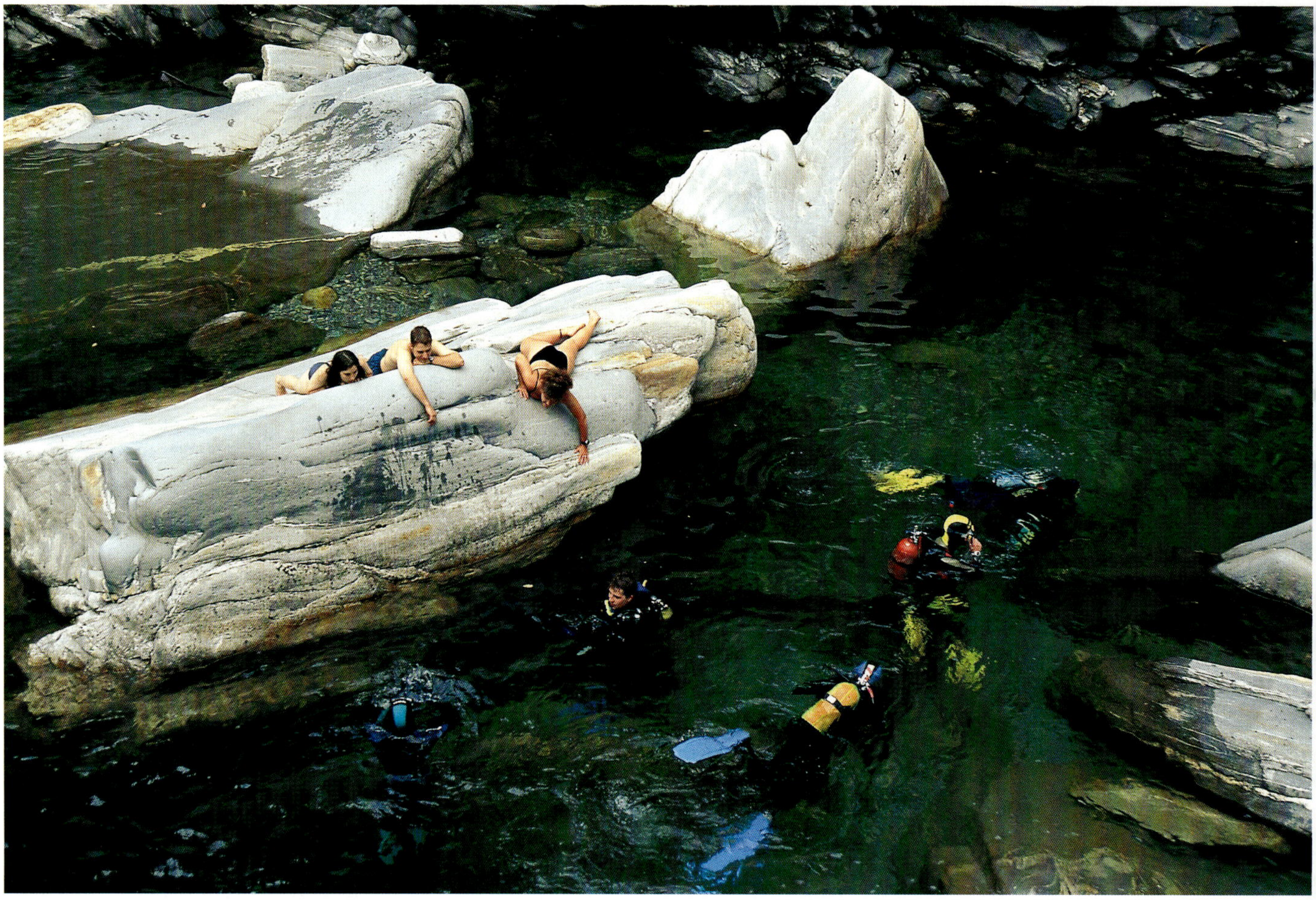

At the point where the Centovalli and Maggiatal diverge lies the village of Ponte Brolla, named after a Roman bridge which once traversed the valley here.

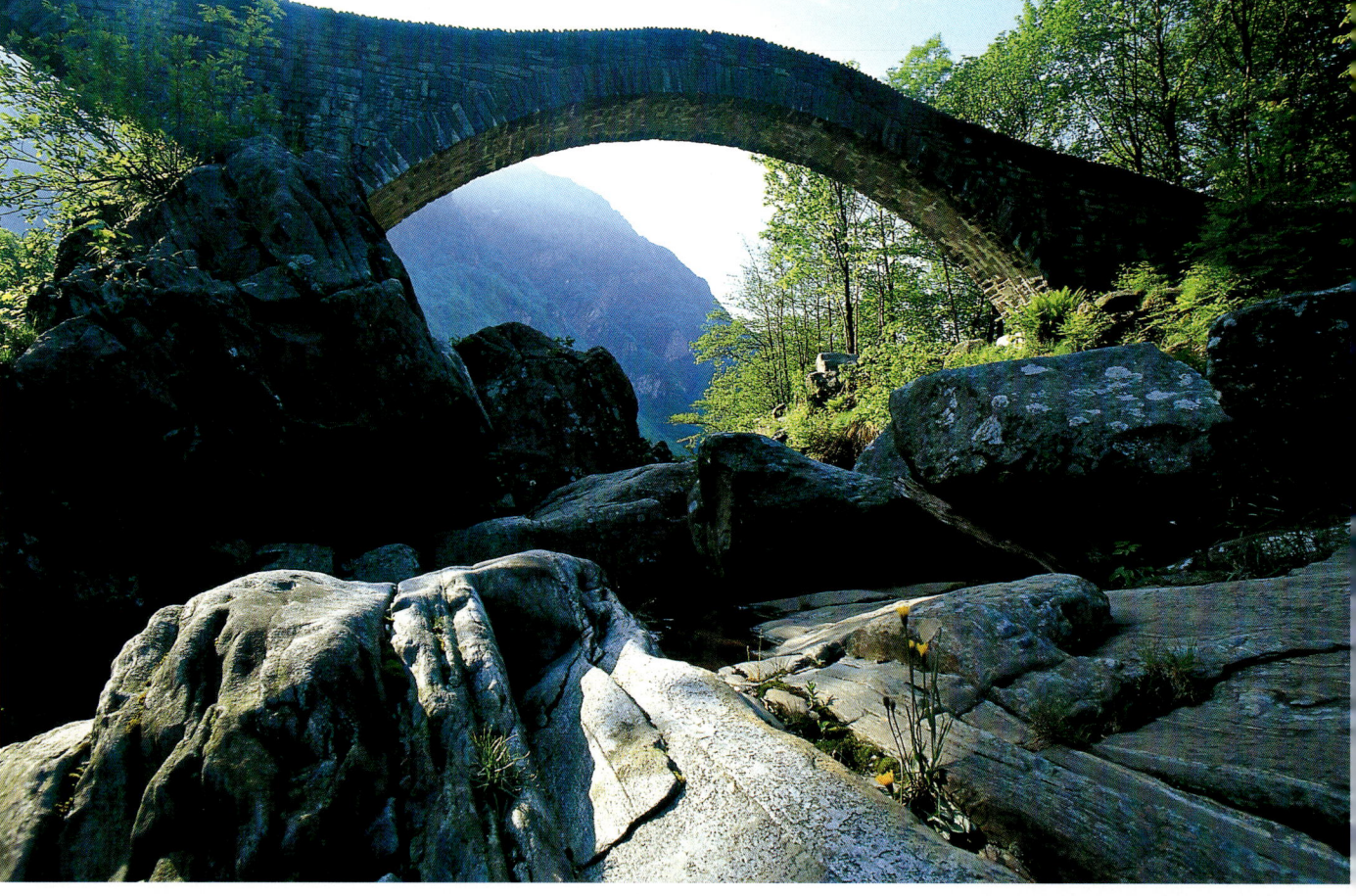

82

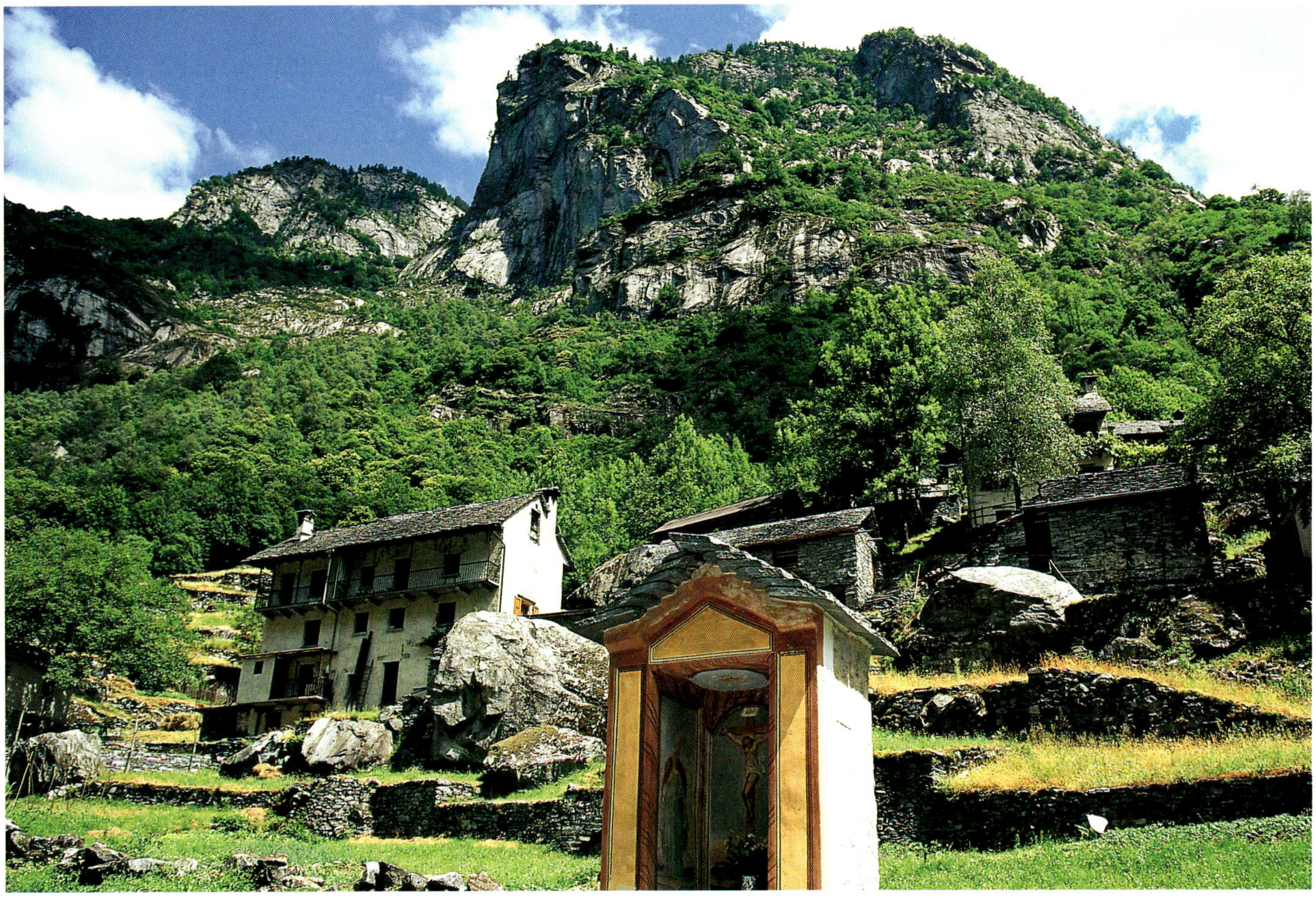

Although German speakers have been in the majority since 1980, the local administration and school in Fontana still prefer Vallader, a dialect of Romansch.

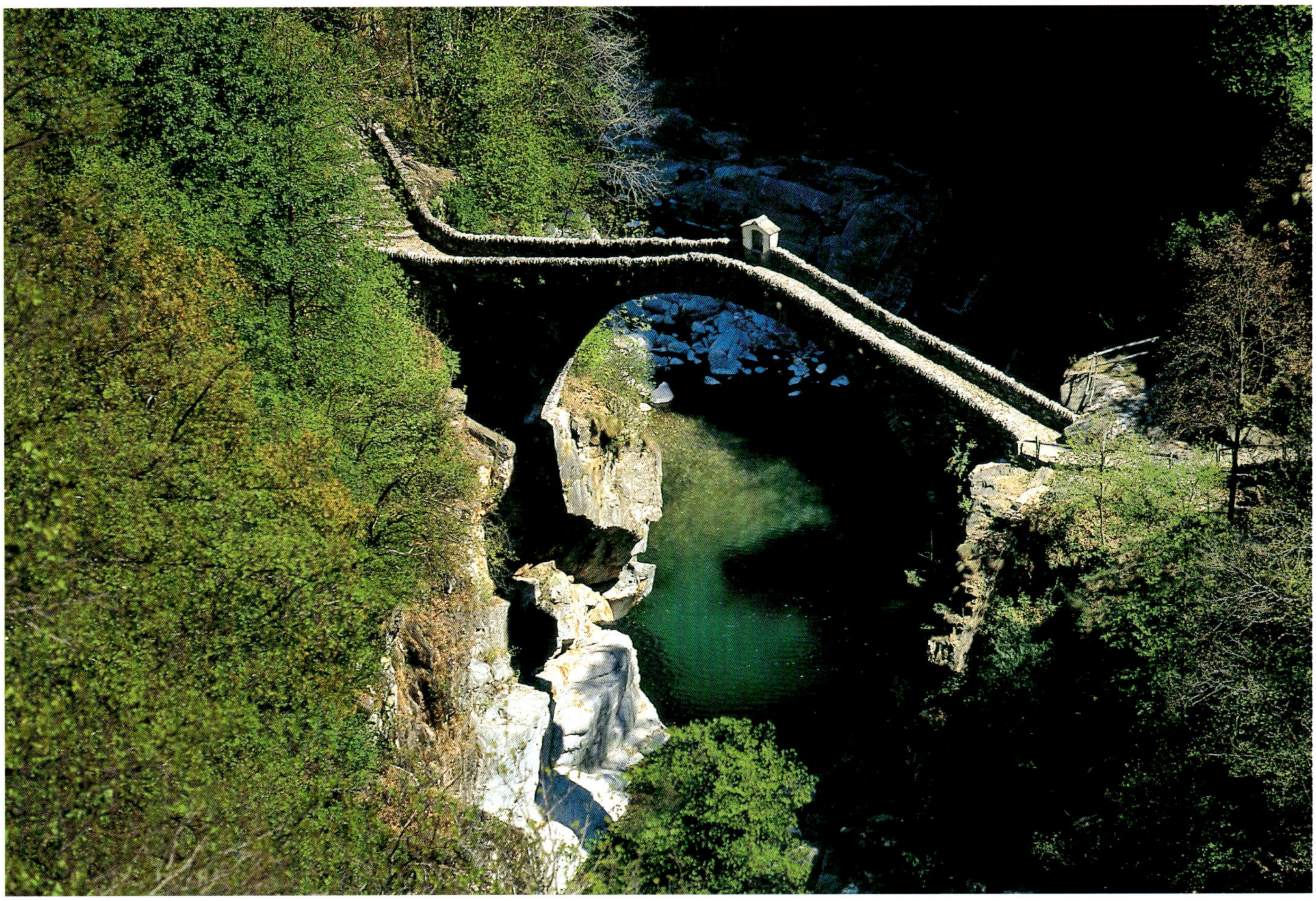

Old and a little narrow but still in service: an arched bridge near Intragna in the canton of Ticino.

83

Locarno elegantly reclines at the top end of the elongated Lake Maggiore. The warmest place in Switzerland – where palms and lemon trees grow – and host to the world-famous film festival, it attracts many visitors each year.

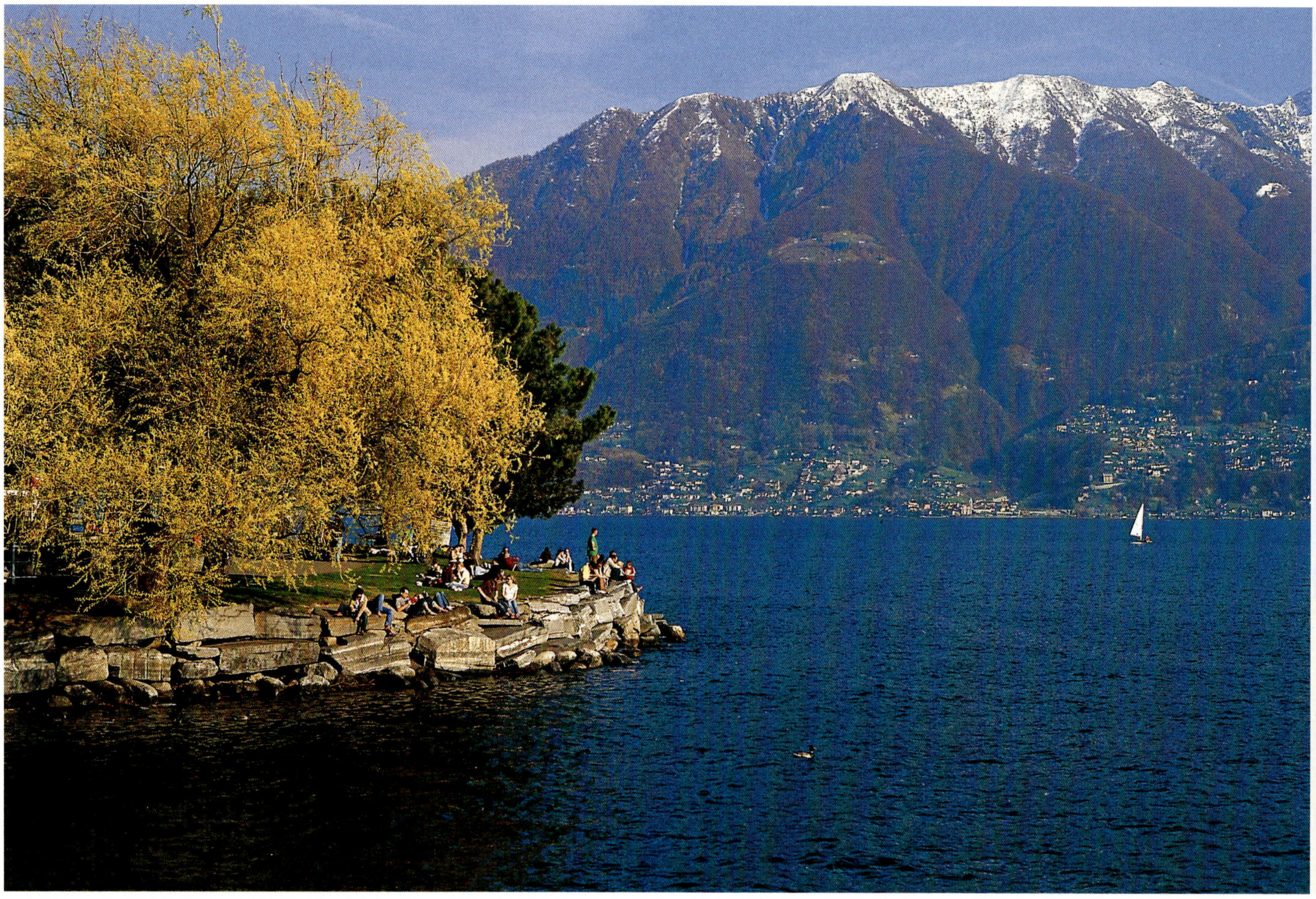

Not far from the northern shores of Lake Maggiore are the Isles of Brissago. In the botanical gardens laid out on the larger of the two in 1885 no less than 1,500 species of plant thrive, among them palms, bamboo and eucalyptus.

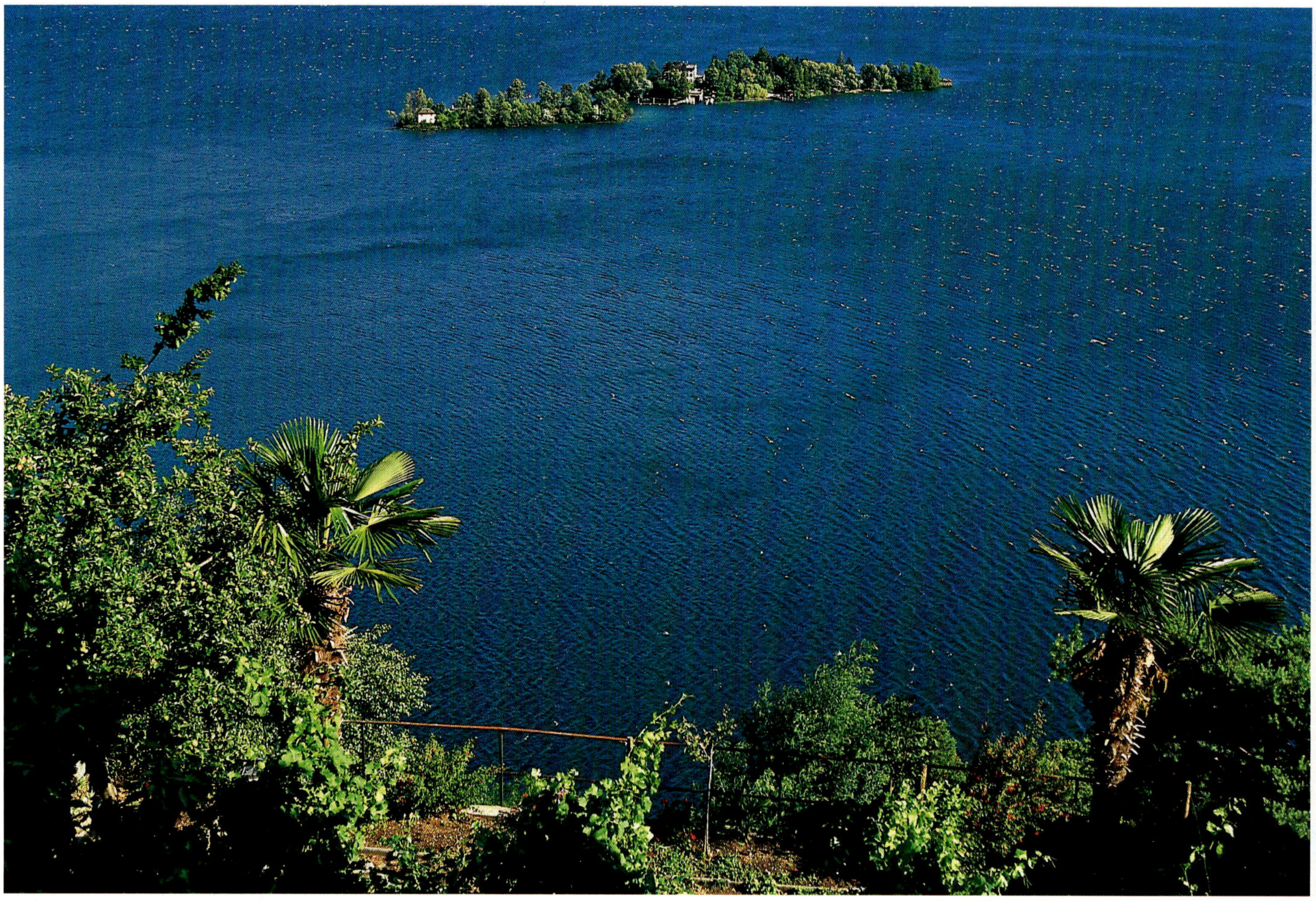

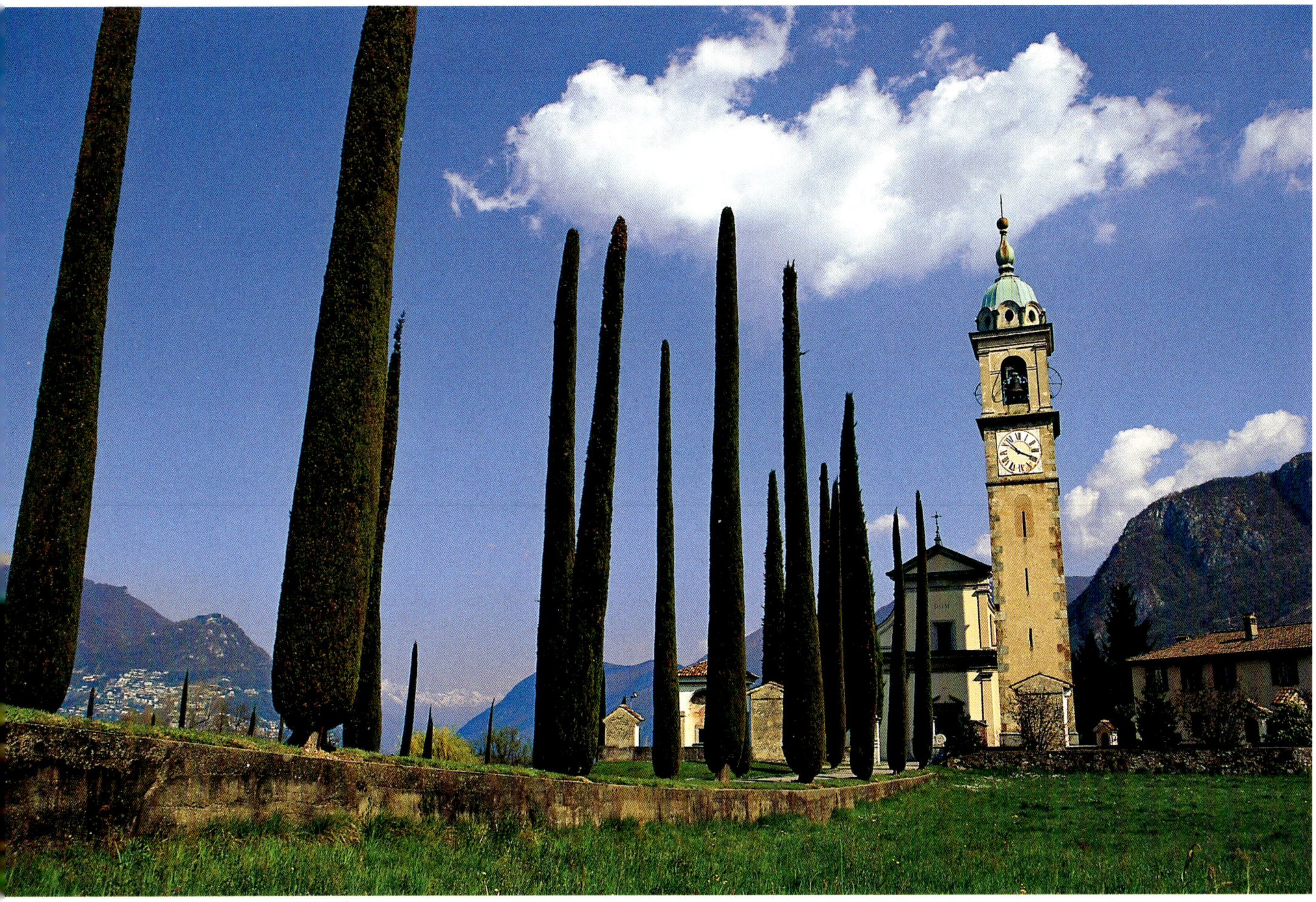

Mediterranean flair near Gentilino. Sant'Abbondio on Lake Maggiore is a melange of 16th and 17th century architecture and its free-standing campanile one of the local landmarks.

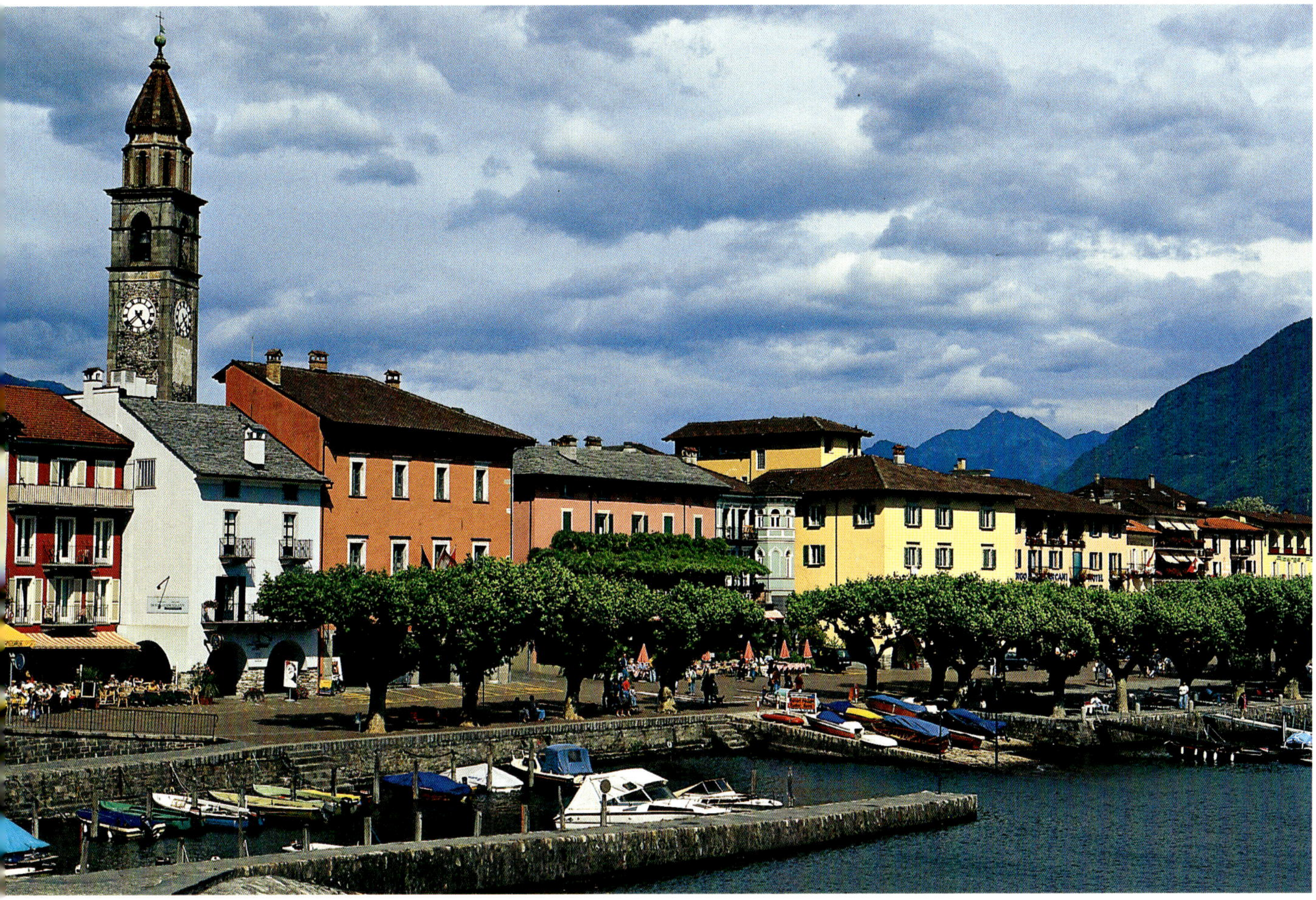

Although the American South is a long way away, each year Ascona stages a yearly New Orleans Jazz Festival. The town hill, Monte Verità, also enjoys a modest fame as an alternative commune where in the first half of the 20th century social dropouts and idealists practised free love, vegetarianism, anarchy and Communism.

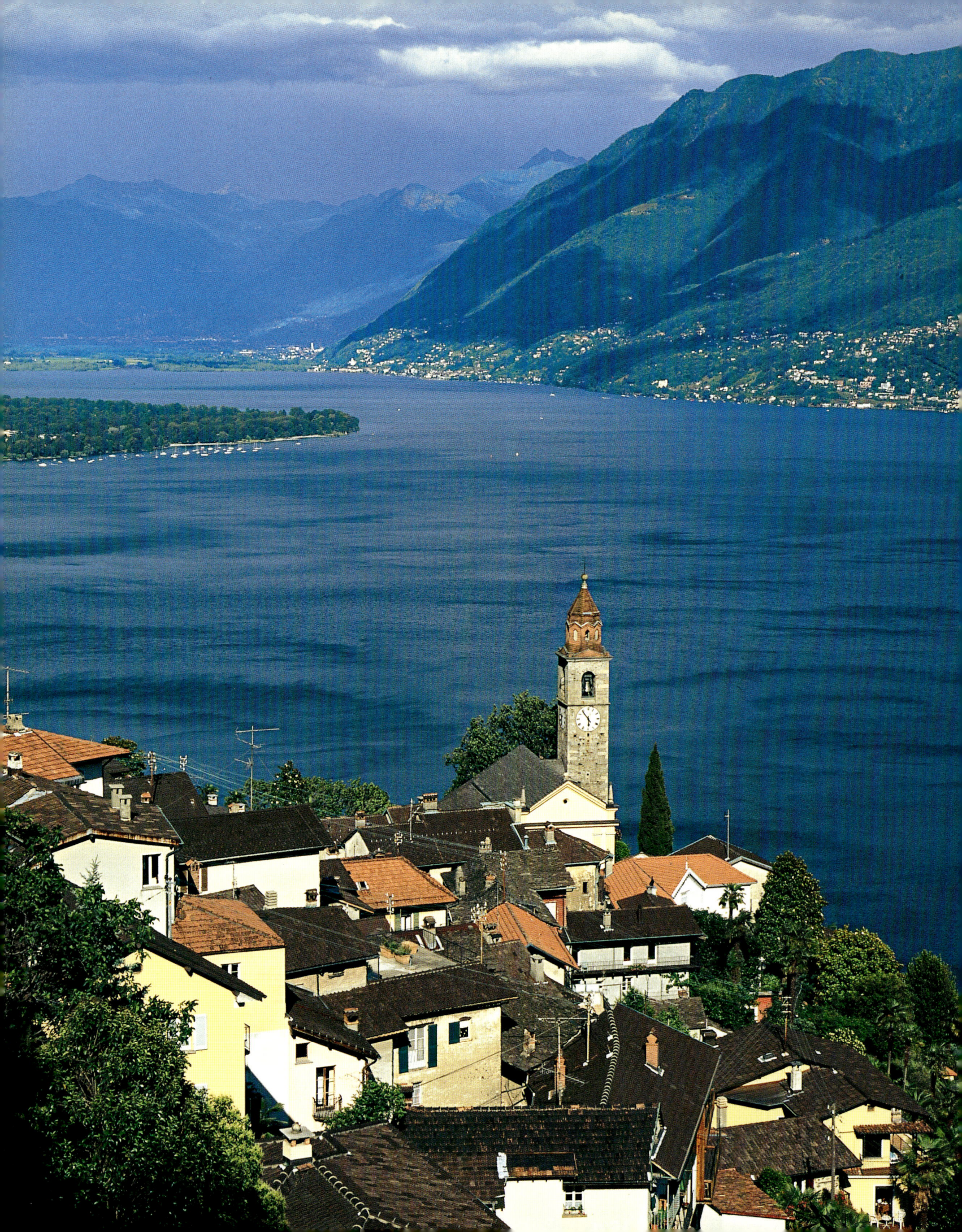

Left page:
Ronco – squashed alongside a mountain road up above Lake Maggiore – provided many people persecuted by the Nazis with a place of refuge. During the 1960s the farming village became a haven for 'refugee' artisans and artists.

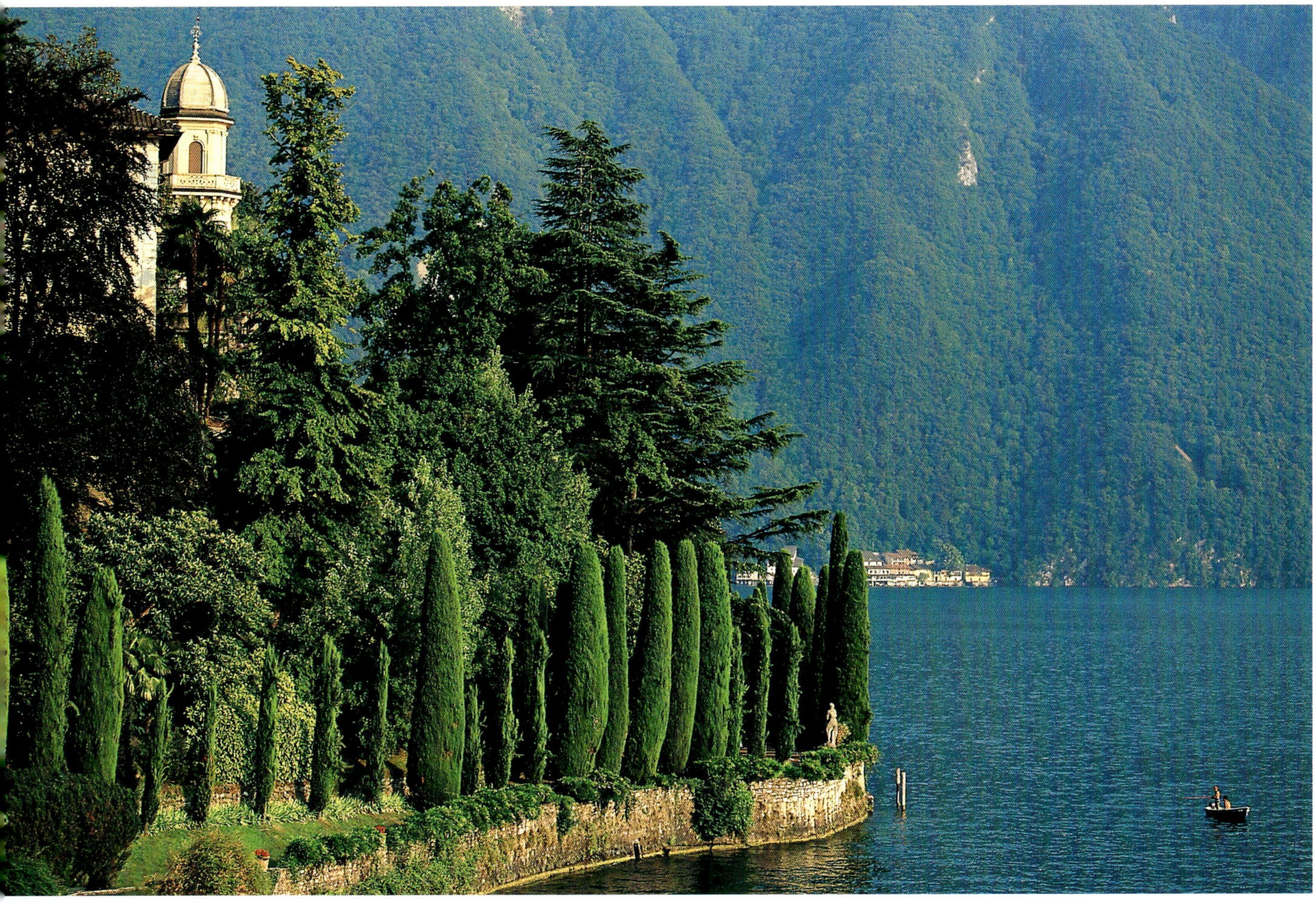

Idyllic Castagnola on Lake Lugano is now part of Lugano itself. The Villa Favorita in the heart of town boasts one of the most beautiful private art collections in Europe, the Sammlung Thyssen-Bornemisza.

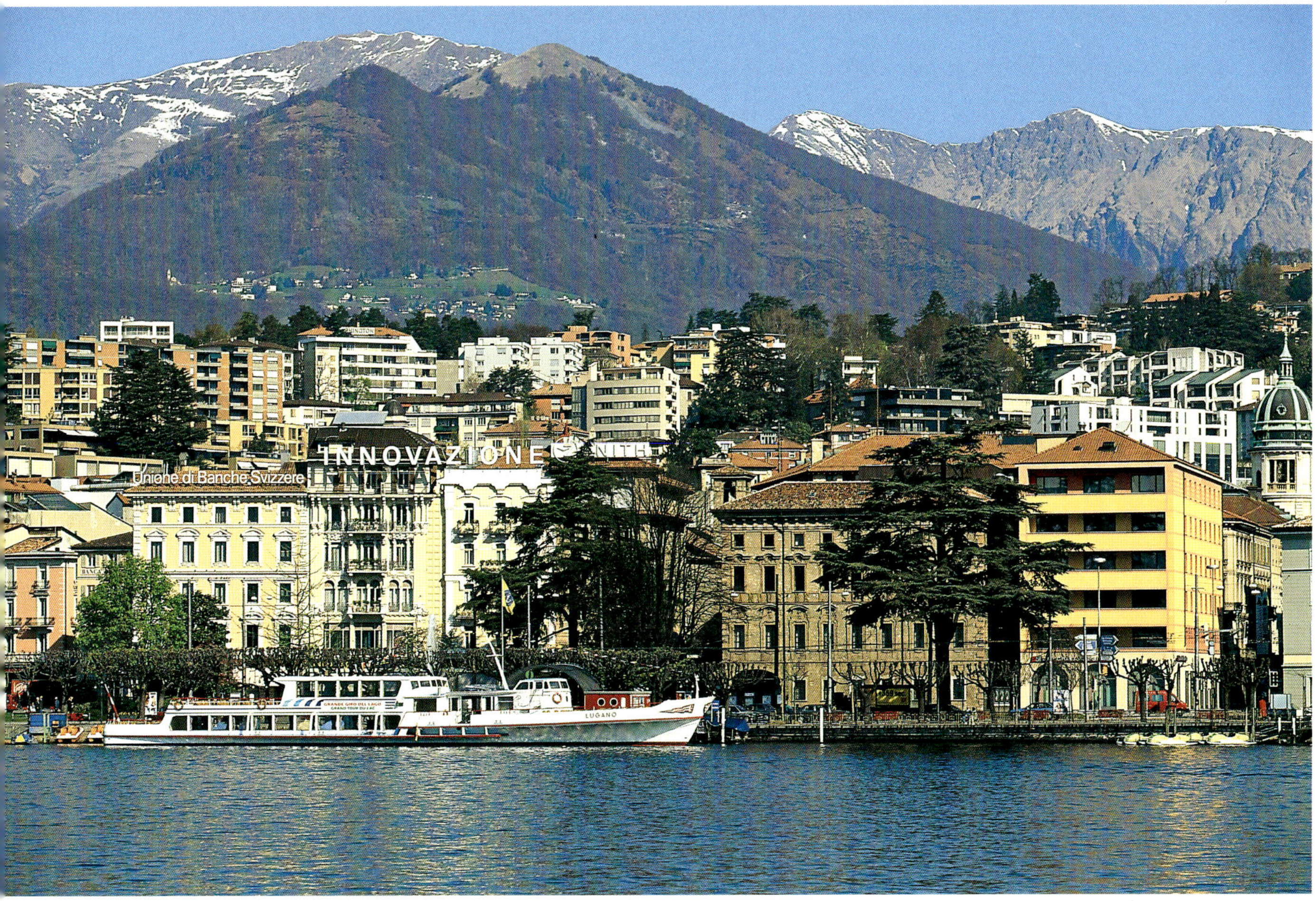

The name Lugano is derived from the Latin "lucus" and means "holy woods". Not much of the forest is left; since its founding the city has mushroomed and now numbers 50,000 with the nine neighbouring communities annexed in 2004 – which increases to 90,000 if you include Lugano's conurbation.

Page 88/89:
The famous mountains which crowd Lake Lugano include Monte Brè (925 metres/ 3,035 feet) in the east, Monte San Salvatore (912 metres/2,992 feet) to the west of Lugano and Monte Generoso (1,704 metres/5,591 feet) on the southeast shore. Tucked in between the south arms of the lake is the UNSECO World Heritage Site of Monte San Giorgio (1,097 metres/3,599 feet) where there are plenty of fossils to be found.

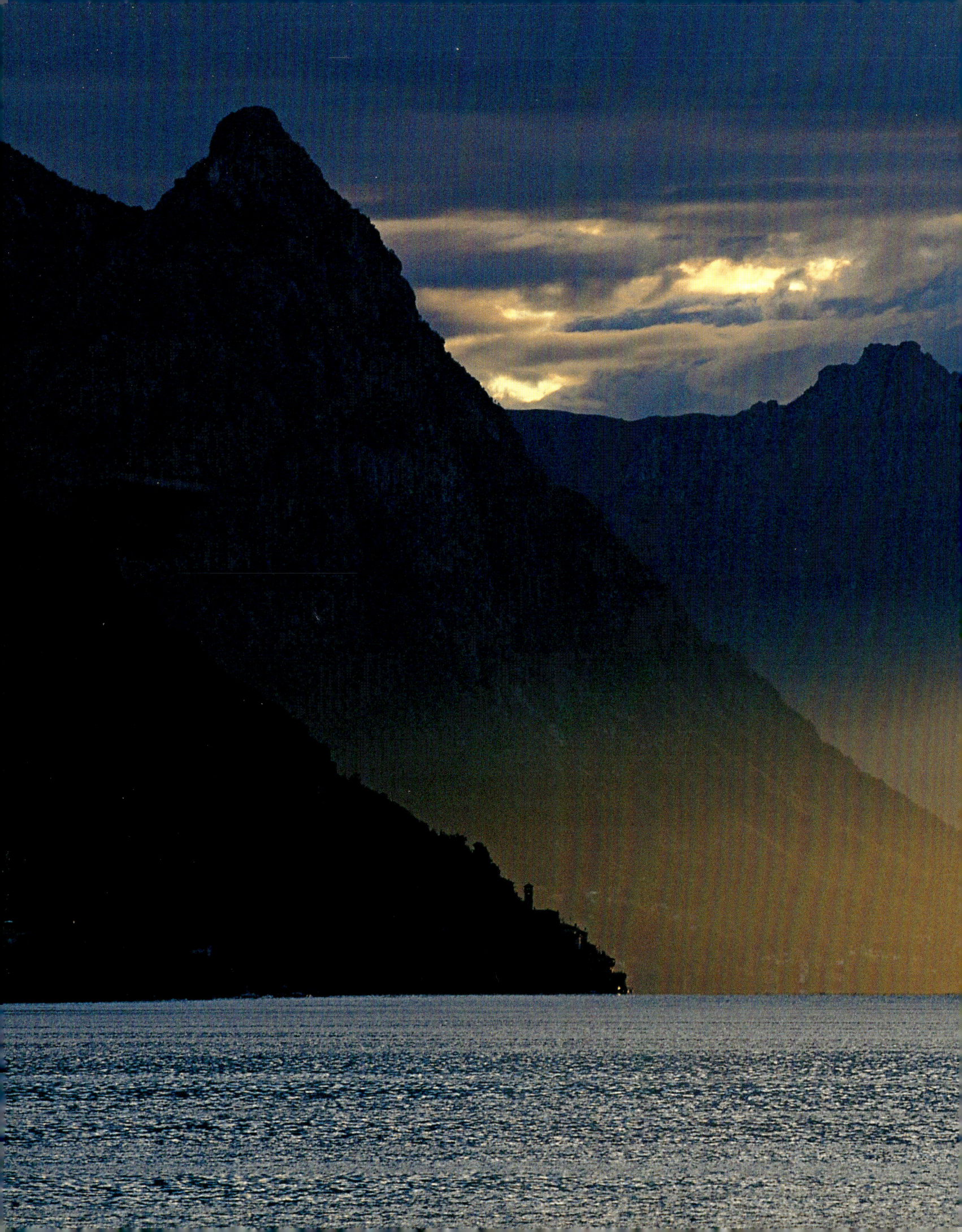

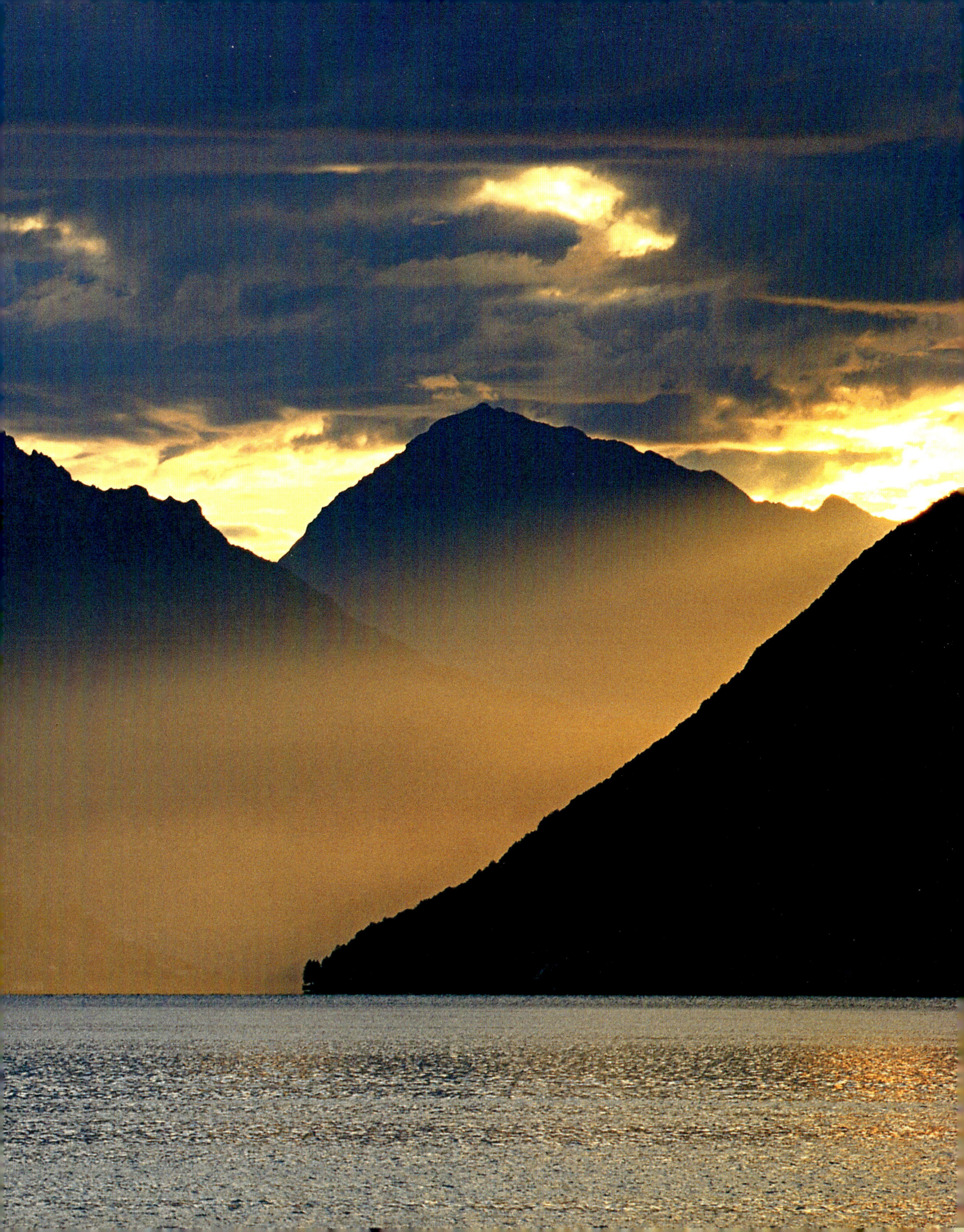

Index

	Text	Photo
Altmann		47
Areuse		30
Arosa		70
Ascona		85
Basle	36	40
Belalp		35
Bellinzona		92
Bern	36	52f
Bière		31
Brugg	36	
Brusio		78
Castagnola		87
Celerina		67
Chillon		26
Chur		43, 68, 72
Churfirsten		43
Corne de Sorebois		34
Eiger		60
Einsiedeln	14	
Fontana		83
Fribourg	20	27
Gandria		78
Garde de Bordon		34
Geneva	16	23
Gentilino		85
Grandson		28
Gruyères		29
Guarda		77
Hundwil		13
Ilanz		73
Intragna		83
Jungfrau		60f
Lauberhorn		60
Lausanne		23
Lavertezzo		82
Le Brassus		31
Le Châtelard		23
Le Landeron		26
Locarno		84
Lötschberg	16	
Lucerne		14f, 62f

	Text	Photo
Lützelflüh		92
Lugano		87
Lumbrein		77
Maienfeld		71
Matterhorn		8, 32, 35
Mönch		60
Mont Crosin		61
Monte Brè		87
Monte Generoso		87
Monte San Giorgio		87
Monte San Salvatore		87
Monte Verità		85
Montreux		23
Morges		27
Morteratsch		16
Moudon		28
Mythen		62
Naters		35
Neuchâtel	20	
Oberhofen		55
Ouchy		23
Pilatus		14
Pohlern		8
Ponte Brolla		82
Riffelalp		32
Riggisberg		37
Ronco		87
Rorschach		40
Säntis		13, 41, 47
Saint-Ursanne		30
Sargans		92
Sasseneire		34
Schwägalp		8, 13, 47
Sils		16
Silvaplana		78
St Gallen		42
St Moritz	66	67, 73
Sumiswald		54
Tarasp		76
Toggenburg		46
Zillis		70
Zürich	36	8, 50

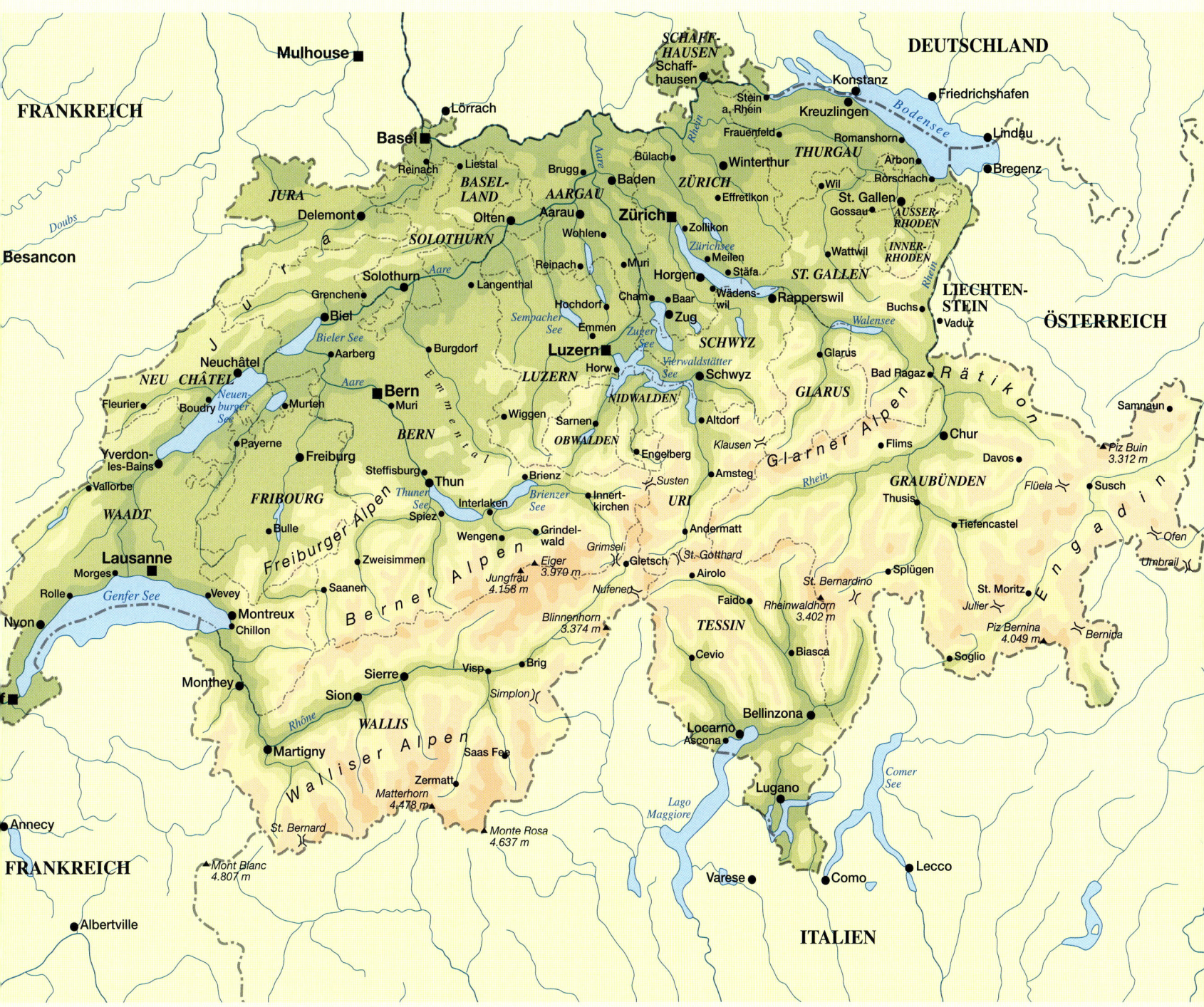

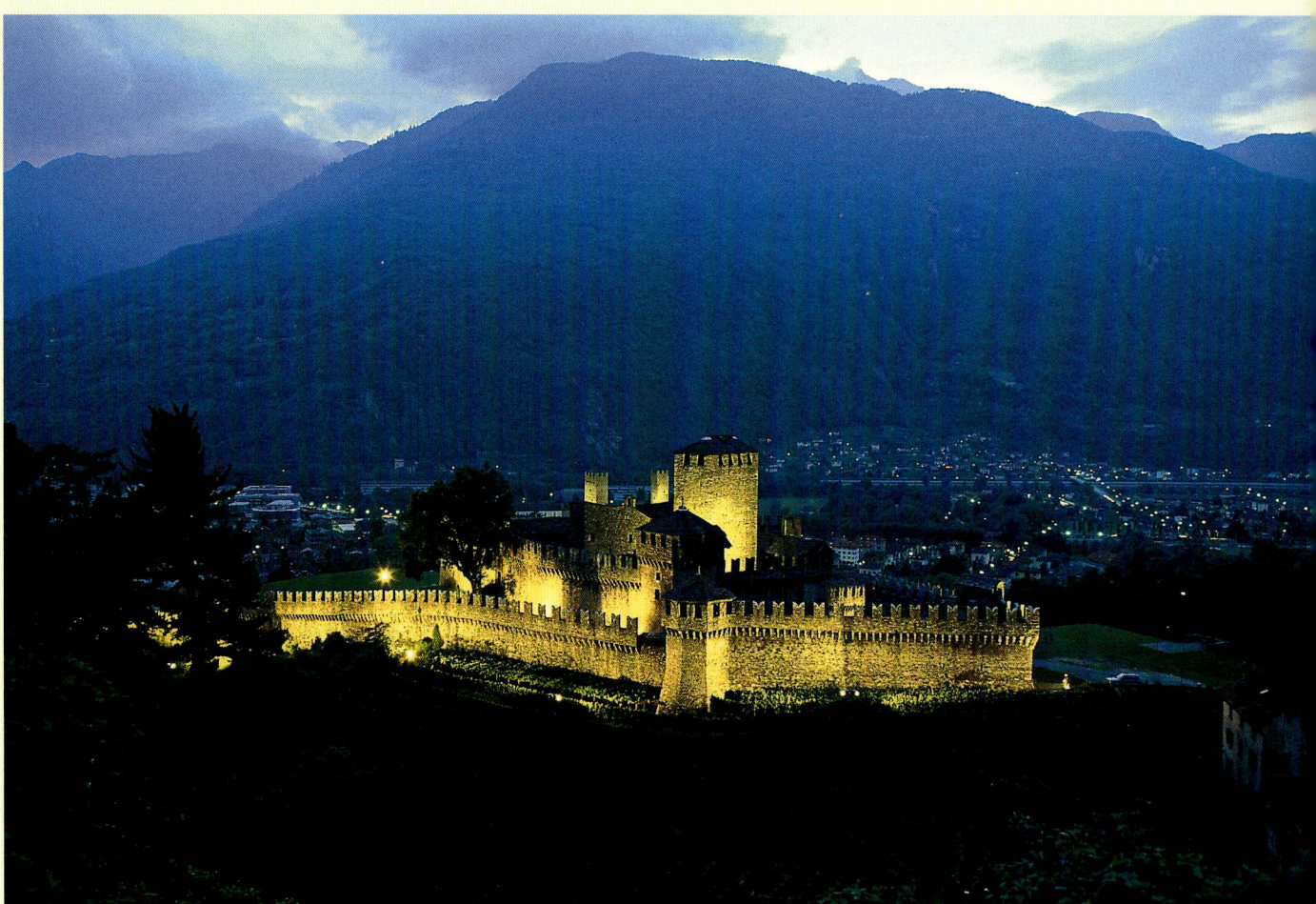

Castello di Montebello is just one of the three castles in Bellinzona. Its oldest parts are 13th century, with later extensions dating back to the 1400s.

Front cover:
Top:
Cows near Lützelflüh in the valley of the Emme where the famous cheese comes from. Poet and Emmental priest Jeremias Gotthelf wrote of his one-time home: "The horizon is crowded by wooded hills at the base of which countless valleys sprawl, fed by babbling brooks gently washing their deposits into the bosom of the River Emme."

Bottom:
Venerable Schloss Sargans in the canton of St Gallen was the administrative pivot of the county of Sargans until 1798. The castle's first tower was erected in c. 1100. Reachable from both the valleys of the Seez and Rhine, Sargans has always provided good access to the Alps.

Back cover:
Lakes are a typical feature of the Upper Engadine Valley in the canton of Graubünden – as is the long winter at elevations of 1,600 metres (5,250 feet) and over. Here it can snow at the height of summer and get down to -35°C in the winter, prompting some locals to joke that for six months of the year it's winter and for the other six it's just cold.

CREDITS

Design
hoyerdesign grafik gmbh, Freiburg

Map
Fischer Kartografie, Aichach

Translation
Ruth Chitty, Schweppenhausen

All rights reserved

Printed in Germany
Repro by Artilitho, Lavis-Trento, Italy
Printed/Bound by Druckerei Ernst Uhl GmbH & Co. KG, Radolfzell am Bodensee
© 2007 Verlagshaus Würzburg GmbH & Co. KG
© Photos: Roland Gerth/Christian Heeb

978-3-88189-666-5

Details of our full programme can be found at:
www.verlagshaus.com

Picture credits

Roland Gerth:
Front cover – top, p. 8–11 (2 fig.), p. 16, p. 18/19, p. 22, p. 23 bottom, p. 26 top, p. 27 (2 fig.), p. 28 bottom, p. 29 top, p. 30 top, p. 31 (2 fig.), p. 32/33 (2 fig.), p. 34 bottom, p. 35 (2 fig.), p. 38/39, p. 52 (2 fig.), p. 53 top, p. 54 bottom, p. 55 bottom, p. 56–59 (4 fig.), p. 60 bottom, p. 61 (2 fig.), p. 68–77 (15 fig.), p. 78 bottom, p. 80–92 (14 fig.).

Christian Heeb:
Front cover – bottom, back cover, p. 5–7 (2 fig.), p. 12–15 (3 fig.), p. 17, p. 20/21 (2 fig.), p. 23 top, p. 24/25, p. 26 bottom, p. 28 top, p. 29 bottom, p. 30 bottom, p. 34 top, p. 36/37 (2 fig.), p. 40–51 (17 fig.), p. 53 bottom, p. 54 top, p. 55 top, p. 60 top, p. 62–67 (7 fig.), p. 78 top, p. 79.

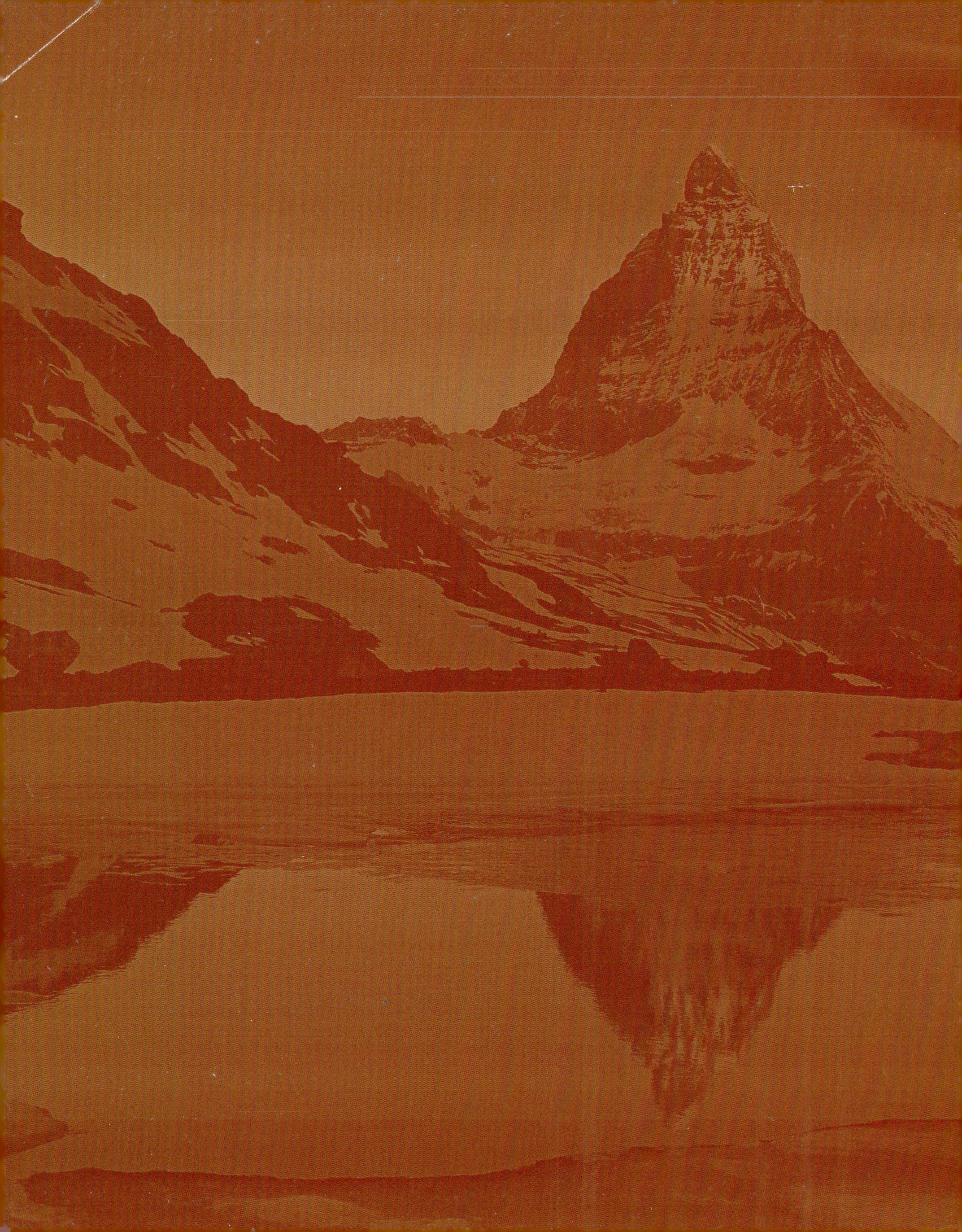